Aug. 2003 —

To Tim —

I hope you
will join us soon
at Croc's /

Until then Enjoy!.

Myra Aron

Thyme in a Bottle

Memories and Recipes

Ingrid Croce

Thanks to the editors, artists, and publishers at Harper Collins, beginning with Shirley Christine, Joanne Moschella, Julia Barfield, Laura Beers, Lisa Zuniga Carlsen, Claudia Smelser, Clayton Carlson, and Lara Starr.

Croce's Web site: www.croces.com

Jim Croce Web site: www.jimcroce.com

THYME IN A BOTTLE: *Memories and Recipes*. Copyright © 1996 by Ingrid Croce. All rights reserved. Printed in the United States of America. No part of this book may be used or reproduced in any manner whatsoever without permission, except in the case of brief quotations embodied in critical articles and reviews. For information address Croce's, 802 5th Avenue, San Diego, CA 92101.

SECOND EDITION. Copyright © 1998 by Ingrid Croce. All rights reserved.

Library of Congress Cataloging-in-Publication Data.

Croce, Ingrid

Thyme in a bottle: memories and recipes / Ingrid Croce.—2nd ed.

0-06-258624-6

1. Croce, Ingrid. 2. Restaurateurs—California—San Diego—Biography.

3. Cookery. I. Title

CONTENTS

FOREWORD

When I had finished devouring this book by my friend Ingrid Croce-Rock, I wasn't sure what had happened. It's part story, part history, part recipe, part restaurant, and part Ingrid. I listened, I laughed, I cried, and I got the munchies—all within a short space of time. There were moments when I was riveted and wanting more, and moments when I drifted between her life and my own, where they touched or ran together side by side through our common traditions. I felt my tears fall softly as details unfolded of our shared sorrows.

This isn't literature, this is life. Between each triumph and through every agony . . . you eat. This is the secret of life—to devour it all with friends and family. And pass on to each succeeding generation the traditions and recipes that make life worth sharing.

Enjoy . . .

—Arlo Guthrie

ABOUT THE RECIPES IN
Thyme in a Bottle

When I grew up, written recipes were nonexistent in our home. The traditions and circumstance of our dinners and their preparation were handed down with explanations like, "A little of this and a little of that." You had to be there, side by side in the kitchen with the cook, to learn the ingredients and their measure and to taste the cook's stew.

That's how my grandmother and my mother learned to cook. There was always room for personal interpretation and creativity. And the aroma in our kitchen, with golden onions sizzling, cinnamon apples steaming, and banana bread baking, made the alchemy they practiced irresistible.

As a teenager, when I married Jim Croce, my husband was the cook in our family. Fueled by generations of the Croces' and Babuscis' scrumptious Northern Italian cuisine, Jim was as passionate about preparing sweetbreads and pastas as he was about playing his songs. Well, almost. But again, nothing was put down in writing. Good food was about trial and error and often depended on the talent or mood of the cook.

I had never used a formal recipe until our son, Adrian James, was born, and Jim Croce's father gave me my first *Fannie Farmer Cookbook.* From that primer, I practiced making bread, roasted colorful legumes for frittatas, prepared hearty vegetable and chicken stocks, mixed organic salads, and baked fresh fruit pies.

During the summer of 1971, I became the chef in our family. Once I'd planted and harvested my first garden of sun-reddened tomatoes, burgundy eggplant, succulent zucchini, peppers, and basil, I was hooked on preparing our meals with gusto. While good food had always been important to me, the bounty that I grew myself and cooked fresh from the garden changed my lifestyle. It was the turning point in the way I looked at food.

As a city girl from Philadelphia who had always thrived on eating out at ethnic restaurants and fancy clubs, I was startled by how ordinary and yet extraordinary growing and preparing my own vegetables could be. Everything I sourced fresh from the soil tasted so delicious. And without making much of a fuss, I could humbly create healthy, tasty meals with ease.

When winter came that year, I was becoming finicky about the nourishment I put into my body. I wasn't satisfied with the frozen and canned options our little Coatesville market offered. So in the spring of 1973, when Jim suggested we move to San Diego, I was excited and thankful for the opportunity to enjoy fresh herbs and vegetables year-round.

As a housewife and a mother, I practiced my cooking and pored over cookbooks as if they were novels. From Marion Cunningham to Fanny Flag, from Alice Waters to Annie Somerville, M. F. K. Fisher, and Richard Sax, I have dripped batter, spattered oil, salivated, and compared notes. As a cookbook junkie, I learned how raw becomes cooked, dredged, minced, and braised.

Then, in 1984, I opened my own restaurant and, out of necessity, started to write down my own family traditions. I costed my menus and wrote recipes, plate presentations, and food descriptions for training my staff.

Over time and with the opportunity for travel and tasting edibles all over the world, I expanded Croce's menus from "home cooking" to include the new and exciting recipes I found on my excursions.

Adding to these the generous contributions of Croce's chefs, staff, family, and friends, I have built a lifetime repertoire of recipes, and these are the ones I share with you in this book. Whether you read all the stories in *Thyme in a Bottle* or just use the recipes, there are a few hints I'd like to offer.

First, there is no substitute for freshness. So follow the seasons and use nature's bounty to determine which meal to prepare.

Before you begin to cook, take time to source your markets for the quality foodstuff available. Then pick out your meal. Using the best recipes and good intentions won't work at all if the ingredients aren't fresh.

Next, there's no need for pretense here. Food is about fun. It must be approachable, embraceable, capturing your heart and your spirit too. So make mistakes and learn from them. I do!

Remember, you have the rest of your life to practice. So relax and take your good old time to learn how to prepare the foods you love to eat. Keep in mind that "cooking time" refers to the length of time a dish takes to prepare. Man-made time has always been a difficult concept for me. So please, adjust the proper cooking time for my recipes to your own personal taste and pleasure. Allow yourself leisure to prepare your meals so you can smile and laugh and enjoy yourself while cooking and eating them too.

Consider the view of *Thyme in a Bottle*. If there's never enough time to do the things you want to do, then why not enjoy the time you have?

My first cookbook gave me courage to go a long way. I hope, in some small way, I can do that for you.

I'd like to thank the following people for contributing these recipes:

Kathleen Daelemans: Baked Bread and Onion Soup, Bruschetta with Sundried Tomato Pesto and Herbed Ricotta Cheese, Grilled Eggplant with Lemon and Basil, Grilled Thresher Shark with Warm Frisee Salad and Yukon Gold Potatoes, Intense Chocolate Cake, Meyer Lemon Tart, Ricotta Gnocchi with Wild Mushrooms and Sage, Santa Barbara Sea Bass with Caramelized Onions and Figs, Blood Oranges, and Anchoiade Vinaigrette, Seared Pork Tenderloin with Garlic Mashed Sweet Potatoes and Michigan Dried Cherry Chutney

Alfonso Morin: Red Snapper Veracruz

Irma Gonzalez: Irma's Tamales

Andy Martinez: Andy's Ceviche, Andy's Salsa Borracha, Casamientos (Mexican-style Rice and Beans), Traditional Mexican Mole

Karen Krasne: French Tart Tatin

Bill Bloomhuff: Spicy Thai Salad with Chicken and Thai Bird Chiles, Tandoori Chicken with Cucumber Raita and Chutney

Nancy Fontes: Osso Bucco con Porcini Funghi

ACKNOWLEDGMENTS

Thyme in a Bottle is dedicated to the four most important men in my life. Kindly and generously they have stirred in the stuff it takes to prepare and build a prosperous restaurant and a joyous life. Oodles and oodles of love.

To the memory of Sid Jacobson, who by example as my father and a general practitioner taught me to trust, commit, respect, and value good health, good work, and a good heart.

To the remembrance of my late husband, Jim Croce, who wildly excited my passion, generosity, laughter, and song.

To our son, Adrian James Croce, who inspires my greatest faith, purpose, forgiveness, and joy.

And, most deservedly, to my devoted husband, Jim Rock, my hero, who valiantly shares and enhances my life, and teaches me the grace of relationship, ritual, and love every day.

My heartfelt thanks to my family, friends, and my old blind dog Jenny, who have taught me life's lessons and given me tales to tell.

Gracias and praise for our hardworking managers and staff, the terrific folks who keep Croce's delicious and alive, at our restaurants and bars.

Thanks to my friends at Waterside Productions, Bill Gladstone and David Fugate, and to Kira Kane at The Cooks Bookshop in San Diego, who serendipitously introduced me to my publishers.

This book owes special appreciation to my enduring and multitalented assistant, Caroline Joyner.

And to everyone who has collaborated, in some distinctive way, to give nourishment, flavor, and meaning to my life, thank you for making the "good times roll" and the good meals still coming.

INTRODUCTION

Hi, I'm Ingrid Croce and *Thyme in a Bottle* is my life story in a cookbook. It is filled with the recipes, friends, and opportunities I experienced for building a family and a home that magically found itself taking the form of a restaurant.

In *Thyme in a Bottle,* I go back and try to figure out how that all happened. I start at the ethnic epicenter of south Philadelphia where I grew up with people who were as passionate about Sinatra and linguine as they were about politics and religion. This "hotbed" of humanity is where my love for food, family, and hard work began, sixteen years before I met and married Jim Croce.

From the moment Jim and I fell in love, good food and music graced every facet and nearly every moment of our lives. Through the folk movement of the sixties, we promoted our Capitol album *Jim and Ingrid Croce,* often playing for our suppers in small clubs and eating our way across the country from college concerts and collard greens to Maine lobster at The Ship's Fare.

When our music failed to get acclaim, we moved to the country, where Jim drove a ten-wheeler and I planted zucchini and thyme. In between writing "You Don't Mess Around with Jim," "Operator," and "I'll Have to Say I Love You in a Song" there were blueberry blintzes, homemade gnocchi, and squash-blossom frittatas to be enjoyed. And then the greatest gift of all, our son Adrian James, came to us, just two short years before Jim Croce topped the music charts and his plane crashed in Natchitoches, Louisiana.

When Jim died in 1973, his music played on and his words "There never seems to be enough time to do the things you want to do" rang even truer than before.

While I was busy raising our son and protecting Jim's and my music rights in court, I kept trying to clarify and redefine my personal vision for family and a home. With no road maps to guide me, I followed many circuitous routes. I sang my own songs, opened a school, even sat on the board of the Woman's Bank.

Then using my heart and my stomach, I surfed south to Costa Rica with Adrian James, to polenta con natilla and mango pie. From blinchiki and Stroganoff in Leningrad, to pizza and spaghetti alla Bolognese, street vendors and five-star chefs blessed our palates.

After A. J. took his rites of passage at the Wailing Wall, I did my darnedest to run off the hummus and falafel at the Stockholm Marathon. I was still blindly following my dream.

In 1985, unable to sing after a failed vocal chord operation, I was looking for a good job with good people and a worthwhile, fun place to work. The result was Croce's Restaurant & Jazz Bar, which I opened as a tribute to Jim Croce and his music, and as a stage for our son to practice and play his songs.

Little did I know back then that my hard work in building our restaurant and bars would lead me to my wonderful husband, Jim Rock. Or that my work as a restaurateur would finally impart to me a powerful opportunity to do all the things I love to do best: serve, eat, and toast to good times and life's blessings.

In the end, Croce's is my prize. My business passionately stokes my entrepreneurial spirit and at the same time embodies my vision for family and community in a wonderfully ordinary way. While it's hard work, there's a lot of love here at Croce's and no limit to the good people, food, and entertainment we are able to bring to our everyday lives.

In my autobiographical cookbook my life stories, garnered over nearly five decades, are punctuated by the meals that nourished and encouraged me along the way. My recipes are a collaboration of kind friends, generous chefs, and family traditions that have been enjoyed at Croce's and served in our home.

Thyme in a Bottle tells how my dream came true. It brings us to the hearth of Croce's, where in addition to feeding the tummy, we enhance the spirit and offer times that are not "saved in a bottle" but enjoyed in the moment with family and friends. I hope you can come and visit us too!

MY HISTORY

From the earliest time I can remember, I was hungry.

Ingrid Croce, 1949.

Photograph by
Sid Jacobson

Though weighing only three pounds, four ounces at birth, I was energetic, ambitious, and always passionate about food. I adored mealtimes and all the circumstance, ceremony, and people that went along with them. As a child I believed, and later pretended, that anyone who dined with us was family. This sensibility has become the aura of hospitality that permeates my restaurants and bars to this day.

My father, Sid Jacobson,
with my twin sister, Phyllis (left),
and me (right), April 1947.

Ingrid and Phyllis, cowgirls at age three.

Photograph by Sid Jacobson

Twelve minutes after I was born, to everyone's astonishment but my own, my sweet twin sister arrived. Phyllis and I were opposites from the start. She weighed a comfortable six pounds, six ounces, and had a round pretty face, dark curly hair, and an apple-pie disposition.

When Phyllis and I were five, our parents divorced. My mother, Shirley, went to get help with her alcohol and drug addiction. My father, Sidney Jacobson, a general practitioner, stayed with us in west Philadelphia, where he practiced medicine from an office in our home.

Shortly after my mother left, my father thought it best for Phyllis and me to stay with my Aunt Ruth's family in northeast Philadelphia. They lived in this wonderfully safe little row home, and there were more kids in the neighborhood than I'd ever seen before. After school, I played and played until the aroma of Aunt Ruth's apple cake or kamish brite (a Jewish biscotti) baking in the oven would call me home.

After my dad's office hours, he always came to share our evening meal. From this time on, mealtime was not only delicious, it symbolized trust and commitment too. Before he tucked us into bed each night, he'd make up the most wonderful stories, metaphors for many of the recipes of my life.

When we were seven, my dad met my stepmother, Florence, an Orthodox Jew from Brooklyn. Shortly after they got together, they married, and Phyllis and I moved home with them. Though Florence did not keep a kosher kitchen, I vividly remember lighting candles with my "new" mom and repeating mysterious Hebrew prayers over plates of golden capons or tender brisket with kasha and varnishkas. I loved Florence, and her customary Jewish fare had me looking forward to the Sabbath every Friday night. Family and religion took on new meaning.

When Phyllis and I were eight, our parents' custody battle forced us to leave my father and Florence and move in with our natural mother for what was promised to be a two-month "trial separation."

Shirley, only twenty-six at the time, lived with her mother, Mary, in a fancy apartment on Rittenhouse Square. My mom had her own local TV show, *The Magic Lady*, on which she played the piano and sang nightly. She was a beautiful, provocative woman with a wonderful sense of humor, all of which made her very popular with the men.

I'd wait up until after her dates for her "Chinese-Jewish" stir-fry

My mother, Shirley Jacobson, at age twenty-one, 1949.

and the wonder of her 3:00 A.M. kitchen sweeps. On nights out together, she always tried to make the occasion very special. We'd go to fancy restaurants like Bookbinders for lobster or to popular clubs to see classic performances by Sinatra, Belafonte, or "Larry, Curly, and Moe." Best of all, when my mom and I were alone, I loved how she'd play a solo Gershwin piano tune, and I would sing it, just for her.

The two-month trial separation from my father became permanent.

I wanted to be with my father and Florence, but I was only a kid. Overnight, my personal menu changed from my father's domesticity to my mom's indulgent permissiveness. I kept trying to balance between these two contrasts: the respectability of *Father Knows Best* and the seductiveness of Ingrid Bergman, for whom I was named.

Always busy with studying, field hockey, gymnastics, and performing in school plays, I found that time moved quickly and before I knew it I was a turned-on teenager. It was 1960 and I was immersed in rock and roll, glad to be living only blocks away from *American Bandstand*, Chubby Checker, and the twist.

In addition to my mother's eclectic tastes and the opportunities I had to cook with her, my love of culinary diversity came from the delicious aromas and flavors of the Russian, Jewish, and European meals my Grandmom Ida made for us on our weekend visits with my dad. My grandmother's recipes traced back to her childhood in Kiev. The rituals that had been handed down to her through generations were served to me in a bowl of steaming chicken soup with matzo balls. Working at a little tin table in her humble kitchen, Ida prepared kreplach, knishes, hamantaschen, and incredible potato pancakes with sour cream.

My other grandmom, Mary, also instilled a love of good eating. After school she would send a cab for us girls and we would join her down on South Street at Mary Greenberg's Dress Store. I distinguished early on between the solitary hard work of Grandmom Ida's cooking, cleaning, and caring for a home and the active struggle of Grandmom Mary, a businesswoman who worked full-time at managing her store.

Forever attracted by the aromas and delights of Ida's homemade meals, I was also lured by the diverse and exotic South Street food vendors near the dress store. The prospect of devouring a South Philly cheesesteak, Chinese egg rolls, and Italian cannoli, *all in one day,* had its own special appeal. Even better, I didn't have to wash a single dish!

In 1963, at only thirty-six, my sweet mother passed away and my sister and I moved in with Father and Florence. Shortly after the move, when I was sixteen, I met Jim Croce, who was then a junior at Villanova University. Our music brought us together at a hootenanny in Philadelphia where I was a folksinging contestant and Jim was the judge. Jim had been playing guitar and singing in a college group called The Coventry Lads. After we met, we became a duo, singing folk songs at local coffeehouses and colleges and spending every minute we could together.

Three years later, Jim's parents still weren't happy about our "lust" or about their eldest son throwing away his college education to become a folksinger and marry a nineteen-year-old Jewish girl studying to be an artist. God forbid!

But after my first Sunday meal at the Croces'—with all the aunts, uncles, cousins, laughter, and antipasti—I refused to go away. Though I was very young, my love for Jim and the marriage of his mother's roasted garlic and peppers assured me that our union was going to be a good thing.

Our marriage, which began on August 28, 1966, was an adventure every moment. Feasts and famines, the loving friends and unforgettable times are still powerfully evoked by the fragrant aromas of the meals we shared. My memories of the highs and lows remain vivid. Jim Croce certainly lived by his motto, "Excess is best."

In 1968 Jim and I moved to New York to record our first album, *Jim and Ingrid Croce,* on Capitol Records. To promote sales we toured the United States and Canada in our ancient vw, and became "Truck-Stop Gourmets." We sampled the wayside diners and small-town fare, but best of all we enjoyed the homemade meals of generous fans across the country, where my love for all styles of American cooking flourished.

In 1969 and 1970 we worked very hard to make our music careers successful by promoting our album on the college circuit, playing to audiences of two to two thousand. But when our success in the music business seemed unattainable, we moved to the countryside in Pennsylvania and opened our home and hearts to our community. Here we played our music just for fun.

For one hundred dollars a month, which included all the flowers and vegetables our kind landlords allowed us to "rescue," we rented a three-room "smokehouse" apartment in an old farmhouse in Lyndell, Pennsylvania. Here Jim wrote

"New York's Not My Home," and slowly we let go of our disappointment at our first record's lack of recognition and "found us a home."

To make ends meet, Jim worked construction and played funky bars, while I sold my paintings and pottery and planted our garden by day. Since we had little money, our homegrown veggies and new songs were a godsend for entertaining, throwing parties, and getting to know our neighbors.

Living in the country, away from the music business, Jim was revitalized. His old buddy and foreman, Billy Reid, came over to our house many days after work to play bluegrass and country music. In addition

The Croces, from the cover of *Jim and Ingrid Croce*, Capitol Records album, 1969.

Photograph by Summerwind, Nik Venet

THYME IN A BOTTLE

to the music Jim and I continued to write and sing, Jim was intensely moved and inspired by the haunting songs and classical and electric guitar accompaniment of our new young friend Maury Muehleisen, who later became Jim's "one-man band" and our best friend.

All this music made us very hungry. And as Jim's hands were full with his guitars, I became the chef in our family. If I wanted something good to eat, I had to cook it.

It really didn't take long, especially for someone who loves to eat good food as much as I do, to learn how to satisfy that need. I even invited Jim's mother, "the Flower," to our home to test my treats. It was then I discovered that the humble dishes I made were my inheritance, filled with emotions and stories, and I *thoroughly* enjoyed offering them to our guests.

Hospitality was our art. Whether it was young musicians like Arlo Guthrie, The Manhattan Transfer, and Bonnie Raitt, or construction workers, groupies, lawyers, Hell's Angels, and the parish priest (all of whom were part of our extended community at that time), it seemed that everyone found his or her way to our kitchen. Though I didn't know it back then, this was the Original Croce's Restaurant.

When we found out we were going to have a baby in 1971, Jim gained a new sense of urgency. Fearful that this was his last chance to "make it" in the music business, he

Jim, Ingrid, and "the Flower," Jim's mother, Flora Croce, testing my apple pie at our kitchen table in Lyndell, Pennsylvania, 1971.

Photograph by James Albert Croce

wrote "Time in a Bottle." And that same week he composed and recorded "Operator," "You Don't Mess Around with Jim," and "Photographs and Memories" onto a cassette to send to his producers in New York City.

Shortly after they received his new songs, Jim was back in Manhattan recording his first gold album. His producers introduced him to BNB Management, and ABC Dunhill Records recorded his first commercial hit, "You Don't Mess Around with Jim." Things were moving quickly. On September 28, 1971, Jim helped deliver our son, Adrian James. A week later he was off on the road.

From 1971 to 1973 Jim played about three hundred concerts a year, and promoted his songs all over the United States and Europe. By the spring of 1973 his second album, *Life and Times,* had topped the charts and, finally, he got a week off to come home and get to know A. J., his "little old man."

Not long after this visit I discovered that I was pregnant again, and we decided to make a move. With all Jim's travelin', I wanted to leave the lonely farm, move closer to an airport, and be in a place where I would have next-door neighbors and could grow vegetables year-round. There were also offers of sound tracks, movie deals, and talk shows for Jim in Hollywood, so California became our new home.

While Jim was on tour in Europe, serious complications during childbirth caused the death of our second son, Max. Deeply saddened by our loss, Jim returned a new man and devoted himself to A. J. and me. In September 1973 we were reunited in San Diego for the best time together I could remember in a long while. We walked on the beaches and downtown along the harbor. We were so happy catching up on the past two years, planning our future and our family, and looking for a good place to eat. (Croce's wasn't around yet, but this was a sign of good things to come.)

Then Jim left for a week to do a quick tour, anxious to return for Adrian's birthday party. On September 20, 1973, just a week before A. J. turned two, Jim died in a plane crash while on tour in Natchitoches, Louisiana. I was devastated. As a widow and a single parent at age twenty-six, I had absolutely no idea what I was going to do.

Soon after Jim died his very first royalty check (after two gold albums!) arrived. It was for more dollars than I had ever seen. I couldn't understand why the money for which he worked so hard had come after his death, so I asked for an audit.

All I wanted was an accounting of our songwriting and performance royalties. But before I knew it I was embroiled in a terrible fight to win a series of litigation battles that lasted a decade: a wrongful-death suit in Texas; estate disputes with attorneys in New York and Los Angeles; contract and fiduciary claims over rights and royalties in New York and California.

Then when A. J. turned four, he suffered a terrible illness that almost took his life and left him blind. This was the worst time of my life. There were days back then when life hurt so much I didn't want to go on. But Adrian James was so brave and so smart, his example inspired me.

In 1974 I opened a children's school, and the following year I developed a "Headstart" program in Costa Rica. I wrote a children's book called *Mirondome* (Looking at Me), encouraging young people to trust themselves. From 1977 to 1981 I served as Vice Consul for Costa Rica in Southern California, promoting my beliefs.

The mid-seventies to the mid-eighties were terribly litigious times. I was building our home and continuously fighting for our rights. I won't pretend they were easy times. But I seriously question the spiritual and ethical life of anyone who won't work for what he or she believes in. So I did, even though it caused us a whole lot of trouble and despair.

Every opportunity we had, A. J. and I made travel our prize. We visited many countries, exploring diverse lifestyles, cuisines, and cultures. We wandered and learned together, and my "little old man" always gave me hope and imparted his great understanding of how to enjoy life right now.

In 1978 I recorded an album, *Reaching Out,* with Jimmy Horowitz (of Riva Records and the Rod Stewart Group) in Los Angeles, and then in 1980 a second with Nik Venet, titled *In an Unfamiliar Way.* While on tour in 1983 promoting my music, I developed vocal chord problems that resulted in a failed surgery.

Unable to sing, I went in search of where my passion led me—and ended up "right back where I started again": preparing the Russian, Jewish, and European cuisine that had given me comfort and nourishment when I was a child.

With my experience in art, music, business, international relations, litigation, education, and motherhood, I was ready to find a job or start my own nation. Not knowing which, I invited my friend Joanne Kerr to our home one night to help me write a résumé.

After an evening of discussing "work" possibilities, I still didn't know how I could put my time, talent, energy, and resources to their best use and still enjoy my life without making music. It was late and we were hungry, so I offered Joanne some of my Most Delicious Blintzes with fresh blueberries and sour cream. I kept the blintzes in the freezer to be armed and ready for unexpected guests. After the snack, Joanne told me that she knew exactly what I should do. Open a restaurant!

In no time, I wasn't just cooking for my family; I was serving American-International cuisine and live music to the whole world. Croce's was my home away from home. It was a real restaurant and bar right in the heart and soul of downtown San Diego.

With only my vision, and no formal training in the restaurant and club industry, I built my own structure and personalized our profit-and-loss statements to get "control" of my business. I hired and trained managers and staff and wrote an extensive employee manual explaining my commitment to excellence and challenging everyone to do his or her best. Once human resources were developed, I learned about licensing, public relations, and the red tape and politics of being a restaurateur. When I opened the forerunner of today's Croce's in 1985, I had a dream, an investment, and enormous energy. I also had a new lease on the ground floor of the Keating Building in the historic Gaslamp district of San Diego, and I was determined to make my business succeed.

At my son's suggestion we brought in live, traditional jazz nightly. A. J. played music at our happy hours, and early on he began to cultivate his raspy vocal style and fancy piano playing. At just fifteen, he was honing his act along with the finest local musicians. Music brought a new clientele, and we were just that much closer to being put on the map as a San Diego landmark along with the San Diego Zoo and Sea World.

In 1987, after fourteen years as a widow, I met one of our customers, Jimmy Rock, on table twenty-one at Croce's. Despite the fact that Jim was an attorney, he understood my disdain for the legal profession. We wed on Thanksgiving Day 1988, and my husband, from Pickle City, Iowa—"Where all the housewives are happy"—gladly quit law and began working with me on our next venture, a club for rhythm and blues called Croce's Top Hat Bar and Grille (named after Jim Croce's song).

A. J. accompanied us on our honeymoon to Thailand, India, and Nepal. We climbed the Himalayas and got a chance to see the most incredible campfire cooks ever. Our diminutive guides—carrying on their backs hundreds of pounds of foodstuffs, tableware, camping and cooking gear up the steepest mountains—prepared five-course dinners every night, with tablecloths and candlelight and always with a smile. They were a great inspiration. After this trip, my workload looked easy.

In subsequent years the three of us went on safari in Africa, feasting on the most beautifully decorated buffets throughout Kenya and Tanzania and by the light of the "Kilimanjaro Moon" on the night train to Mombasa. We dined our way through the Netherlands, France, Turkey, and Italy. Then, having experienced various cultures and cuisines abroad, we brought our understandings and recipes back to Croce's restaurants and bars.

In 1988, fifteen years after Jim Croce's death, a fan letter from a student in Natchitoches, Louisiana, spurred me on to write the life story of Jim Croce with my husband, Jim Rock. This was a difficult endeavor, writing a biography of my first husband with my present husband. Though the book has not yet been published, the four years we worked together to uncover the past cleared a wonderful path for our future.

In 1995, after a dozen years in the restaurant business, and many attempts to publish the Jim Croce Story, I decided it was time to write my own story. I knew that "Thyme In A Bottle" would have to embody the people, anecdotes, and the meals of my life. And, it seemed perfect to offer my autobiographical cookbook here at Croce's Restaurants and Bars, where many of the recipes can be enjoyed and where live music and new stories are being made every day.

In the last chapter of "Thyme In A Bottle", *The Life of a Restaurateur,* I tie together my first fifty years and talk about the restaurant business. I reveal how change, our most reliable variable, has been managed at Croce's and how my past experiences have empowered me to succeed.

In this updated printing, I add the highlights of 1996 through 1998 and tell how our Croce's story finally got produced on *VH-1, TNN,* and *The Today Show*. I admit how my cooking experiences on *QVC*, with Philadelphia's "Book and the Cook" and on *The Food Network* in New York City challenged me. And, I share how working hard and taking risks has brought rewards.

Over the years, with the help of wonderful people and the gift of national media, Croce's Restaurants and Bars, my tribute to Jim Croce, has enjoyed success. Our business has given me the opportunity of great livelihood and purpose that fills my heart and offers a fun place for fans and patrons to experience Jim Croce's spirit and hospitality.

I hope you enjoy my stories and practicing the recipes in my cookbook. And if you ever come to San Diego, please stop by and visit us, or you can drop me a line at www.croces.com. We have a saying that has served us well over the years, at Croce's we say, "When you're not home be here", and we mean it!

Time in a Bottle
Italian Family Recipes

In the early sixties, defying a racist teacher at my high school became my quest. I was determined to overcome prejudice at Springfield High by joining every club and sorority I could, shaming "them" into allowing me to be their first Jewish cheerleader and pledge. So I gave up my dream of becoming a famous gymnast, joined the cheerleaders, and at the same time started singing folk songs with two popular Irish Catholic boys.

We Three, as our folk group was called, soon learned enough songs to perform at the Pennsylvania Military College. We drew attention from a group there called The Rumrunners. And not only did I get a date with one of the cadets, but best of all I got asked to join the group, which was looking for "a strong female singer."

🍴

On a snowy night two days before Christmas in 1963, I was auditioning with The Rumrunners to be a contestant in an upcoming hootenanny at WDDS radio station in Philadelphia. Close to the station's parking lot, our old clunker had gotten stuck in the snow, and for fear of being late, I had jumped out to push our car while my band members, six husky military cadets, sat inside the sedan, teasing and chiding me on.

Program cover: Jim Croce and The Coventry Lads (Villanova University), January 25, 1964.

Top row, far right, Jim Croce; *top row, far left,* Tim Hauser of The Manhattan Transfer; *bottom row, far left,* Tommy (Picardo) West.

Ingrid Jacobson and The Rumrunners, from program of the "Giant Hootenanny," Convention Hall, Philadelphia, January 25, 1964.

After the automobile was liberated, I looked up and saw this handsome, curly-haired guy staring at me from inside his VW beetle. At sixteen, I wanted so much to impress him by looking older and cooler than I was. But instead I waved at him impulsively, like a little kid wearing mittens. He smiled back sweetly, waved, and drove on.

Once inside the studio, as I stood before the microphone tuning my guitar, I had a funny feeling that someone was watching me. I looked through the smoky glass into the control booth and there he was again. That cute guy from the parking lot was the judge for the audition! He introduced himself as Jim Croce, a college student at Villanova University who was in a group called The Coventry Lads. He and his friend Tommy Picardo were there that night for our audition. I noticed Jim staring at me with the biggest, saddest brown eyes I'd ever seen. He looked shy and sensitive, yet at the same time he was impish. I felt like he was undressing me with every glance.

Self-consciously I began to sing. Then, trying to impress my perceived critic, I decided to improvise. Without apprising my band of my new introduction, I performed an unexpected opening to the folk song we had rehearsed.

In a husky, sexy voice, I mimicked the words, a cappella, to Marilyn Monroe's tune from the movie *Some Like It Hot.* "You've heard of instant coffee/You've heard of instant tea/Well you just cast your little ol' eyes on little ol' instant me." I went with it completely, body language, gestures, and all, and when I finished, my band, though staring at me dumbfounded, picked up their instruments and joined me promptly in our unrelated folk song, "The Midnight Special."

Next we played "The Cruel War" and completed our audition with Pete Seeger's "Where Have All the Flowers Gone?" When we finished, "my" audience smiled at me sheepishly and Jim Croce came into the studio, clumsily tripping over the microphone chord to reach me. "I like your voice," he managed. "Maybe we could sing together sometime."

That night I passed the audition and made the first cut. I also fell madly in love with Jim.

Two weeks after our audition, the hootenanny was held at Convention Hall in Philadelphia. I was determined to look cool. I borrowed a sexy dress from an older friend—a tight, white sheath with a black stripe up each side.

Before the show began, Jim searched me out and located me practicing my guitar. I thought I'd melt when I saw him. He was dressed conservatively in a highly starched light blue oxford shirt, navy blue V neck, and light beige jeans with pressed creases. He looked so grown-up.

Before I could catch my breath, he planted his foot firmly in his mouth and bantered, "That's a nice dress you're wearing. You look like a little skunk!"

Humiliated by his comment, I withdrew, put down my guitar, and lowered my chin to my chest. Gently moving closer, Jim apologized for embarrassing me. Realizing he had also hurt my feelings, he jumped back and told me, "You look so pretty, Ing," and then, very politely, he asked if he could play me a song. I had no idea of the treat I was in for. He tuned my guitar and then sang me a haunting, traditional blues ballad called "Cotton-eyed Joe." I was mesmerized. His warm, sincere voice and his music healed my wounds. That night we won the contest and my heart was his. We were off to a great beginning.

ROASTED PEPPERONATA SALAD

3 yellow peppers
3 red peppers
3 green bell peppers

1 clove garlic, minced
1/2 cup olive oil
1/4 cup balsamic vinegar

2 jalapeño peppers, seeded and minced

2 ripe tomatoes, seeded and cut
    into julienne strips (not peeled)

Salt and pepper, to taste

PREHEAT THE OVEN TO 325°F. Rub olive oil on the peppers and jalapeños. Put them on a baking sheet in the oven for 20 to 30 minutes. Remove the peppers and jalapeños from the oven when their skins have blistered, and sweat in a sealed container or bag for 15 minutes—this loosens the skin. Remove the peppers from the bag and cut them in half. Rinse under cold water to remove the skin, stem, and all seeds. Slice the peppers and jalapeños into thin julienne strips. Arrange the peppers and tomatoes in a shallow serving dish.

Mix together the garlic, olive oil, balsamic vinegar, and salt and pepper and sprinkle over the salad. Allow the pepperonata salad to marinate overnight.

SERVES 6 TO 8

O ur first practice and first date was a Sunday afternoon at my house. Jim was shy and uncomfortable when he first arrived. I answered the door dressed casually in jeans and a baggy sweatshirt and there was Jim, standing with a guitar case in each hand, dressed stiffly in a brown three-piece suit with a biting, starched, button-down collared shirt. He apologized immediately for his attire, explaining that he was just coming from his cousin Patty's wedding. Which, of course, he was not.

Having heard that my father was a psychiatrist, he had some strange notion that if he acted weird or dressed funny, my dad would get "the net." Of course, he was joking. (At least, I think he was.)

But Jim, when I met him, was a formal kind of guy. He was here to court me, and woo me he did! His sweetbreads were the first I ever tasted. The recipe went something like this.

SEARED SWEETBREADS
WITH MUSHROOMS DUXELLE

⁂

2 pounds veal sweetbreads

Iced salted water

1/2 cup lemon juice

1 teaspoon salt

1/4 teaspoon black pepper

Flour, for coating

4 tablespoons Clarified Butter
   (see page 174) or vegetable oil

1 teaspoon garlic, minced

1 medium yellow onion, chopped

2 cups mushrooms, sliced

3 tablespoons shallots, minced

1/2 cup white wine

1/4 cup all-purpose flour

1 cup half-and-half

1 cup chicken stock

Lemon juice, to taste

Salt and pepper, to taste

2 tablespoons parsley, chopped

AFTER REMOVING excess fat and membranes, soak the sweetbreads for 1 hour in a bowl of iced salted water and 1/4 cup lemon juice. Drain the sweetbreads and weight them down with a heavy plate or dish and put them in the refrigerator for 2 hours, or overnight if you have the time. For crisp outsides and creamy centers, it's important to remove their liquid.

Preheat the oven to 200°F. Pat the sweetbreads dry and season with salt and pepper. Coat them lightly with flour. Heat 2 tablespoons of Clarified Butter or oil in a skillet with the minced garlic. Sauté the sweetbreads over moderate heat in two to three batches for 4 to 5 minutes, until they are golden brown all over. Transfer to a warm uncovered platter in the oven.

Heat the remaining butter in a skillet over medium heat and sauté the onions, mushrooms, and shallots until the onions are golden brown and the mushrooms have sweated. Deglaze with white wine. Allow the mushroom mixture to reach the boiling stage, then reduce to medium-low heat and stir in the flour, half-and-half, and chicken stock and bring to a boil. Stir and simmer for 2 minutes. Remove the sweetbreads from the oven and cut them into 1-inch squares, transferring the sweetbreads and the juices from the platter into the skillet. Stir gently and remove from the flame. Adjust seasoning with lemon juice, and salt and pepper. Remove from the heat and serve over soft polenta, toast points, or bruschetta. Garnish with parsley.

SERVES 6 TO 8

Jim and I went to my room to practice, and the moment his guitar was in his hands he relaxed and took control. He told me stories about the Great Depression, the Dust Bowl, and Woody Guthrie. Then he taught me some of Woody's songs. "Green Pastures of Plenty" was the first one we sang together, and our voices blended like pasta and cream. From that moment on, making music with Jim was like making love. The physical feelings we held in check thus far were played out when we sang.

Though only sixteen, I knew in my heart I wanted to marry this man and have his babies.

GREEN SPINACH TORTELLINI IN PORT WINE CREAM SAUCE

1 pound dry tortellini
1 tablespoon Clarified Butter
*   (see page 174)*
1/2 tablespoon garlic, freshly minced
1/2 cup sundried tomatoes,
*   coarsely chopped*
1/4 cup fresh basil, thinly sliced
1 cup port wine

1 1/2 cups chicken stock
2 cups heavy cream
Salt and white pepper
1/2 cup roux, if needed
A few teaspoons olive oil
2 tablespoons Parmesan cheese,
*   freshly grated*

COOK THE SPINACH TORTELLINI according to the instructions on the package; drain the pasta and set it aside. In a medium-size saucepot heat the butter. Sauté the garlic, 1/2 tablespoon of the tomatoes, and 1/2 tablespoon of basil for 1 minute. Deglaze with port and reduce by half. Add the stock and cream. Mix well. Bring to a boil and reduce the heat to a simmer. Continue cooking for 10 minutes. Add remaining basil, sundried tomatoes. Season to taste with salt and pepper.

To adjust sauce consistency, thicken with roux (a mixture of 2 parts butter and 3 parts flour cooked slowly until they froth together for 2 minutes), incorporating it with a wire whip to prevent lumps. In another medium-size pot bring salted water to a boil. Add the tortellini and cook until tender but still firm. Drain the tortellini in a colander; add small amount of olive oil to prevent sticking.

When ready to serve, add the tortellini to the heated port wine sauce and cook 2 to 3 minutes, or until desired consistency. Garnish with Parmesan cheese.

SERVES 4

Jim picked me up in his little vw bug and took me for my first visit to the Croce family home. I was most nervous about meeting Jim's mom. I had spoken to Flora or "the Flower," as Jim often referred to her, several times on the phone and she had always been curt with me. But, parked out in front of his house, I could smell the aromas of their cooking all the way to the street. I took the roasted garlic as a sign of a loving God and was enticed to go in.

When I walked through the door, Aunt Ginger's smiling face was waiting for us. Jim introduced me and she gave me a big welcoming hug. Jim's brother Rich and Rich's girlfriend, Dian, were there, and Jim's father, a tall, handsome, silver-haired man, came over and shook my hand warmly. But Jim's mother was nowhere to be seen.

Then I spotted a small middle-aged woman darting back and forth between the kitchen and the dining room. She seemed purposely to ignore me. She was wearing a cotton plaid sheath skirt and a sleeveless blouse in the dead of winter, and I assumed (correctly) that the Flower was going through her "changes." I was petrified even to say hello. Though I was dying to try her alluring plates of antipasti and her pasta pomodoro, I hung close to Jim.

Tagliatelle Pomodoro

1 pound dry tagliatelle pasta
20 whole garlic cloves, roasted
1/2 cup extra virgin olive oil
2 cups tomatoes, seeded and chopped
1 1/2 tablespoons garlic, minced
1/2 cup white wine
1/2 cup chicken stock
1 tablespoon butter, cut into small pieces

1 cup snow peas,
    cut into julienne strips
2 tablespoons Parmesan cheese,
    freshly grated
1/2 cup basil leaves,
    sliced thin (chiffonade)

Cook the pasta in boiling salted water until al dente. Rinse and stir in a little olive oil to prevent sticking.

Preheat the oven to 325°F. In a shallow pan, mix the garlic cloves with half tablespoons of olive oil until they are covered and roast until light brown, about 15 minutes. Set aside. Over medium-high heat, heat the rest of the oil in a large pan. Add the roasted garlic, tomatoes, and minced garlic. Cook for 1 minute, stirring constantly. Deglaze with the wine, then cook for 2 minutes. Add the stock and the tagliatelle to the pan and cook until desired consistency. Add the butter. Stir in the snow peas and adjust seasonings.

Garnish with 1/2 tablespoon Parmesan and 2 tablespoons basil per serving.

Serves 4

___

At the Croces' house, there were shiny glass hutches filled with delicate porcelain. Crucifixes and religious icons hung from the red-and-gold antique-brocade walls. Everything was pastel, red, or gold, it was all covered in plastic, and there was not a speck of dust anywhere. Since our meal was of great interest to me, my eyes were naturally drawn to the dining room table, and while I drooled over the broccoli rabe with garlic and olive oil and the osso buco, I couldn't help but notice that on top of the lace tablecloth, under the platters, was, again, the plastic.

If Jim Croce was intimidated by a psychiatrist's net that he imagined my father would drop on him, I was terrified by his mother's plastic, and the perfection and purity it implied to me. With pictures of the Virgin all around, I knew I could never live up to the Flower's expectations.

And of course, at least initially, I did not. To start with, I was Jewish, I was young, and I was hot for her son. But my greatest flaw was that I supported Jim's dreams to become a full-time musician.

Jim was the eldest son in a traditional Italian Catholic family. The first to go to college. The first to graduate. His parents wanted Jim to use his hard-earned education wisely. "Don't throw it away on music." "Get a good nine-to-five job with a pension."

It was fine for Jim to sing at family gatherings, or at church or school when he was young, but he was a grown man now. And he should act like one. "The Beatles have ruined this world" believed Flora, and "The people in the music business are gypsies. They aren't any good anyway."

Now we get down to the meat of the situation. Down to the bone. This osso buco is traditional. It's familiar and comforting too.

Osso Buco con Porcini Funghi

&ε ε∂

1 cup dry porcini mushrooms
3 carrots, peeled, ends removed
6 stalks of celery, leaves removed
1 large red onion

2 cups red wine
8 cups beef stock
2 cups tomato sauce
Zest of 1 lemon

THYME IN A BOTTLE

6 cloves fresh garlic
1 cup all-purpose flour
8 veal shanks cut 2 inches from
    the center of the hind leg
1/4 cup olive oil

2 anchovy fillets
2 tablespoons butter
1/4 cup fresh Italian parsley
Salt and black pepper, to taste

THIS RECIPE is by Nancy Fontes of Fio's Cucina Italiana in San Diego. Soak the porcini mushrooms in hot water until soft. Remove them from the water and reserve the liquid. Wash the mushrooms under warm water to remove any sand. Pat dry with a towel, and chop fine, along with the carrots, celery, onion, and half the garlic.

Flour the veal shanks completely and in a roasting pan heat the oil over medium-high heat. Brown the shanks on both sides for about 10 minutes. After the shanks are done, remove them from the pan and set aside.

Pour off any excess oil in the pan and add the mushrooms, carrots, celery, and onions. Sauté the vegetables until soft, about 10 minutes. Deglaze with the wine and reduce completely. Preheat the oven to 350°F.

Put the veal shanks back in the pan on top of the sautéed vegetables. Add the stock and the tomato sauce and strained liquid from the mushrooms, cover the pan with foil, and cook in the oven for 1 1/2 to 2 hours.

Ten to 15 minutes before you are done, chop the zest of 1 lemon, the remaining garlic, and the anchovies. Melt the butter in a small saucepan, add the anchovies and garlic, and cook for 2 minutes. Remove from the heat and add the lemon zest and the chopped parsley. Stir until combined, then add it to the veal shanks when done. Season with salt and black pepper.

SERVES 6 TO 8

Personally, I loved the Beatles, but Flora had a strong point to make about the people you met in "the music business." On my first visit, Jim took me into the kitchen and uncomfortably stood me next to his mom. We were three strong-willed people and Jim was postured firmly between us to depolarize our energies. He introduced me to his mother, and Flora's response was "Uh-huh." She had a very, very dry sense of humor and I wasn't getting it.

I was as polite as I knew how to be, but there were no hugs for me. Not much more was said between us that night. But I observed a lot. First off, this woman could cook. Her food was awesome, it was a "family" thing.

I also recognized that Jim and his mom had a private admiration for each other. Not demonstrative, on her part, but very deep and sometimes difficult to express. They were similar in their command for attention, Jim with his stories and his music and Flora with her dry, cutting sense of humor and, of course, her *delicious* food.

You'll get lots of hugs with this risotto.

SPRING RISOTTO WITH SEARED SCALLOPS, CORN, ASPARAGUS, AND TOMATOES

6 cups chicken stock
6 tablespoons olive oil
1/2 cup onions, diced
1 tablespoon fresh ginger, minced
1 1/2 cups arborio rice
1/4 cup shiitake mushrooms
1 cup tomatoes, diced
1/2 cup asparagus tips (if unavailable,
  use broccoli florets cooked al dente)

1/2 cup fresh English peas
1/2 cup corn kernels
3 tablespoons cold butter
1 pound large scallops
1/4 cup white wine
1 tablespoon fresh lemon juice
4 tablespoons Parmesan cheese,
  grated
Salt and pepper, to taste

BRING THE CHICKEN STOCK to a hard simmer. In a separate pot, heat 3 tablespoons olive oil. Add the onions and cook until soft, about 5 minutes. Add the ginger and cook 1 minute more. Add the rice and stir until well coated. Begin adding the broth, 1/2 cup at a time. When the rice has absorbed most of the liquid and is almost dry, add an additional 1/2 cup of stock. Continue this process until the rice is creamy yet still firm. This will take approximately 30 minutes. Watch the risotto carefully and stir often.

While the risotto cooks, begin preparing the vegetables and scallops. Heat the remaining 3 tablespoons olive oil in a separate medium-size pot or large skillet. Add the mushrooms and cook until soft, about 5 minutes. Add the tomatoes, asparagus, peas, and corn to the pan and cook 5 minutes. Add this vegetable mixture to the risotto during the last 5 minutes of cooking. In the same large skillet as you cooked the vegetables, add 1 tablespoon of the butter, heat, and then add the scallops to the pan. Cook quickly, about 1 minute per side. Add to the risotto just before you serve. Add wine and lemon juice to the risotto. Adjust the seasonings. Add the remaining butter and cheese and serve.

SERVES 4

Jim and I began dating heavily when I was a junior in high school and he a junior at Villanova University. We sang together as a duo and practiced every day after school. Our dates usually started early. First we'd rehearse our songs and then listen to records of Bob Dylan, the Beatles, or Bessie Smith. After dinner, at his house or mine, Jim would tutor me in history and geography. Then we'd park in the lot of the Baptist church down the street from my house. Still not very good at memorizing facts, I learned my geography quickly in the backseat of Jim's VW bug. After my lesson, we'd make out until my eleven o'clock curfew interrupted our fun. "We were only kids, but then/I've never heard it said/that kids can't fall in love/and feel the same. I can still remember the first time I told you 'I love you'" (Jim Croce, "Alabama Rain," *Time in a Bottle*).

In spite of Jim's parents' concerns, our love persisted. After several visits to Jim's home for family get-togethers, I wasn't going to leave. It was then that I developed my "impressive" recipe for Ingrid's Vegetarian Lasagna. It didn't necessarily win Flora over, but she ate every bite.

Alabama Rain

Lazy days in mid-July
country Sunday mornings
dusty haze on summer hiways
sweet magnolias callin
now & then I find myself thinkin of the days
when we were
walkin in the Alabama rain

Drive-in movies Friday night
drinking beer & laughin
somehow things were always right
~~Kids~~ just don't know what happened
still I cant forget
the way you said my name   when we were
walkin in the Alabama Rain

we were only kids, but then
Ive never heard it said
that kids cant fall in love
and feel the same
I can still remember the 1st time
I told you I love you

on a dusty mid July
country ~~summertime~~ evenin.
weepin willow sang a lullaby
and saw (shared) our secret

& I go wooooo — just
like James Brown

Original words to "Alabama Rain,"
handwritten by Jim Croce.

INGRID'S VEGETARIAN LASAGNA

❧ ❧

This has been a favorite comfort food at Croce's since we opened. Because it takes a lot of time to prepare (two to three hours), I often make at least two lasagnas at the same time, even at home. Lasagna always tastes best after it has had a chance to settle. It can be assembled ahead of time for company and baked when you are ready to serve it.

Marinara Sauce (see directions below)
Lasagna Noodles (see directions below)
Breaded Eggplant (see directions below)
12 to 14 thin slices Provolone cheese
Lemon Ricotta Mixture (see directions below)

12 to 14 thin slices of mozzarella cheese
1 cup Parmesan cheese, grated
1 cup basil, freshly chopped

PREHEAT OVEN to 350°F. In the bottom of a 9 x 13-inch baking pan, spoon 1/2 cup of Marinara Sauce. Cover it with a layer of 3 or 4 spinach Lasagna Noodles to cover the bottom of the pan. Pour 1 cup of Marinara Sauce over the pasta, followed by 1 layer of Breaded Eggplant (about 8 slices). Cover the eggplant with a layer of Provolone, about 6 to 8 slices, and spread the Lemon Ricotta Mixture evenly over the top. Cover with a layer of semolina lasagna noodles (6 to 8) and place a mantle of sliced mozzarella on top of the noodles and cover with the rest of the Marinara Sauce. Top with Parmesan cheese and fresh basil.

Refrigerate the lasagna until ready to bake. Bake for 45 to 55 minutes until bubbly and golden brown. Allow 15 minutes for the lasagna to set before cutting into large squares and putting on a plate. Allow the lasagna to cool before refrigerating, and cover securely.

If you are freezing your "extra" lasagna, cut the cooking time to 30 minutes, allowing it to cool before covering it tightly and freezing.

Marinara Sauce

1 tablespoon extra virgin olive oil

1 medium yellow onion, diced

3 cloves garlic, finely minced

Salt and pepper, to taste

1 cup mushrooms

1 1/2 cups zucchini, diced

1 1/2 cups yellow squash, diced

1/2 teaspoon thyme

1/2 teaspoon oregano

1/2 teaspoon dried basil

2 cups fresh tomatoes, diced

30-ounce jar of your favorite
tomato sauce

1/2 bay leaf

HEAT THE OLIVE OIL in a large nonreactive saucepan. Sauté the onion, garlic, salt, and pepper until tender. Stir in the mushrooms and sauté for 2 minutes. Add the zucchini, yellow squash, thyme, oregano, and basil and sauté for 5 minutes. Add the tomatoes and cook 5 minutes more. The vegetables should be tender, but not browned. Remove to large saucepan and add the tomato sauce and 1/2 bay leaf if desired. Simmer the sauce for about 30 minutes or until it has thickened and the flavors are blended. Remove from the heat, season to taste with salt and pepper, and set aside.

This recipe makes 7 to 8 cups of marinara sauce.

Lasagna Noodles

1 tablespoon plus 1 teaspoon olive oil

12 to 14 semolina lasagna noodles

12 to 14 spinach lasagna noodles

BOIL A LARGE POT of salted water and add a tablespoon of olive oil. Gently lay a couple of lasagna noodles in the briskly boiling water and remove them when they are al dente, about 1 minute. Place them in a bowl of cold water with a teaspoon of olive oil to prevent further cooking and to keep the noodles from sticking together.

Breaded Eggplant

2 medium eggplants

Salt

2 eggs, beaten

1 clove garlic, crushed

3 tablespoons extra virgin olive oil

2 cups dry panko crumbs (Japan-

1 cup milk or half-and-half   ese bread crumbs) or
Pinch salt and pepper   unseasoned bread crumbs

WASH THE EGGPLANT, cut off the top, and slice crosswise. Sprinkle with salt and
arrange the slices on a plate at an angle. Put a weight on top of it to sweat the
"aubergines," allowing the juices to drain for 1 to 2 hours. Dry the eggplant slices
with a paper towel.

Preheat the oven to 375°F. Mix the eggs, milk, and salt and pepper in a bowl. Stir
the crushed garlic into the olive oil in a cup. Lightly coat a baking sheet with the
garlic-olive oil mixture.

Dip each slice of eggplant on both sides in the egg batter and then into the
bread crumbs. Tap in the bread crumbs with your palm to get a good adherence to
the surface. Shake off the excess crumbs and place breaded slices of eggplant on the
baking sheet. Bake for about 10 minutes on each side until the eggplant is tender.

LEMON RICOTTA MIXTURE

2 pounds ricotta cheese   Juice of 1 lemon
3 eggs, beaten   Salt and pepper, to taste
Zest of 1 lemon

PUT THE RICOTTA in a medium-size bowl and stir in the eggs; add the remaining ingredients and mix together.

MAKES 2 LASAGNAS, EACH OF WHICH SERVES 6 TO 8

For entertainment, besides playing our music, we'd go down to The First Ward
Italian Club near Passyunk Avenue and Tasker Street in Philadelphia and
watch "Pa," Jim's maternal grandfather, Massimo Babusci, play bocci with his
cronies, and we'd dine on the daily offerings. While the regulars at the club were
at home and seemingly unaffected by the excellence of their cuisine, I was trans-
fixed by the rich aromas, the stinky stogies, and the hotheaded conversations.

Linguine with Clams, Arugula, and Roasted Garlic

಄ ฾

1/2 cup garlic cloves, roasted

1 cup plus 1 tablespoon olive oil

12 ounces dry linguine

1 cup white wine

1 cup clam juice

1 tablespoon garlic, chopped

32 raw clams

4 tablespoons butter

2 cups loosely packed arugula

Salt and pepper, to taste

Parmesan cheese, for garnish

Chopped parsley, for garnish

PREHEAT THE OVEN TO 350°F. Mix whole garlic cloves with 1 tablespoon olive oil. Roast on a sheet pan for 10 to 15 minutes or until light brown. Set aside, and peel when cooked.

While the garlic is roasting, cook the pasta in salted boiling water until al dente. Rinse and set aside.

In a large pan, heat the remaining oil over medium-high heat. Add the wine, clam juice, roasted garlic, and chopped garlic, and bring to a boil. Add the clams. Cover and steam until all the clams are open. Remove the clams from the pan and set aside. Reduce the liquids in the pan until slightly thickened. This will take 5 to 7 minutes. Add the clams, butter, and linguine and cook 2 to 3 minutes more. Just before serving, add the arugula and seasonings to taste.

Garnish with Parmesan cheese and parsley.

SERVES 4

When Jim asked me to marry him, I was a freshman at the Rhode Island School of Design. We drove to Cape Cod for our first romantic weekend together. On a windy winter's night Jim played a melody he had written for me called "Ingrid." He placed a diamond engagement ring on my finger, one he had saved for with great pride. When we awoke in each other's arms the next morning, I was filled with love and I was absolutely starving.

Newlyweds. Jim is on his way to Fort Jackson, South Carolina, for Army National Guard boot camp, September 1967.

Photograph by James Albert Croce

Downstairs in the lobby, I drank my first cup of coffee ever. Aroused by the pleasure of sharing breakfast with my fiancé for the first time, I reveled in our meal. And then we went back upstairs for dessert. . . .

In 1966 Jim Croce and I were married at my family's home. We exchanged our vows under a huppah, a traditional Jewish wedding canopy, in what was once Dick Clark's backyard. While I was away at college, Jim had studied with Rabbi Kaplan and, on his own, decided to convert to Judaism. During Jim's personal "excommunication," my dad and Jim had spent many long hours discussing psychology, philosophy, and religion and were becoming father and son.

At the same time Jim was becoming a Jew, I was away at the Rhode Island School of Design investigating Italian cooking and Christianity. In many ways we were trading places. I was intrigued by "Mystic Pizza" and the secrets of the Catholic Church. Jim was drawn to the

Jim on patrol at Fort Jackson, 1967.

freedom of questioning authority and the lifestyle of continued education that my heritage encouraged.

Our opposites were engaging us, and we were "stirring the stew."

¶¶

When Jim graduated from Villanova in 1965, he traveled for the State Department as a "musical" cultural liaison and then, the week we were wed, he went away to Fort Jackson, South Carolina, with the Army National Guard. We missed each other terribly, but we exchanged love letters every day, and our passion and admiration for each other were intensified by distance.

Then in December my dear father passed away and Jim was given "heartship" leave from completing his obligation with the guard. When he came home, to keep his commitment to my dad that he would support me through college, Jim took a job teaching special education to some "wild-ass" junior high school students in Chester, Pennsylvania. While his scholars were slashing his tires and bashing our car, I transferred from the Rhode Island School of Design to Moore College of Art in Philadelphia and studied painting, pottery, and education.

I was the "celebrity" in our family: painting and potting at art school, winning fellowships to Mexico, and applying to graduate school at Yale.

My husband was so good to me. Every night he'd come home from the student war zone, prepare delicious meals, and pick me up at the Media train station for dinner. While Jim Croce was famous for his extraordinary musical repertoire of over two thousand songs, in the culinary arena his skills were just as impressive.

STUFFED ARTICHOKES

❧ ☙

1 teaspoon salt

2 tablespoons white vinegar

1 cup mortadella cheese,
    chopped

4 large artichokes
1 lemon, halved
1/2 cup onions, minced
3 tablespoons unsalted butter
1 cup mushrooms, sliced
1 cup zucchini, chopped
1 egg

Juice of 1 lemon
1/2 cup plus 2 teaspoons Parmesan
    cheese, freshly grated
2 tablespoons extra virgin olive oil
1 clove garlic, minced
2 cups flavored bread crumbs
1/2 cup balsamic vinegar,
    for dipping

PREHEAT THE OVEN TO 400°F. In a covered stainless-steel saucepan large enough to hold the artichokes, put 2 cups salted water and the vinegar and bring to a boil. Slice about 1 inch off the tops of the center cone of the artichokes and cut the stalks so that they will sit flat. Rub the surfaces with one of the lemon halves. Put the artichokes in the water and simmer, covered, for about 30 minutes. When the leaves pull off easily, put the artichokes on a rack; cool and drain them upside down. Remove the center leaves and the choke with a spoon and cut the tips off all leaves.

You will need a deep casserole skillet that can later accommodate the standing artichokes. Sauté the onion in 1 tablespoon of butter over moderate heat, stirring until translucent, 3 to 5 minutes, then transfer to a bowl. Sauté the mushrooms and zucchini in the remaining butter over moderate heat. Add the vegetable mixture to the bowl. Mix in the egg, mortadella, the juice of 1/2 lemon, and 1/2 cup Parmesan. In a separate large saucepan heat the olive oil with the garlic and add bread crumbs. Remove from the heat and stir in the completed vegetable and bread crumbs mixture. Stuff the artichokes with the mixture. Set the artichokes upright in a baking dish with water below the first leaf, about 1 cup. Sprinkle the juice of 1/2 lemon and 1/2 teaspoon Parmesan cheese over each artichoke. Bake them, covered, for 30 minutes.

Serve with balsamic vinegar for dipping.

SERVES 4

Jim Croce's charm and intelligence could have landed him almost any job, but his heart was still in music. To make ends meet, he took a second job with a black-music radio station, WDDS. Jim began writing commercials and was soon promoted to selling airtime. But after the third threat on his life by a pool shark in Fu-Fu's Bar, Jim left his sales ambitions in the 'hood and went back to driving a truck with his good buddy Billy Reid in the country. Jim's "character development" during these times later inspired him to write his standards, "You Don't Mess Around with Jim" and "Bad, Bad Leroy Brown." He'd take sandwiches of Broccoli Rabe on crusty Italian bread to work with him—this was Jim's all-time favorite lunch.

Broccoli Rabe with Olive Oil and Garlic

Be sure to use broccoli rabe that is bright green with small florets and tender stalks.

2 pounds cleaned broccoli rabe, washed and trimmed
1/4 cup extra virgin olive oil
2 teaspoons garlic, finely minced
2 tablespoons lemon juice
1/2 teaspoon salt

1/8 teaspoon pepper, freshly ground
1 cup water
1 Meyer lemon, sliced thin, for garnish

Separate the leaves and the flowers of the broccoli rabe and chop them into 3-inch pieces. In a 3-quart saucepan that will hold all of the broccoli rabe, sauté the olive oil and garlic over moderate heat for about 1 minute to flavor the oil. Add the broccoli rabe and toss with tongs to keep the greens from browning. Add the water, lemon juice, and salt and pepper and cook 1 minute longer. Garnish with the lemon slices and olive oil if desired.

Serves 6

Every opportunity, we would indulge Jim's passion by singing our songs in local bars and coffeehouses, secretly planning our future. In addition to our busy daytime gigs, four nights a week we played for our supper and twenty-five bucks at a funky little club in Lima, Pennsylvania, called the Riddle Paddock. Here we'd offer up our new songs to the unruly crowds, consoled by the great response and by believing that someday Jim would make music his career.

🍴

Once Jim and I were married, Flora and I became a team. After breaking her washing machine, flooding her floor, burning her bread, and giving up on being as neat and clean as she, I learned to appreciate her ways, not copy them.

Mom (now eighty-three) and I are still good friends who appreciate each other's differences. She's still the matriarch of the family, and though she'd never admit it, under her curmudgeon facade she's a wonderful person.

This next dish is for the Flower.

FRIED ZUCCHINI BLOSSOMS

8 to 10 zucchini blossoms
1 cup all-purpose flour
1 tablespoon extra virgin olive oil
Water as needed
1 tablespoon dark sesame oil
1 clove garlic, minced
1 cup zucchini, finely diced

1 cup coarse-textured bread crumbs
1 tablespoon parsley or cilantro, chopped
Vegetable oil, for deep-frying
Salt and pepper, to taste

WHEN I GREW my own squash, and got intimate with zucchini, I learned the difference between the male and the female flowers and found the male stalk to grow the finest blossoms (the female stalk is too busy growing the fruit).

Cut the stalk close to the flower and remove the pistils. Mix the flour and olive oil, adding enough water to keep the batter from becoming "runny" and refrigerate, covered, for 30 minutes.

While the batter is refrigerating, quickly heat the sesame oil in a saucepan and sauté the garlic, zucchini, bread crumbs, and parsley (or cilantro) for 2 to 3 minutes over medium heat. Allow the mixture to cool. Fill each blossom with as much of the mixture as it can hold, closing the flower around the stuffing.

While you heat the vegetable oil over medium-high heat to almost boiling, dip each stuffed blossom into the batter. Fry until golden on all sides, 2 to 3 minutes. Season with salt and pepper and drain on paper towels. Serve immediately.

This makes an excellent first course or side dish.

SERVES 4

In September 1968 we settled into a wonderful two-hundred-year-old townhouse in Media, Pennsylvania, that I had proudly scored for one hundred dollars a month. Soon after, we got a portentous phone call from Jim's college buddy Tommy Picardo, who had moved to New York to become a record producer. Tommy was familiar with the music Jim and I were performing at local bars and coffeehouses, and he called to ask if we could move to New York to record an album for Capitol Records.

The next day we moved into an apartment on the Upper East Side with Tommy and his first wife, Pat Rosalia. After signing contracts, we went into the studio and a week later we'd recorded our first album, *Jim and Ingrid Croce,* co-produced by Cashman, Pistilli, and West and the famous Nik Venet, who produced such artists as Bobby Darin, the Beach Boys, and Linda Ronstadt.

After the record was released, we toured the United States and Canada from one college to the next, driving Jim's old rusted-out VW that we fondly called The Raisin. While traveling over 100,000 miles that year, we mostly lived on good ole American blue plate specials at colorful truck stops and cafés. Jim and I were young, broke, and so much in love, we weren't dismayed about the modest gigs we played or the roadside cuisine we suffered, as long as we were doing it together.

Sometimes we got lucky and found culinary paradise in the most unexpected places. Before fast food took over like the plague, folks could savor the finest of family recipes sitting on a stool at a corner café.

Other times we were welcomed in by generous fans. This was my favorite part of traveling. What a treat to be invited home by people you'd never met before. Along with the comfortable fare of Southern fried chicken, bone-marrow sandwiches, hush puppies, and grits, these were invitations to visit the hearts of people all across America. Their invitations filled us with great joy, and provided Jim with his wonderful songs and stories.

🍴

Finally, after a year on the road, we returned to a tiny rented apartment in an enormous dirty old building in the Bronx. It was awful. It even had bars on the windows, so you wouldn't jump out!

Without any gigs or money, there we remained, cooped up, practicing and writing every day, patiently waiting for our careers to skyrocket. We lived on toasted bagels and cream cheese, saving every penny we had for gas to get into the city and search for work.

At Easter we treated ourselves to San Gennaro, the "Italian Feast" in Greenwich Village, stuffing our faces with roasted pepper and egg sandwiches on crusty Italian rolls and creamy homemade Italian cannoli. Feasts, but mostly famine, filled our days. Food was precious. A fleshy red pomegranate was my Christmas surprise from Jim that year. They've been a special reminder of my good fortune ever since.

🍴

In the summer of 1970, Jim and I wrote about thirty original American folk songs for a children's show we were commissioned to do in Boston, only to discover that Hoagy Carmichael had gotten our job. Several of these songs, along with cuts from our Capitol album and some unreleased sides, have been remastered for the *Jim Croce Anthology—Fiftieth Anniversary* CD: "Spin, Spin, Spin," "Vespers," "Big Wheel," "And I Remember Her," "Cottonmouth River," "More Than That Tomorrow," "The Migrant Worker," "Child of Midnight," "Stone Walls," "King's Song," "Walkin' Back to Georgia," "Hey Tomorrow," and "Age."

About this time, we were joined in our tiny Bronx apartment by John Stockfish, Gordon Lightfoot's former bass player, and his wife, Pat, from British Columbia. We practiced our new music and later that summer we toured together on Cape Cod. One of the restaurants where we played, The Ship's Fare, served the most delicious stuffed lobster tail ever. As part of our payment for performing, I was offered langostino for breakfast, lunch, and dinner. I took their proposition seriously and ate a lifetime's worth in a week and a half.

Though this New England circuit was fun and filling and a great respite from the city, the fact was that our hearts were broken. After all our traveling there was no support from our record company, and careerwise, the failure of our first album was imminent.

Finally we decided it might be time to move back home to Pennsylvania, out to the country. Jim gladly gave up the little work he had playing backup for commercials, singing some "oohs" and "aahs" in New York studios. Ready to get out of the city, we left to find ourselves a home.

🍴

Jim was distraught by his failure in the music industry. A tempest of despair surrounded him as we packed our things. With his adrenaline pumping, he carried our air conditioner down seventeen flights of stairs. Attempting to vent his anger by throwing the heavy weapon on the landlord's front step, sadly he missed, and with his toe throbbing, his back aching, and all our possessions piled high on the truck, he performed his final act of defeat. He heaved his bicycle up on top of our pile of belongings only to have it reverse direction and plummet down, catching his ear in the spokes of a wheel.

This was not a good day. As the blood was coagulating on Jim's ear and tears of pain were welling up in his big brown eyes, our friend Gene Pistilli wished us luck and hugged us good-bye.

We drove the rental truck with our old red Saab in tow. Without enough money to pay the toll to New Jersey, I threw a handful of pennies in the basket and Jim drove like a bat out of hell across the border. We felt like fugitives in our own land.

Once we reached the HoJo on the other side of the bridge, I looked back at the imposing skyline. It was majestic all right, but it had never felt like home.

This pasta tastes like home. It was so popular on our menu, we had to remove it for a while so our guests who got "focused" on it would try our other specialties too.

CROCE'S FETTUCCINE ALFREDO

☙ ❧

24 ounces dry semolina fettuccine
3 tablespoons olive oil
4 teaspoons garlic, chopped
5 cups heavy cream

1/2 cup Parmesan cheese, grated
Salt and white pepper, to taste
Chopped parsley or arugula, for
    garnish

PUT A LARGE POT of salted water on to boil. Cook the fettuccine while you're preparing the sauce. Heat a large saucepan until hot. Add the olive oil and garlic. Wait until garlic "blooms," that is, when it releases its aroma, then add the cream. When the cream comes to a boil, add the Parmesan and reduce for 2 to 3 minutes. Add the fettuccine, salt, and white pepper. Reduce the sauce to proper consistency. Garnish with the parsley or arugula.

SERVES 6

The Original Croce's Restaurant

Veggies, Greens, and Grains

Once home in Lyndell, Pennsylvania, Jim was stumped by the phone calls and threats we were receiving from his old friend and producer Tommy Picardo (now known as Tommy West) and our attorney, Phil, who also represented the publishing, management, and record company. They told Jim that no matter where we'd go, or what we'd write, it belonged to them forever, in perpetuity! And they had contracts to prove it. So much for friendship.

Being honest and poor, we just didn't know how to fight back. It was very confusing.

Try our Broccoli Almond Quiche; it's not confusing or confrontational at all. Just friendly.

Jim and Ingrid Croce in Lyndell, Pennsylvania, September 1971.

Photograph by Paul Wilson

Broccoli Almond Quiche

෴ ෴

2 tablespoons olive oil
6 cups raw broccoli, chopped
6 green onions, chopped
1/2 teaspoon salt
1/4 teaspoon white pepper
1 cup almonds, sliced
Pâte brisée dough (a French short
    dough, available in most
gourmet food stores;
    regular pie dough may also
    be used)
1 1/2 cups Swiss cheese or
    Gruyère, grated
Custard (see directions below)

HEAT THE OLIVE OIL in a medium-size sauté pan over medium heat. Add the broccoli and green onions. Stir constantly. Cook until the broccoli turns bright green. Season with salt and pepper. Remove from the heat. Add the almonds.

Flour your work surface and cut the dough into squares to fit individual tart pans. Press the pastry into greased tart pans and trim off the excess. The crust should be 1/4 inch over the edge of the pan.

Preheat the oven to 325°F. Spoon the filling equally into the tart pans. Place the grated cheese on top of the broccoli filling. Ladle the Custard into the tart pans to the top. Bake for 30 to 45 minutes, or until golden brown and the Custard has set. Remove from the oven and cool on a rack. Serve with a mixed green salad and Champagne Vinaigrette.

Custard

6 eggs
1 quart half-and-half
1 teaspoon salt
White pepper, to taste
1/4 teaspoon nutmeg

IN A LARGE BOWL stir the eggs well with the half-and-half, salt and pepper, and nutmeg.

MAKES 6 INDIVIDUAL QUICHES

The early seventies were a boom time for entrepreneurs, but Jim was not a businessman. He just wanted to make music, even if he couldn't make it pay. Always strapped for cash, he was continually conjuring up ways to make something happen. While driving trucks, Jim took his tape recorder in his cab and dictated a manual on "Buying and Selling Guitars." Better yet, he did one on "How to Succeed in the Music Business." At least his humor was intact!

Jim explored all kinds of notions, but when he wanted to put a weasel farm in our kitchen, I intervened. I was sure our kitchen was better served by simmering Summer Ratatouille than by raising weasels.

SUMMER RATATOUILLE

1/2 cup extra virgin olive oil
1 yellow onion, cut into
quarters and sliced coarsely
6 cloves garlic, minced
3 medium eggplants, sliced in half length-
wise and cut on the diagonal
into 1/2-inch pieces
2 medium bell peppers, seeded, deveined,
and chopped into 1/2-inch pieces
1 bay leaf
1 pound zucchini, sliced lengthwise
and cut on the diagonal into 1/2-inch pieces

2 cups vine-ripened tomatoes,
peeled, seeded, and chopped
1 cup tomato sauce
1/2 teaspoon salt
1/4 teaspoon pepper
3 tablespoons fresh basil,
finely chopped
1/2 teaspoon fresh oregano,
finely chopped
1/2 teaspoon thyme
1/2 cup Parmesan cheese, grated

HEAT THE OLIVE OIL over medium heat in a large skillet. Add the onion and garlic and sauté for 5 minutes. Stir in the eggplant and bell peppers and sauté for 8 to 10 minutes with the bay leaf. Add the zucchini, tomatoes, and tomato sauce with salt and pepper and stew the vegetables 15 to 20 minutes, or until tender. Remove the bay leaf and sprinkle the ratatouille with fresh basil, oregano, and thyme and serve on a bed of grilled polenta (see the recipe for Polenta del Pueblo, page 227) with Parmesan cheese.

SERVES 4

Living in the country, Jim was revitalized by his good friend Billy Reid and his other buddies, Frank, Emil, and Reds, a colorful bunch of rowdy, beer-drinkin' truck drivin' hard workin' construction guys. After work, the men brought their guitars and banjos to our house. They'd play country and blue-grass, brag about their outrageous escapades, and tell stories of one-upmanship, the likes of which were immortalized in "Rapid Roy" and "Roller Derby Queen" and stories I couldn't tell in public.

Jim's frail young accompanist, Maury Muehleisen, often our houseguest, inspired Jim in a different way. Songs like "Time in a Bottle," "Operator," and "Photographs and Memories" were conceived while Jim and Maury practiced

Jim Croce and his pals Reds and Emil at a construction site, testing some homemade dande-lion wine.

THYME IN A BOTTLE

together. Our young friend from Trenton, New Jersey, evoked Jim's deepest feelings. And Maury's sensitive, intelligent, and powerful guitar licks enhanced Jim's songwriting and arrangements. While Billy brought out the machismo in Jim, Maury brought out the sweetness and helped Jim to express his feelings in his songs.

Our tapenade is pungent yet delicate, served best with crisp bruschetta or soft fresh bread.

Tapenade with Bruschetta

1/8 cup capers, drained and rinsed
4 anchovy fillets
1/2 teaspoon fresh thyme
2 tablespoons brandy

1/8 cup extra virgin olive oil
2 cups black Niçoise olives, pitted
1 tablespoon orange juice
Bruschetta (see directions below)

Combine the capers, anchovies, thyme, brandy, and olive oil in a food processor and process until just blended. Add the olives and orange juice and pulse until well combined yet fairly coarse.

Bruschetta

Twelve 1 1/2-inch slices Italian bread
1/4 cup extra virgin olive oil

2 cloves garlic, peeled

Preheat the broiler. Using a pastry brush, coat the bread on both sides with olive oil. While the bread is hot, rub each side lightly with the garlic cloves. Serve immediately with the tapenade.

Serves 4 to 6

For weekends, and often for weeks, our friends and their "entourages" would come out to the country and stay with us. Jim loved having company, and sometimes Joe "Sal" Salvioulo, Gene Pistilli, Pat Rosalia, Erin Dickens, Marty Nelson, and Tim Hauser (the original Manhattan Transfer) would visit too. With a houseful of guests, we'd all sit around the living room and entertain ourselves for hours, taking turns practicing our new songs and "raps" and joining in.

I'd often raid my summer garden for plump, purple eggplants and fresh basil leaves for our guests. Today, Kathleen Daelemans makes this recipe for us.

GRILLED EGGPLANT WITH LEMON AND BASIL

1 eggplant, peeled or not, sliced lengthwise or crosswise into 1/4-inch slices

1 Maui, Vidalia, or Walla Walla onion, sliced very thin, or sliced thicker and grilled, as you prefer

1/4 cup olive oil, as needed

1 Meyer lemon, juiced

1 Meyer lemon, sliced paper thin

1 large very ripe tomato, diced

1/4 cup basil or flat-leaf parsley or a combination of the 2 cut into chiffonade (to cut into chiffonade, roll the leaves together tightly and cut in narrow slices in one direction only, to get narrow strips)

Black pepper, freshly ground

Salt, to taste

GRILL THE EGGPLANT SLICES. Grill the onion if you choose. The eggplant and onions can be grilled under the broiler. Put the slices on a cookie sheet and broil until they begin to brown. Turn and repeat for the other side. Drain on paper towels. Brown in a nonstick skillet with olive oil as needed.

In a small bowl, combine the olive oil, lemon juice, sliced lemon, tomato, and the herbs. Begin to layer the eggplant and onions in a shallow dish by starting with a layer of eggplant. Drizzle the oil/lemon mixture over the eggplant. Put down a layer of onions, drizzle more of the oil/lemon dressing. Continue to layer the vegetables alternately; be sure to drizzle the dressing on the vegetable layers as you construct the salad. Serve cold or at room temperature.

Variation I: Grilled eggplant is great drizzled with a little olive oil and balsamic vinegar, salt, and freshly ground pepper and served at room temperature.

Variation II: Follow the original recipe but omit the lemon slices and substitute 1/4 cup more or less of balsamic vinegar for the lemon juice.

SERVES 4 AS AN ENTRÉE OR 8 AS AN APPETIZER

On rare occasions when there were just two of us in the house, Jim Croce's perfect morning meant waking up early and doing his own thing: brewing a pot of strong Italian espresso, sitting down at the kitchen table with a couple of good books, a pad of paper, a tape recorder, and a six- and twelve-string guitar.

An hour or so later, when I was still asleep in our cozy bed, Jim would wake me gently with a traditional demitasse of thick, black Italian coffee topped with a lemon zest and a kiss. This wake-up call from my best friend meant he wanted to make love, or guests had unexpectedly arrived and Jim wanted me to give *them* my attention.

Our neighbor George Spillane, who absolutely adored sharing time with Jim and his music, anticipated my husband's morning routine. He would allow a polite amount of time to pass after hearing the sound of Jim's guitar, and would then be at our back screen door, coffee cup in hand, ready for some morning music and conversation. Jim never minded interruptions. I always did! (Nothing personal, George.)

You can interrupt me anytime you want with our Vegetable Frittata with Pancetta. This recipe is dedicated to George Spillane, for being such a wonderful friend.

Vegetable Frittata with Pancetta

3 ounces pancetta or slab bacon

1 to 2 tablespoons butter (or vegetable oil)

1/2 cup scallions, chopped

2 small zucchini, sliced thin

1/2 cup green pepper, sliced thin

1 cup mushrooms

Salt and pepper, to taste

10 eggs

6 tablespoons Gruyère or Parmesan cheese, grated

Sprinkle of fresh parsley or arugula

PREHEAT THE OVEN TO 325°F. Put the pancetta or bacon in a heavy-bottomed skillet and fry until crisp. Remove from the pan, put on paper towels to drain, and crumble. Save the bacon fat for later.

In a clean skillet, melt the butter or oil and sauté the scallions, zucchini, green peppers, and mushrooms. Season with salt and pepper. Beat the eggs and crumbled bacon in the bowl. Heat a large saucepan and add 2 teaspoons butter and the egg mixture. Use a rubber spatula to pull the egg mixture into the center of the pan. Do this until the eggs are lightly cooked.

Pour the vegetable mixture on top of the eggs and cook for 3 minutes until light brown. Tip the frittata over onto a flat lid and slide it back into the pan to brown the other side. Remove from the heat while the center is still moist and reserve in the oven until the center of the frittata is firm.

Slice in wedges, "pizza-style," and serve hot or at room temperature. Grated Gruyère or Parmesan cheese may be sprinkled on top while the frittata is hot. Garnish with fresh parsley or arugula when you're ready to serve.

Serve with red potatoes with prosciutto and chives.

SERVES 8

One of my painting professors, Harold Jacobs, and his wife, Berénice, from Paris, lived down the road from us in an old restored mill house with a pond. Our friends invited us to their home for dinner one night, and when we arrived I felt like Jim and I were entering an artist's chateau in southern France.

Harold's large canvasses and sculptures filled the white stuccoed walls and niches with sensual forms and color, and the aroma of Berénice's fancy five-course dinner and French apple tarts baking in the oven brought tears to my eyes.

As a young artist, I was struck by the enormous amount of time Berénice poured into her sophisticated and intricately prepared banquet. And I was naively saddened to think that while a painting was tangible and timeless, a meal seemed elusive and fleeting. Today, my paintings are long forgotten, but my first homemade French meal stands out as a highlight and as a critical ingredient in my selection of work and my quest for excellence.

This recipe for a French apple tart, offered by pastry chef Karen Krasne, of Extraordinary Desserts in San Diego, tastes a lot like the one that changed my life.

FRENCH TART TATIN

৪৯ ৪৯

Prebaked tart shell
   (can be a store-bought puff pastry)
1 egg, lightly beaten
4 tablespoons unsalted butter,
   room temperature

8 golden delicious apples,
   peeled, cored, and halved
1 cup plus 2 tablespoons sugar

PREHEAT THE OVEN TO 375°F to 400°F (depending on the oven). Cut out a 10-inch circle of the puff pastry dough. Paint the dough with the egg, prick it with a fork, and place it on a greased baking sheet. Bake for 15 minutes.

Rub butter on the bottom of a 9- or 10-inch sauté pan. Cut the apples so that each of their bottoms is flat and will fit on the skillet bottom evenly. Arrange a layer of apples in a circle on top of the butter, putting one next to the other tightly. Spread the extra ends, which have been cut off, over all the other apples. Sprinkle with the sugar and place the skillet over a low flame on the stove. Leave on the stove for approximately 45 minutes.

When the sugar and butter have caramelized and the apples are tender, take off the stove and cool for 5 minutes. Invert onto the baked tart shell. Serve with crème fraîche or vanilla ice cream.

SERVES 8

I believe the trait of generosity is inherited and wonderfully contagious. I have never met a more charitable group of people in my life than the Croces and the Babuscis (Jim's mom's family). These folks can't do enough for you, and food is an offering they present like a sacrament. At our home, morning began with "baptism"—that is, welcoming the day with friends, food, and song.

Once I arrived in our kitchen, it was time to make bread, bake muffins, and pick some squash and herbs from our garden. Jim would head down the road to Frank's Folly general store for eggs, thick-slab bacon, a six-pack of beer, and Frank's local chatter.

If George hadn't joined us by then, it was certain our good friend Sal or Maury had stayed the night and would be playing music at our kitchen table. Soon, my best friend, Judy Coffin, would surely follow, bringing something beautiful, strange, or funny to add to our bounty, along with her young sons Andy, Jake, and Ed, and there would always be big hugs all around and lots of delicious small talk about our neighbors.

These were times when "Give us this day our daily bread" had real meaning.

CHALLAH FRENCH TOAST

3 eggs
1/4 cup half-and-half

8 thick slices challah
(egg bread)

Pinch salt

1 tablespoon vanilla extract

1 tablespoon Cointreau

4 tablespoons butter

1/2 cup confectioners' sugar

Maple syrup, warmed

BRISKLY STIR THE EGGS, half-and-half, and salt in a medium-size bowl with a fork. Transfer the mixture to a wide, shallow bowl and add the vanilla and Cointreau. Lay the slices of bread on a cutting board and pierce the surface of each piece of challah several times with the tongs of the fork to encourage the bread to absorb the egg mixture. Dip the bread into the egg mixture coating both sides. Remove from mixture and set aside.

Preheat the oven to 250°F. Melt 2 tablespoons of the butter in a large skillet that will hold 3 slices of bread at a time. Fry the challah bread over medium heat, until lightly brown, turning once. Place the warm French toast on a large serving plate and heat in the oven (do not stack the French toast). Fry the remaining slices and add them to the serving plate in the oven until all the French toast is thoroughly cooked but not dry. Sprinkle with confectioners' sugar. Serve with warm maple syrup.

SERVES 4

I was an enormous optimist. At every turn I felt that financial prosperity and success were right around the bend. Though fame and fortune kept eluding us, we were so damn happy that money became an issue only when our health insurance premiums were due, or we ran out of cigarettes. (Yes, health-conscious me smoked back then. It just seemed so "cool." And I was dreadfully addicted.)

Then one day I got tired of waiting for our ship to come in on the farm. I decided it was way past time for Jim to quit his day gig and work on his music full-time again. There had to be a way.

I wrote down my first recipe for my delicious Mama's Cheese Blintzes and sent it in to a Pillsbury bake contest that was offered on the flour wrapper. Thinking the prize of ten thousand dollars would be enough for us to live on for the rest of our lives, I just knew I had to win it! Funny how things happen; the check never came, but instead something even more wonderful did.

I remember when I told Jim we were going to have a baby. The look on his face was a combination of utter fear and sheer ecstasy. Though he was excited about building a family, his big brown eyes registered panic and "Oh my God, more responsibility!" But once Jim got over the initial shock of becoming a father he found a new sense of urgency to make his career successful as a singer and songwriter.

From the moment he learned I was pregnant, Jim felt this was his last chance, before the baby came, to make music his profession and provide for his family too. That night, he sat down at our little kitchen table and recorded the haunting melody and the words for "Time in a Bottle." The next morning, he played it for me.

> If I could save time in a bottle
> The first thing that I'd like to do
> Is to save every day like a treasure and then,
> Again I would spend them with you.
> But there never seems to be enough time,
> To do the things you want to do, once you find them.
> I've looked around enough to know,
> That you're the one I want to go through time with.
> (I hope she's kind with you.)

That very week Jim also completed "New York's Not My Home," "Operator," "You Don't Mess Around with Jim," and half the songs on his first gold album. This time, when Jim sent a cassette of his music to Tommy (Picardo) West, his producer, things really started to happen. From that point on, Jim's obscurity was over, and although fortune never came to him while he was alive, fame was just around the corner.

I discovered in 1971 that small zucchini are best. I like to buy or grow them about four inches long. I learned this firsthand when I planted my first garden outside our kitchen door.

I watched the squash grow and grow, and when they were looking as plump and as pregnant as I was, I picked one excitedly and dragged it up the hill to my landlord, John Kaltenbach. I was so proud.

I flaunted it to big John, thinking that he'd be amazed by my green thumb. But he just took one look at my "prize" and told me, "Stuff it!"

STUFFED ZUCCHINI

2 gigantic zucchini
Salt and pepper, to taste
2 teaspoons vegetable or olive oil
1 large onion, chopped
1 medium tomato,
   peeled, seeded, and chopped
1/2 cup canned chickpeas
   (garbanzo beans)

1 tablespoon parsley, chopped
1/2 teaspoon cinnamon
1/2 teaspoon cumin
1/3 cup basmati rice
3 cups Light Tomato Sauce
   (see page 87)

CUT THE ZUCCHINI in half lengthwise and scoop out the pulp. Roughly chop the scooped portion for the stuffing. Sprinkle the boat-shaped shells with a pinch of salt and pepper, and set aside.

Heat a saucepan with 1 teaspoon of vegetable or olive oil. Add the onion and cook until golden. Add the zucchini pulp and sauté for 5 minutes. Add the tomato and cook 5 minutes more. Remove from the heat and quickly stir in the chickpeas, parsley, cinnamon, cumin, and salt and pepper to taste. Stir in the uncooked basmati rice.

Preheat the oven to 350°F. Oil one large casserole dish. Cover the bottom of the dish with 1 cup of tomato sauce. Arrange the hollowed zucchini boats in the dish on top of the sauce. Stuff each boat evenly, cover loosely with foil, and bake for 30 to 40 minutes or until the rice is cooked through. After baking the zucchini boats, spoon the balance of the tomato sauce over each "boat" to moisten.

SERVES 4

Jim postponed his touring so he could help deliver our son. Though Jim suggested we do the Lamaze method, he refused going to class and opted for teaching me himself. On the delivery table while I practiced breathing in between singing "Yankee Doodle," the only song that came to mind, Jim was by my side with his guitar in hand, keeping time.

Two weeks after Adrian James was born on September 28, 1971, Jim took to the road. Then, overnight, "You Don't Mess Around with Jim" was being played everywhere. And Jim was out there promoting his hit single all over the world while I was in Lyndell, Pennsylvania, eating crow.

After eight years of performing and being with Jim constantly, I found the separation very painful. I missed him terribly.

Waiting at home with A. J., I was so lonely. Being the wife of a travelin' man is a difficult job to master, especially with a family to raise. To save money I did whatever I could to stay busy. I made Jim's shirts, batiked and tie-dyed place mats, and even made my own baby food as a regular part of my day. Once Adrian James was weaned, I would put a portion of whatever I cooked for myself into a small handheld food processor for him. Greens, grains, and pot roast were his favorites.

Couscous Salad
with Cucumbers and Tomatoes

⚘ ⚘

2 1/2 cups water (or stock)
Pinch salt
2 tablespoons unsalted butter
2 cups quick-cooking couscous
3 tablespoons extra virgin olive oil
2 cloves garlic, peeled
1 medium onion, finely chopped
1 cup cucumbers, finely chopped
1 cup tomatoes, finely chopped
1 cup sliced almonds, toasted

1/4 cup parsley, chopped
1/2 tablespoon fresh mint,
    finely chopped
3 tablespoons white wine vinegar,
    to taste
Salt and freshly ground pepper,
    to taste
1 bunch parsley or arugula,
    chopped, for garnish

IN A SAUCEPAN bring the water, salt, and butter to a boil. Put the couscous in a large mixing bowl and pour the boiling liquid over it. Cover it tightly for 5 minutes. Fluff the couscous gently with a fork. Stir in 1 tablespoon of the olive oil and allow to cool completely.

In a saucepan over medium heat, sauté the garlic and onions in the remaining olive oil for 5 to 7 minutes, until the onion is translucent and soft. Remove from the heat and fold in the cucumbers, tomatoes, almonds, parsley, and mint.

In a serving bowl, whisk together 2 tablespoons of the olive oil and vinegar, and gently toss the couscous with the dressing. Add all the ingredients from the saucepan and season with salt and pepper. Serve hot or cold, garnished with parsley or arugula.

SERVES 6

Though Jim was truly humble and never acted puffed up, fame is a double-edged sword, and it cut like a knife into our relationship. The longer he stayed out on the road, the more we felt the strain on our marriage. What we needed was some good time together like we used to have, around our own kitchen table, to share a meal and focus on what was really important.

Two years later, in 1973, Jim's second album topped the charts and he finally came home to relax with his family. We settled in to enjoy our time alone together, and the next day we were joined by an entire film crew! Fifteen people from Acorn Productions descended upon our house, unannounced to me, to record a promotional film of "Jim Croce at Home on the Farm."

Of course, I spontaneously squeezed fresh orange juice, baked banana bread (my original "poppers" recipe), prepared a vegetable frittata, grilled gingerbread pancakes, and ground the beans for freshly brewed coffee and espresso with lemon zest. The crew all stayed for lunch and dinner too, and then Jim generously invited them back the next day for some more.

Some things never changed. But sharing those days around our kitchen table started to mend some of the hurt feelings we'd both had while he was out on the road. Our warm Banana Bran Nut Poppers have a way of making difficult times feel okay.

THE ORIGINAL
BANANA BRAN NUT POPPER

శ్రీ ళ్య

2 cups whole-wheat flour
2 cups all-purpose flour
2 cups Quaker quick oats
2 teaspoons baking soda

2 teaspoons vanilla extract
1 cup brown sugar
1/2 cup butter or margarine,
    softened

10 very ripe bananas	*1 cup sour cream*
6 eggs	*1 cup walnuts, chopped*

PREHEAT THE OVEN TO 375°F. Measure the dry ingredients into a large mixing bowl and blend.

Mash the bananas in a separate bowl. Gently stir in the eggs, then add the vanilla, brown sugar, and butter. Slowly fold in the dry mixture, a little at a time. When all dry ingredients have been added, slowly fold in the sour cream, alternating with the walnuts.

Spray the popover pan with a vegetable spray, such as Pam, to prevent sticking. Bake poppers for 40 minutes, or until a straw inserted in the center of a popper comes out dry.

MAKES 16 POPPERS

After the film crew left, I questioned Jim about our finances. After a year and a half of Jim working hard on the road, we were barely making ends meet, but Jim wouldn't talk about it. He hated questions as much as he hated confrontation. He stormed out of our bedroom and went down to the kitchen table to brood.

The next morning he woke me gently by singing his new song. "Every time I tried to tell you/the words just came out wrong/so I'll have to say I love you, in a song."

When we were living in our little town of thirty-seven people, in Lyndell, Pennsylvania, I had no idea just how "big" Jim Croce had gotten. Certainly our bank account didn't show it. I'll never forget my first trip to Los Angeles when we went to the accountant's fancy offices. I felt so out of place and nearly got a stiff neck looking up at the tall buildings in Century City with their offices way at the top.

Then Elliott Abbott, Jim's road manager, took us for a ride up Sunset, and just as we were approaching Doheny Drive, Elliott told us to look up again. There was Jim's face, a thousand times bigger than life, on a double billboard above the street. The record company was promoting his second album, *Life and Times.* No wonder people stared at us wherever we went. I was so self-conscious and insecure being around all those professionals in their Gucci three-piece suits and fancy shoes, I thought it was just me and my Levi's they were staring at. But of course it was Jim, in his.

These Phyllo Purses will fit in anywhere. Ritzy or not.

PHYLLO PURSES
WITH BRIE AND SUNDRIED TOMATOES

⅋ ℔

2 tablespoons pine nuts
1/2 cup Sundried Tomato Pesto
   (see page 265)
2 tablespoons basil, chopped

1 1/2 pounds Brie cheese
9 sheets phyllo dough
1/8 cup olive oil

ROAST THE PINE NUTS in a saucepan over medium-high heat for 2 to 3 minutes, turning once.

Purée the Sundried Tomato Pesto with the basil and pine nuts in a food processor and set aside.

Preheat the oven to 350°F. Cut the Brie into 6 even triangular pieces. Place 3 sheets of the phyllo dough on a cutting board and brush each lightly with olive oil. Stack the sheets on top of each other and cut the stack in half widthwise forming 2 smaller rectangles. Place one wedge of the Brie on the lower edge of each stack of the cut phyllo dough. Top the Brie with 2 tablespoons of the tomato pesto filling. Carefully wrap the phyllo dough over the cheese, forming tightly wrapped triangles. Repeat the process two more times.

Coat a baking sheet with vegetable cooking spray. Put the 6 phyllo purses on it and bake to a golden brown, 5 to 7 minutes. Serve immediately.

SERVES 6

Once "You Don't Mess Around with Jim" reached number one on the charts, Jim started getting a whole lot of recognition, not just in the industry but also in the streets. By now he was a real star, and there was hardly anywhere he could go that someone didn't recognize his face or his name. As grateful as he was for the acceptance of his music, Jim was rather shy about being famous. When we were together he avoided crowds and conspicuous places, opting for unpopulated beaches or staying home.

Though he had renown, Jim's pockets were still empty. The fact is, he hardly had any pockets at all. By now we had moved to San Diego; one weekend, we went down to a thrift store in Ocean Beach to outfit him for the road.

As we were roaming the aisles of used jeans, the store clerk walked clumsily up to Jim to help him find stuff. When the clerk got a good look at Jim, his eyes bugged out and he spoke in a slow, stoned drawl.

"Hey man, you look just like Jim Croce, man. You could make a lot of money pretendin' to be him, man."

"Do ya think so?" Jim queried, and walked on shyly with a pair of used, faded blue jeans in hand, heading toward the counter.

A. J. Croce and his dad, 1972.

Photograph by Ingrid Croce

After paying for the Levi's with his last dollar, Jim was about to leave the store when the unsuspecting salesperson stopped Jim again.

"Hey man, I mean it. You look just like Jim Croce. He must be some kinda millionaire or something. You should try it, man."

We weren't aware of any millions. In fact, we were livin' on small potatoes, and deeply in the red.

After Jim Croce's first two albums were released and "You Don't Mess Around with Jim," "Time in a Bottle," and "Bad, Bad Leroy Brown" had topped the music charts, A&R man and close friend Corb Donahue played some of Jim's music to a young artist named Jimmy Buffet. Jim and Jimmy met first in L.A., then down in Florida, and later, whenever they could. They had a lot in common and their love of music, good stories, and crazy on-the-road lifestyles bonded them like brothers.

Jim had just written "Five Short Minutes of Love" in honor of young groupies (including the Plaster Casters), and Buffet's "Why Don't We Get Drunk and Screw" was Jim's favorite Buffet tune at the time. That should have given me a clue! But I was trusting of Jim and personally insecure. While Jim was away, I stayed home doing my best to take care of our marriage and our son, hoping to join him on the road when I could.

One special time Jim surprised me with a ticket to meet him in the Florida Keys. When I deplaned, Jimmy Buffet was there to meet me, explaining that he was to take Jim's place. My husband, I was told, had been stranded at his last gig. I'd traveled the whole way there just to be with Jim, but it seemed that he was "de-laid."

Buffet welcomed me to his home in the Keys. He took me to lunch and I had my first margarita ever. He was the perfect Southern gentleman, polite, witty, and totally charming. Then he invited me to go sailing with him. He promised we would be absolutely safe, that "pontoons *never* tip over."

A veteran sailor, Jimmy had us flying across the water until a storm wind took over and a towering wave took us down. When we came to the surface we found ourselves side by side, bellies up against the fiberglass pontoon, trying our damnedest to turn the boat upright and get back to shore.

My husband never did show up that weekend. Jimmy and I spent that Sunday sucking Key limes and tequila and painfully picking slivers of fiberglass from our own sunburned bellies.

I never did find out the whole story of Jim's "de-lay." Buffet kept his secret well. But whenever I taste a Key lime, I smile out there at Jim Croce and remember our long-ago weekend apart. And I forgive him. Well, almost.

Adrian James and I moved to San Diego in August of 1973 while Jim was on the road. A month later Jim came home unannounced and surprised me. His arms were teeming with presents for us and his heart was filled with regret. He was anxious to make things right again, as if he knew there wasn't much time.

He walked in the front door and kissed me and said, "I'm guilty," with this big shit-eating grin on his face. And "It won't happen again." He handed me an "S," a surprise, as he always did when he came home. This time it was a Japanese pottery book that Cheech Marin had suggested. He promised that the "rock and roll" craziness was over, vowed to be faithful, and pleaded for forgiveness.

Jim joked that whatever I thought he'd done on the road wasn't half as much fun as I imagined. I told him, "I doubt that!" but he only grinned some more.

That night, Jim wanted to make it all up to me. He asked me on a date, and it was the best "date" we'd had in a long time. We walked on the beach in downtown San Diego, along the harbor, catching up on two years, planning our future, and looking for a good place for dinner. I had my first sushi that night and eventually became a big fan.

Croce's version of sushi is still one of my favorite meals.

Seared Hawaiian Ahi with Japanese Salsa

⚘ ⚘

2 pounds ahi tuna (sushi grade),
    cut into 6 portions
Pinch salt
1 tablespoon cracked black peppercorns
2 tablespoons olive oil
1/2 cup shiitake mushrooms,
    sliced and stemmed
1/2 cup white mushrooms, sliced
1/2 cup sherry
1/2 cup green onions, chopped
2 tablespoons pickled red ginger

1 cup Teriyaki Glaze
    (see directions below)
1 cup Beurre Blanc
    (see directions below)
1/2 cup Japanese Vinaigrette
    (see page 255)
Salad greens
Optional: 3 teaspoons
    white sesame seeds, for
    garnish

SEASON THE AHI with the salt and cracked peppercorns. Put the olive oil in a sauté pan over medium-high heat. Place the ahi in the heated oil and sear quickly until medium rare or to your liking (about 1 minute per side). Set the ahi aside. In the same pan, over high heat, cook the mushrooms. Deglaze the pan with sherry and reduce to medium heat.

Put all the mushrooms and sherry in the sauté pan and reduce slightly. Add the green onion, ginger, Teriyaki Glaze, and Beurre Blanc to the pan and cook until combined and slightly thickened, about 3 minutes.

Slice the ahi into strips and set aside. Pour the Japanese Vinaigrette over the greens, toss, and place in the center of the plate. Arrange the ahi around the greens and pour the mushroom sauce over the ahi strips. Garnish with white sesame seeds.

TERIYAKI GLAZE

6 tablespoons soy sauce
2 tablespoons brown sugar
2 teaspoons white sugar

2 cloves garlic, minced
1 teaspoon fresh ginger, minced
1 teaspoon arrowroot

6 tablespoons Japanese vinegar
3 tablespoons sake or sherry

1 tablespoon water

COMBINE THE SOY SAUCE, brown and white sugar, Japanese vinegar, sake or sherry, garlic, and ginger in a heavy-bottomed saucepot. Bring to a boil (the sauce will flame as the alcohol burns off). Dissolve the arrowroot in the water. Reduce the sauce to a hard simmer and add the arrowroot mixture. Simmer hard for 5 minutes more.

This recipe makes 1 cup of Teriyaki Glaze.

BEURRE BLANC

1 cup white wine
1 tablespoon shallots, chopped
2 tablespoons rice vinegar

1 cup cold unsalted butter
  (2 sticks), cut into
  small pieces
Salt, to taste

COMBINE THE WINE, shallots, and vinegar in a small saucepan. Bring to a boil over medium-high heat. Continue boiling until 1 tablespoon of liquid remains. Lower the heat and whisk in the butter. When the butter is completely incorporated, remove from the heat. Add salt to taste.

This recipe makes 1 cup of Beurre Blanc.

SERVES 6

Before Jim's songs hit the charts, his dad passed away. James Albert Croce, Sr., who had discouraged his son from making music his career for fear of his failure, never lived long enough to see Jim's success. But shortly before he died he had listened to "You Don't Mess Around with Jim" and with encouragement he had told his son, "Honestly, Jim, I think it's a hit!"

At a concert about six months after his funeral, a fan came backstage and told Jim she'd met his dad in the audience. She described him perfectly, about six feet tall with thick gray hair, dressed neatly, with silver-rim glasses, a flannel shirt, and a big smile. When she told Jim his father had said, "I knew 'You Don't Mess Around with Jim' would make it," Jim was so proud. He called me right away to tell me this story, so gratified that his father knew.

Jim senior never did like veggies much. Whenever I'd go to dinner at the Croces', he'd say, "Just a few green beans, Mommy." So this heavenly recipe is dedicated to Jim's dad, James Albert Croce.

Roasted Corn and Green Bean Salad with Pine Nuts

4 medium ears of sweet corn
2 teaspoons Tabasco sauce
Pinch salt and pepper
1 pound green beans, trimmed
3 tablespoons olive oil

4 tablespoons roasted pine nuts
1/2 cup red onion, chopped
4 to 5 tablespoons red wine vinegar

PREHEAT THE OVEN TO 400°F. Pull the husks back from the corn, but do not detach. Baste the sweet corn with Tabasco and salt and pepper and cover the corn back up inside the husks. Roast the corn on a cookie sheet in the oven for 50 to 60 minutes.

Cool in the husks, shuck the corn, and cut the kernels off the cob. In a saucepan, bring salted water to a boil and simmer the green beans for 5 to 7 minutes, until they are crisp but tender. While the beans cook, heat the olive oil in a skillet over moderate heat and add the pine nuts, stirring for 3 to 5 minutes until they are golden brown. Add the roasted corn, green beans, and red onion to the skillet and toss with the nuts. Add the red wine vinegar and remove from the heat. Season with salt, pepper, and Tabasco to taste. Serve hot or cold.

SERVES 6

Before Jim left us that last weekend, he told me he couldn't stand the strain anymore. "Here we are, Ing, after all my work, two years, three albums, and we're still broke. I don't want to go back on the road again. I hate this. I've got to get away!"

I told him he couldn't just "go away." "Talk to them. Make them listen," I said. But he couldn't.

"Not to worry," he told me, avoiding my suggestions. "You'll hear from me in about six months." And then he left for what was to be a one-week stint. Every night that week, he called me and declared his love. He talked and sang to A. J., and he spoke on and on about our future and the family he wanted to be with and watch grow up. Jim was at a crossroad. And he was doing his damnedest to find his way home.

I remember when the phone rang very early that Friday morning, only two weeks after we'd moved to San Diego. I'd been dreaming a strange dream all night long. Something about my son and my life and my work.

In my dream, I was sitting at my potter's wheel, a precious gift my husband had just bought for me. It was deadly silent and all I could hear was the spinning of the wheel and our baby's sweet voice in the next room. Suddenly, something was missing. I kept trying to find it in my illusion, but I was caught on this wheel that kept going 'round and 'round, not letting me finish my dream.

The phone rang again and I picked it up. It was my stepmother, Florence, in Philadelphia. Her voice was sad and strained. "Hello, Ing," she said cautiously. "Did I wake you?" She paused. "Did you hear the news?" I had been sleeping and was confused, but I got this terrible feeling that I knew what was wrong.

"There was a plane crash, Ing," she told me.

"And Jim is dead, isn't he?" I said before she could tell me. He was the one missing from my dream!

"Is Maury dead too?" I asked, referring to our best friend.

"Yes, all five passengers and the pilot went down last night in a field in

Natchitoches, Louisiana. No one survived the crash. I saw it on *The Today Show* this morning. Hasn't anyone called you yet?"

While I held the phone to my ear, I got out of bed and walked toward a photograph of Jim that hung at eye level in our little bedroom. I was lost in his big brown eyes. As if he were somewhere inside the picture and if I just stared long enough I could find him and be with him forever.

Jim Croce and his one-man band, Maury Muehleisen, in a private aircraft, 1973.

SINGLE PARENTING
Homemade Meals

Sometimes things happen that you just have to think about. Like back in Lyndell when I got pregnant and this friend of ours, Danny, who read horoscopes told me there were three things he could see clearly in my future. First, I'd have a son and he'd be born with a strange mark. Second, our boy would have only one parent by the age of two, and third, there was money in our future. Though Adrian James was born with a blue bottom and Jim died when A. J. was two, I couldn't really believe that money was in the cards. But I did think about it.

When Jim passed away, I didn't have much of a clue about our finances. I guessed by the tons of time Jim was out on the road that there must have been some money for A. J. and me to live on. And I knew there was life insurance—Jim's father had insisted on that. I was told that everyone from attorneys to publicists got their piece of Jim's earnings before he did. But with Jim's popularity and the extensive radio airplay he was getting, I thought there should be something "left over" for his family.

The day of Jim's funeral, my husband's "businesspeople" had me "sign on the line" and put them in charge of the estate. "Not to worry," they assured me. They'd handle everything.

They started the ball rolling by filing a wrongful-death suit in Texas, where Jim's plane was headed the night of the crash, and they also were working on settling Jim's estate.

I knew so little back then, but it just seemed logical to me that if they were going to oversee Jim's legacy they should know its worth. So, innocently, after I returned from Philadelphia to San Diego with A. J., I called them back in New York and asked for an audit. By their response, you might have thought I was asking them for millions of dollars. In fact, I was, but I didn't know it at the time.

This is my Shepherd's Pie. I sure could have used a shepherd to watch over me back then!

I use my Meat Loaf with Garlic Mashed Potatoes in this casserole.

SHEPHERD'S PIE (SPICY MEAT LOAF WITH GARLIC MASHED POTATOES)

1/2 pound ground lamb
1/2 pound ground pork
1 pound ground beef
1 cup fresh bread crumbs
1 cup onion, finely chopped
1/4 cup parsley, chopped
2 eggs, lightly beaten
1/4 cup water
1/2 teaspoon salt
1/2 teaspoon white pepper

1/4 teaspoon dried thyme
1/2 teaspoon nutmeg, grated
1 teaspoon Tabasco
1/4 teaspoon Worcestershire sauce
1/2 cup hot chili
6 cups Garlic Mashed Potatoes
  (see directions below)
Optional: Green chile strips,
  for garnish

PREHEAT THE OVEN TO 350°F. Combine all the ingredients in a large bowl and mix thoroughly with your hands. Lightly oil an 8 x 10 x 2 1/2-inch baking dish. Put the meat loaf mixture into the pan and press it down lightly. Do not lean on it or the meat will become too compact and dry. Bake the meat loaf, uncovered, for 1 hour.

To assemble the Shepherd's Pie, cover the meat loaf evenly with the Garlic Mashed Potatoes, creating small peaks. Paint with the milk, if desired, to brown the top. Return to the oven an additional 20 minutes. Garnish with the green chiles and allow to cool for 15 minutes. Serve like lasagna, with fresh cooked spinach or seasonal greens, fresh tomatoes, and vinaigrette.

GARLIC MASHED POTATOES

3 pounds Idaho potatoes,
*   peeled and quartered*
Salt, to taste
4 tablespoons unsalted butter
1 egg, beaten
1 cup half-and-half or milk

1/2 cup sour cream or yogurt
2 to 3 cloves garlic, roasted
1/2 teaspoon white pepper,
*   freshly ground*
Optional: 1/4 cup milk

PUT THE POTATOES, with water to cover, and a pinch of salt, in a 2-quart saucepan and bring to a boil. Simmer, covered, until the potatoes are soft, 20 to 30 minutes. Drain well in a colander.

Combine the butter, egg, half-and-half or milk, and sour cream or yogurt, and heat in a separate pan. Put the potatoes in a food processor with the roasted garlic, salt, and white pepper and pulse the ingredients together, maintaining the density. Return the potatoes to the original pot. Over medium-low heat, gradually add the warm milk mixture to the potatoes, stirring constantly with a wooden spoon to avoid browning, until the potatoes are thick and creamy.

SERVES 8

To get through the anger, sadness, and utter abandonment I felt at age twenty-six after my mother's, father's, baby's, and now Jim's death, I had to work hard on spiritually surviving my losses. My agenda included a lot of deep breathing, yoga, and long walks to clean out my head and heart. It was a bad time all around: disco was king and I was barely hangin' in there, just "Stayin' Alive, Stayin' Alive."

A. J. was my godsend, my reason to search for and find a sense of humor. He was my motivation to get up every morning, just to make breakfast, lunch, and dinner. Mealtimes put continuity back into my life, and preparing my first single-parent Thanksgiving turkey and stuffing gave me "Reason to Live." I was thankful for the work and my guests were happy for the meal.

Thanksgiving Turkey with Mushroom and Onion Bread Stuffing

&⁕&

The day before Thanksgiving I begin the festivities by preparing a double batch of my Chicken Soup (see page 113). It sets the tone for the festive events and the stock can be used in many of the preparations.

Before preparing the turkey, make your stuffing. Since my guests have enjoyed this dressing immensely over the years, I prepare enough to fill every opening of a large bird and a casserole on the side. If you have vegetarian guests (we always do), separate one-third of the ingredients from the start, omitting the chicken stock and livers. Serve the vegetarian dressing in a separate casserole. I have also substituted spicy sausage for chicken livers, for the finicky eaters in our family who won't eat liver. But you can omit all meat and the stuffing is still hearty and engaging.

20-pound turkey	*1/4 teaspoon salt*
6 tablespoons extra virgin olive oil	*1/8 teaspoon pepper*
2 cloves garlic, finely minced	*1/2 lemon*
1/4 teaspoon paprika	*Mushroom and Onion Bread*
1/4 teaspoon rosemary	*Stuffing (see directions below)*

1/4 teaspoon sage   *4 cups chicken stock, for gravy*
1/8 teaspoon thyme

WARM THE OLIVE OIL in a small saucepan with the garlic, paprika, rosemary, sage, thyme, and salt and pepper. Set aside. Remove the innards, neck, and gizzard from the turkey and boil in 4 cups of water over moderate heat. Reduce to a simmer, cover, and cook about 1 hour until the giblets are tender. Reserve for the gravy.

Rinse the fresh turkey inside and out under cold running water. Rub the inside of the breast cavity of the turkey with 1/2 lemon. Rub the inside and outside of the bird with half the olive oil mixture. Reserve the rest for basting.

Preheat the oven to 425°F. Stuff the turkey body and neck with the mushroom and onion bread stuffing and sew the cavities together with a needle and thread. Gently separate the skin from the body and insert more dressing deep inside the skin on the breast or wherever you can stuff it.

Add 1 to 2 cups water or chicken stock to the turkey pan and set the turkey, breast down, on a roasting rack, inside a large roasting pan. Put in the oven and bake for 45 minutes, basting with the oil mixture every 20 minutes. Reduce the heat in the oven to 350°F and turn the turkey over with the breast up. Add water to the bottom of the pan, if necessary, to avoid burning. Bake the turkey for 15 to 20 minutes per pound. Bake hens (8 to 16 pounds) for 20 to 25 minutes per pound. When using these measures, insert a thermometer in the thigh without touching the bone to determine the exact temperature (at least 30 minutes ahead of scheduled doneness) to allow for variations in oven temperature. When the dense thigh registers 180°F, remove from the oven immediately and allow the turkey to cool 20 minutes before carving.

Each Thanksgiving I try to prepare my fresh turkey so the meat will be tender and moist and the skin crispy and golden brown. Make sure your bird has a healthy history, and if you take the time to baste it every 20 minutes during roasting, you will get wonderful results. Remember to save the neck, gizzard, and heart for the stock and gravy.

While the turkey is standing, prepare the gravy. Remove the giblets from their stock and chop them finely. Pour the pan drippings into a 1-quart glass measuring cup and remove the yellow fat at the top. Use equal parts giblet stock, chicken stock, and defatted pan drippings for the gravy. Measure 4 cups of mixed stock or water. Set the roasting pan on top of two stove burners on moderate heat. Sprinkle in the flour and whisk, scraping up brown bits from the bottom of the pan.

Reduce to a simmer and add the giblets if desired. Whisk until you reach desired consistency. Season with salt and pepper. Serve warm.

MUSHROOM AND ONION BREAD STUFFING

8 to 10 cups chicken stock
    or vegetable broth or water
5 tablespoons butter
2 large yellow onions, sliced
1 1/2 cups zucchini,
    chopped into small pieces
1 cup chicken livers
    (or precooked, decased spicy sausage)
6 cloves garlic, minced
1 1/2 cups white or assorted mushrooms

Salt and pepper
3 tablespoons olive oil
8 to 10 cups bread cubes (2 to 3
    boxes store-bought variety)
Optional: 2 cooked carrots
    from the soup stock, chopped
Optional: 2 ribs cooked celery
    from the stock, chopped

SET ASIDE prepared chicken stock. Heat 3 tablespoons of the butter and sauté the onions with the sliced zucchini in a medium skillet for 7 minutes. In a separate pan, sauté the chicken livers in 1 tablespoon of butter with 1 clove of minced garlic until brown. Chop the chicken livers and garlic into small pieces and reserve.

In a third large skillet, sauté 1 tablespoon butter with 3 cloves of minced garlic, the mushrooms, and salt and pepper for 3 minutes. Combine the onion mixture to this pan. In a large flat-bottomed stockpot, stir the olive oil with 2 minced garlic cloves. Over medium-low heat, add 3 cups bread cubes and stir with a wooden spoon, browning the cubes for 2 minutes. Add half the onion/mushroom mixture and 2 cups stock and continue to stir.

Repeat until all the ingredients are evenly mixed. Stir in the carrots and celery. Add the chicken livers or sausage to the bread stuffing, if desired. Add more liquid if needed to moisten the mixture before stuffing the turkey or putting the stuffing in a covered casserole. Set the stuffing aside to cool.

SERVES 20 TO 24

CRANBERRY, ORANGE, AND MANGO CHUTNEY

ॐ ৯৯

1 medium navel orange
1 cup fresh cranberries
1 ripe mango, peeled,
    seeded, and chopped
1/4 red onion, chopped

1 teaspoon jalapeño pepper,
    minced
1/4 cup fresh lime juice
2 tablespoons sugar
1/4 cup walnuts, coarsely chopped

REMOVE THE ZEST from the orange and set aside. Peel the orange and cut the orange pulp into chunks. Simmer the cranberries in water for about 10 minutes, or until they pop.

Pulse the orange chunks, cooked cranberries, mango, onion, jalapeño, lime juice, and sugar in the food processor. Add the walnuts and pulse the mixture quickly—the consistency should be crunchy. Refrigerate and serve chilled with turkey or pork.

MAKES 3 CUPS

BRUSSELS SPROUTS WITH BALSAMIC VINEGAR

ॐ ৯৯

1 1/2 pounds brussels sprouts,
    washed and trimmed
2 to 4 tablespoons unsalted butter

1/4 cup balsamic vinegar
Salt, to taste
Black pepper, freshly ground

To AVOID uneven cooking of brussels sprouts, remove the loose outer leaves, cut the sprout stem as close to the head as possible, and cut an "X" about 1/4 inch deep into the stem end of each sprout. Drop the brussels sprouts in a large kettle containing several quarts of salted boiling water. Bring to a boil again over high heat and cook for 5 to 8 minutes, depending on the size and age of the sprouts. Drain in a colander and refresh with very cold water, then pat dry.

Melt the butter in a large skillet, add the sprouts and shake them over medium heat for 2 to 3 minutes. Pour the balsamic vinegar over the sprouts and shake them, covering completely. Season with additional salt and cracked black pepper and serve hot.

SERVES 6

My agenda for the seventies was getting under way. First, I was concerned about gaining an understanding of our finances, to assure some security for A. J. and me. Next, I was determined to keep Adrian close to his family. When I could, we'd go back east to visit, so A. J. didn't lose touch with the Jacobsons, the Croces, and the Babuscis. My next priority was finding some friends in our new hometown to help us build a new life together.

The night before Jim died, we'd visited some folks Jim knew in San Diego. They included a disc jockey named Larry Himmel, Bobbi Hansen and her young son Theo, and a surfer dude named Cliff. They all lived in the funky little cottages at the end of the Ocean Beach Pier, where shades of the sixties continued to flourish. Since they were the *only* people I'd met in San Diego besides our wonderful real estate broker Louise Phillips and her husband, Bill (and my cousin Judy and her family), it seemed like a good place to start.

Between reading and playing with Adrian and concocting gallons of fresh fruit and veggies in my new juicer, I'd also put an ad in the paper to find a handyman to do some work around our house. Tom Scheuring, a new California import, answered the advertisement, got the job, and also became my very good friend. Tom was in his late twenties, and after reckoning with his sexuality, he had left his home, wife, and daughter in Ohio to follow his heart. He loved his daughter dearly, but he had come to San Diego to make a new gay life for himself.

All of us were searching for extended family. And I felt like Dorothy in Oz, gathering up my new compatriots to face the great unknown. For me, having

THYME IN A BOTTLE

folks to our home for dinner signified kinship. So I made a party for my new friends with Roasted Pork, Rosemary and Thyme, and a fresh California Salad.

GARLIC ROASTED PORK
WITH ROSEMARY AND THYME

One 5- to 7-pound boneless pork loin
6 cloves garlic, peeled and all but
    2 slivered
1/4 cup fresh parsley, finely chopped
1/4 teaspoon dried thyme
1 tablespoon olive oil

Salt, to taste
1 cup dry white wine
Freshly ground black pepper, to
    taste
1 teaspoon rosemary

IN THE BOWL of a food processor fitted with a steel blade, or a blender, process the garlic cloves, parsley, thyme, olive oil, 1 teaspoon of salt, and 1 tablespoon of the wine into a smooth paste. With a sharp knife, make small slits on all sides of the meat. Force generous quantities of the slivered garlic into the slits. Rub the remaining mixture all over the roast. Put the pork in a roasting pan and pour over 1/2 cup of the wine. Cover and marinate overnight, turning the meat several times.

Preheat the oven to 425°F. Sprinkle the top of the roast with salt and pepper and rosemary, and roast for 10 to 15 minutes. Lower the oven temperature to 325°F and cook for 30 to 40 minutes per pound, or until the meat is tender and medium rare.

Pour off all but 2 tablespoons of fat from the roasting pan. Add the remaining garlic and sauté gently for 2 to 3 minutes. Deglaze the pan with the remaining wine (about 1/2 cup) over high heat. Adjust the seasoning with salt and pepper. Carve the roast into thin slices and serve with the sauce. (The pork is also delicious served with mint sauce or horseradish.)

SERVES 6

CALIFORNIA SALAD

3 slices bread, cut in half
   (or the crust of a country-style bread)
1 teaspoon garlic, minced
1 tablespoon plus 1 teaspoon capers
1/2 pint red and yellow pear tomatoes

12 mixed lettuces
1 lemon, juiced
Salt and pepper, to taste
3 tablespoons extra virgin olive oil

PREHEAT THE OVEN TO 350°F. Toast the bread and rub with the garlic. Or cut the crust off of a 1-pound country-style loaf, cut into 6 pieces and brush with olive oil, rub with garlic, and bake until crunchy. Put the garlic, capers, bread croutons, and tomatoes in a stainless-steel bowl. Add the lettuce, squeeze on the lemon, and season with salt and pepper. Drizzle with olive oil. Adjust the seasonings and serve.

SERVES 6

The year 1974 began with an important call. My friend Tom Scheuring, who was now renting a room in our home in exchange for his excellent carpentry, had answered the phone. I heard him chatting away as if to an old friend. Then, handing me the receiver, he said casually, "It's Dick Clark."

"How do you know Dick?" I inquired, holding my hand over the phone.

"From television," he said, looking at me as if I were the silly one.

"Hello, Dick," I said. I actually did know Dick Clark. I had met him as a teenager when my father bought Dick's home in Wallingford, Pennsylvania. I also knew him from the times when Jim Croce had performed on his TV shows.

Dick Clark, who was hosting the American Music Awards, told me that Jim had been nominated for Best Male Vocalist of 1973. This was the first year of the show and Dick kindly convinced me to attend. (I took this call with the assurance that Jim had won the award, and he did.)

When I arrived at the awards presentation, Dick was so genuine and encouraging, he made me feel welcome when I proudly picked up Jim's award.

Your guests will feel welcome with my Pennsylvania Pot Roast. This was A. J.'s favorite from the time he could eat it. I'd prepare it for dinner and then puree and freeze baby portions for him. This was my original Croce's Baby Food. And in Jim's memory, I pondered whether I should consider packaging and labeling it with Jim's baby photo. I figured with this picture my product would definitely sell.

Jim Croce as a baby, the inspiration for Croce's Baby Food.

PENNSYLVANIA POT ROAST

3-pound boneless top chuck roast
Salt and pepper
3 cloves garlic, minced
4 cups water
4 carrots
2 stalks celery
1 large onion

Vegetable cooking spray
4 black peppercorns
1 bay leaf
2 tablespoons parsley, chopped
1/4 teaspoon thyme
Sprigs of fresh parsley, for garnish

CLEAN THE ROAST well and dry it with a paper towel. Rub salt, pepper, and minced garlic on all the surfaces. Boil the water in a pot, add the carrots, celery, and onion and cook until the carrots are almost tender. Use a slotted spoon to remove all the vegetables. Set aside 2 carrots and the vegetable broth. Chop the vegetables and add to 1 cup of broth in a food processor bowl or blender. Mix the ingredients, adding liquid as needed to achieve a puree consistency, then set the vegetable puree aside.

Coat a large saucepan with cooking spray and heat the pan over a medium flame. Put in the roast and brown on all sides to a deep mahogany color.

Preheat the oven to 325°F. Place the meat in a roasting pan and cover with the vegetable puree. Pour 1 cup of the vegetable broth in the bottom of the pan with the thyme, peppercorns, bay leaf, and parsley and cover tightly. Cook the beef until tender, about 3 hours.

Remove the bay leaf and peppercorns. Slice the roast, place on a serving platter, and keep warm. Pour the pan juices in a saucepan and reduce, uncovered, to 2 cups.

Serve with Roasted Potatoes (see page 246) and sliced, buttered carrots from the vegetable broth. Garnish with fresh sprigs of parsley.

SERVES 6 TO 8

After I brought Jim Croce's trophy home, my surfer friend Cliff suggested we take a road trip to Costa Rica for the waves. I'd had enough waves in my life, but ironically, Jim's A&R man, Corb Donahue from ABC Dunhill, had called that day and suggested the same thing, a surfing trip to Costa Rica. It all seemed so serendipitous, I decided to go.

Corb explained that shortly before Jim died, they had made a plan to meet up in Quepos, Costa Rica, so our families could do some R&R together. He also reported that land down south was reasonable and it was a good time to buy. This sort of explained Jim's strange comment to me the weekend before the crash when he had said that he wanted to go away and hide and that I'd see him in six months. I was consoled in believing that I was still part of Jim's plan, and traveling sounded like a good idea at the time.

Our first stop was Tijuana for a luscious fish taco. Today at our Ingrid's Cantina & Sidewalk Cafe we serve the best. Watch out Rubios and Taco Bell!

FISH TACOS WITH PICO FISH SAUCE

᪥   ᪥

4 eggs

1 cup flour

2 cups panko crumbs (a Japanese bread
    crumb; regular bread crumbs
    may also be used)

12 pieces fish (2 1/4 pounds of fish—
    any whitefish may be used:
    halibut, pollack, or cod)

1 quart vegetable or canola oil

12 corn tortillas

3/4 cup Blackened Tomato Sauce
    (see page 212)

3 cups cabbage, shredded

1 cup salsa

3/4 cup Pico Fish Sauce
    (see directions below)

12 lime wedges

3 cups cooked rice

3 cups cooked black beans

HEAT THE OIL in a large pot to 350°F. In a medium-size bowl, whisk the eggs with a wire whip. Put the flour in a second bowl and the panko or bread crumbs in a third bowl. Cut the fish into twelve 3-ounce pieces. Bread the fish pieces in this order: first in the flour, then in the eggs, and then in the panko or bread crumbs. Deep-fry the fish three at a time until golden brown. Place on a sheet pan and put in the oven for 6 to 8 minutes, then turn down the oven to 250°F. Heat the tortillas in the oven or on a griddle for a few minutes.

Build the tacos as follows: For each taco, start with a warm tortilla, cooked fish, lightly broken up, 1 tablespoon Blackened Tomato Sauce, 1/4 cup shredded cabbage, 1 tablespoon salsa, and 1 tablespoon Pico Fish Sauce. Serve with rice and beans and lime wedges.

PICO FISH SAUCE

1 cup sour cream

1/6 bottle Pico Pica sauce (available in most stores)

COMBINE THE INGREDIENTS in a bowl and mix well with a wire whip.

SERVES 6

All the way south we were able to take advantage of the local produce, freshly caught seafood, and the most unexpected and fun happenings. At the bay of Concepción, in Baja, Mexico, we were parked on the beach when a shrimp boat pulled up to shore and the men came ashore and offered to take us fishing. On board, my little shrimp, A. J., threw away his last pacifier and his last diaper and puckered up on limón and camarones the whole way. For starters, Ceviche was easy to prepare, and the aroma of our Shrimp Scampi with lemon and garlic brought a lot of hungry *pescaderos* to our fire.

ANDY'S CEVICHE

2 pounds Sierra fish

2 green onions

3 tomatoes, chopped

1 bunch cilantro

2 teaspoons olive oil

1/2 teaspoon salt

1/4 teaspoon pepper

10 lemons, juiced

2 oranges, juiced

6 to 7 small jalapeño peppers

1 small bowl jalapeño chiles

1/4 cup vinegar

MIX THE FISH with all the ingredients and let marinate, covered and refrigerated, overnight.

SERVES 8 TO 10

SHRIMP SCAMPI

જી છે

30 ounces angel-hair pasta

6 tablespoons Clarified Butter

    (see page 174)

2 cloves garlic, minced and mashed

30 medium-to-large shrimp,

    well cleaned and deveined

Kosher salt and white pepper, to taste

1/4 cup scallions, chopped

1/4 cup brandy

1/4 cup dry vermouth

3 lemons, halved

Fresh dill, for garnish

PREPARE THE ANGEL-HAIR PASTA al dente and set aside to keep warm in a bowl. Heat a large sauté pan until hot and add the clarified butter, garlic, and shrimp. Season lightly with salt and pepper and cook for 3 to 5 minutes. Add the scallions and deglaze them with the brandy and vermouth. Squeeze the juice of 3 lemons over the shrimp and stir. Serve over warm angel-hair pasta, and garnish with dill.

SERVES 6

In Guatemala I got a lot of practice with tacos and made my first burritos and tamale pie. I was in charge of the cooking and the guys got the beer. Speaking of which, these beer-batter onion rings should not be forgotten. They are a great side dish or appetizer for any meal.

SPICY ONION RINGS

2 cups all-purpose flour

1 tablespoon Lawry's seasoning salt

1 teaspoon garlic powder

1/2 teaspoon black pepper

1 teaspoon cayenne pepper

1 teaspoon cumin

1 teaspoon dried rosemary

1 cup beer

6 cups canola oil

4 medium red onions,
    cored and sliced 1/3-inch
    thick

COMBINE THE FLOUR, seasoning salt, garlic powder, pepper, cayenne, cumin, and rosemary and mix thoroughly. Add the beer and mix until incorporated.

Heat the oil to 350°F in a heavy-bottomed pot. Dredge the onions in the batter and gently drop into the oil. Cook the onions until golden brown, turning once. Serve immediately.

SERVES 4 TO 6

After a month of easy riding and surfing the warm water south, we arrived in Costa Rica. Quepos was paradise. We were practically the only gringos in town, so it was easy to go native, speaking Spanish and living off the sea and land. What incredible therapy. My new life was extraordinarily primitive, and I felt happy to bring Adrian James into such a wonderful world.

In the morning he'd wake up and pull bananas off the tree or suck on mangoes. And although he was not yet three years old, he and Cliff were surfing the warm waves of the Pacific together, enjoying life. There were underwater caves with fish of luminous colors and brilliant purple-blue butterflies the size of his little head to chase after. Every day we'd collect puka shells to string and sell back on the "mainland." We'd eat when we got hungry. Grab a papaya or tamarindo off the tree in the morning and fish for camarones and pescada at midday.

In the evening, our social agenda included an occasional visit to Sonya and Wiley's, our seasoned gringo neighbors down the road. On Sonya's veranda, while A. J., swinging happily in her colorful hammocks, engrossed himself in conversation with her whimsical parrot, Wiley, a retired surgeon, drank his tequila straight from the bottle and told of his "Jimmy Buffet"-like adventures that had swayed him south.

Sonya, our gracious hostess, offered us perfect pitchers of margaritas to wash down her homemade chips and salsa, and the past seemed to disappear into the surreal sunset while we watched the turquoise Pacific fade to black.

Our bartender Melissa Metroka's Perfect Margarita and Andy Martinez's Salsa Borracha with chips remind me, at the busiest of times, that life is too short not to seize the day.

MELISSA'S PERFECT MARGARITAS

3/4 cup Cuervo Gold tequila
6 tablespoons Cointreau
5 tablespoons lime juice
Margarita mix (or sweet and sour mix)
Orange juice

5 tablespoons Grand Marnier
  liqueur
Lime slices
Salt

MIX IN A 64-ounce pitcher with ice: tequila, Cointreau, lime juice. Fill the remaining pitcher to the top with the margarita mix or the sweet and sour mix. Top off the pitcher with a splash of orange juice and the Grand Marnier. Stir the pitcher vigorously and serve in 12-ounce glasses. Garnish each glasses with a lime wheel. If you like salt on the rim, before pouring a margarita, sprinkle salt on a plate, moisten the rim with lime juice, and turn the glass rim-side down and dip in the salt.

SERVES 5

Andy's Salsa Borracha

꧁ ꧂

7 tomatillos

7 serrano chiles

1 bunch green onions

2 teaspoons olive oil

Juice of 3 lemons

1 bunch cilantro, chopped

1 shot white tequila

Salt and pepper

1 onion, chopped

2 avocados, peeled and diced

     into 1/2-inch squares

BOIL THE TOMATILLOS, chiles, and the white onion in water for 7 to 10 minutes, or until creamy. Put all the other ingredients except the avocado in a medium bowl and mix until creamy. Add the avocado and stir, keeping the salsa chunky.

SERVES 4 TO 6

I suppose I should have stayed in Costa Rica a long, long time. For months I had not even called home to see how the wrongful-death action and the closing of the estate were going. But I was so in love with Quepos I wanted to buy a piece of paradise, and my money was back home. Truthfully, my compulsive nature couldn't leave well enough alone.

When I called the accountants in Century City to get my money, I was sorry to find that they were hesitant to let it go. When I asked about the estate closure, not much progress had been made. No final accounting was even close to being prepared. I purchased the property in Quepos, but something told me I was in deep guava and it was time to go home.

A week later we drove up to our front door in San Diego, just in time for A. J. to begin preschool. From the start, he hated it. He cried for "Mommy" or maybe for the "mañana" style of living we'd left behind. I made him my Mango Almond Apple

Crisp to remind him of our hot times down south. But even this treat couldn't thwart his tears or convince him that school was okay.

MANGO ALMOND APPLE CRISP

2 teaspoons butter
2 pounds mango, sliced
1 pound apples, sliced
1/2 cup sugar
2 teaspoons orange zest
1/4 cup Cointreau
12 almond cookies
1 cup granola or oatmeal

1/4 cup brown sugar
1 teaspoon cinnamon
1/2 teaspoon nutmeg
1/2 cup almonds, chopped
6 tablespoons unsalted butter, softened
2 eggs
1/4 cup lemon juice

PREHEAT THE OVEN TO 350°F. In a large saucepan melt the butter over medium-low heat. Add the mango, apples, sugar, and orange zest and stir for about 3 minutes. Remove from the heat and stir in the Cointreau. In a separate bowl, mash the cookies until they crumble like graham crumbs. Add the granola, brown sugar, cinnamon, nutmeg, and almonds to this bowl. Cut in the rest of the butter, add the eggs, and using your hands, combine the mixture.

Generously butter the bottom of a shallow baking dish and pour the mango and apple mixture into the dish. Mist with lemon juice. Sprinkle evenly with the cookie mixture and bake 30 to 40 minutes, until hot and bubbly. Serve warm with vanilla bean ice cream or whipped cream.

SERVES 6 TO 8

Adrian James was an intense kinda guy. He was so smart. And even at an early age, he had this quirky sense of humor that let you know he was right there taking it all in. As A. J. was growing up, I often felt like *he* was parenting *me*. But school was a place that did not agree with his soul and he continued to fight it like a bandit.

At home I encouraged him to do the things he loved best, and to soothe him after school, I made him his favorite comfort foods, Pork-Stuffed Cabbage with Light Tomato Sauce and warm Rice Pudding.

PORK-STUFFED CABBAGE WITH LIGHT TOMATO SAUCE

1 large head savoy cabbage
(14 to 16 large cabbage leaves)
1/2 cup pine nuts, roasted
1/2 pound ground pork, finely chopped
(may substitute ground veal)
1/2 pound fresh pork sausages,
peeled and mashed
1 teaspoon olive oil
2 cloves garlic, minced
1/2 cup bread crumbs
1 cup prepared kasha or brown rice

3/4 cup Parmesan cheese, grated
1/2 teaspoon thyme, chopped
1 teaspoon parsley, freshly
chopped
2 tablespoons butter
1 small yellow onion, finely
chopped
Salt and freshly ground pepper
Light Tomato Sauce
(see directions below)

BOIL WATER in a large pot with a pinch of salt. Cut out the deep core of a savoy cabbage and discard it. Add the cabbage and cook until you can easily remove the largest leaves, 5 to 7 minutes. Carefully separate the largest leaves and return them to the pot to cook until they are tender enough to roll. Drain and press them flat on a cloth to dry. Remove the hard center stalk to make rolling easier.

Roast the pine nuts in a large pan until golden brown; remove and set aside. Precook the pork and sausage in the olive oil with the garlic for 7 minutes. Remove from the heat. When cool, add the bread crumbs, kasha, Parmesan, thyme, and parsley to pan with the meat. Add the pine nuts evenly throughout the mixture.

Place the stuffing at the base of each leaf, fold over the base, then the sides, and roll up into little bundles. Secure with a toothpick. Melt the butter in a large skillet over moderate heat, add the chopped onions, and sauté 5 minutes over low heat. Arrange the cabbage rolls over the butter and onions and cook, covered, for 20 minutes over moderate heat, turning once. Add water when necessary to keep the stuffed cabbage juicy. Season with salt and pepper and serve in their own juice or top with Light Tomato Sauce.

LIGHT TOMATO SAUCE

2 tablespoons olive oil

1/2 medium onion, chopped

2 cloves garlic, minced

2 1/2 pounds tomatoes, peeled,
*   seeded, chopped, and drained*

3 tablespoons tomato paste

1 bay leaf

1/2 teaspoon oregano

1/2 teaspoon thyme

1/2 teaspoon salt

1/4 teaspoon pepper,
*   freshly ground*

HEAT THE OLIVE OIL in a deep saucepan over medium heat. Add the chopped onion and sauté until golden. Stir in the garlic, tomatoes, tomato paste, bay leaf, and the spices. Cook for 15 to 20 minutes, stirring to avoid burning, until the tomatoes are soft. Remove the bay leaf and put the sauce in a food processor and puree quickly, until smooth.

This recipe makes 2 to 3 cups of tomato sauce.

SERVES 6

RICE PUDDING

4 cups milk

1 orange peel, removed in a spiral

1/2 cup long-grain rice

1/2 cup granulated sugar

2-inch cinnamon stick

1/2 teaspoon salt

1 cup half-and-half

2 large egg yolks

1 teaspoon vanilla extract

1 teaspoon Grand Marnier

Optional: 1/2 cup raisins

3 teaspoons sugar and cinnamon, mixed together, for garnish

Whipped cream

SCALD MILK in a double boiler with the orange peel. Add the rice, sugar, cinnamon stick, and salt and cover the pan over boiling water for 45 minutes, until the rice is tender. Remove the orange rind from the mixture.

Mix the half-and-half and egg yolks together. Add the liquid in a stream to the rice blend and cook an additional 20 to 30 minutes, until the pudding is thick, stirring occasionally. Remove the cinnamon stick and stir in the vanilla and Grand Marnier.

In a saucepan, plump the raisins by boiling them in 1 cup of water for 5 minutes. Drain them and stir into the pudding. Portion the pudding into 6 to 8 individual bowls and allow to cool, or serve warm. Sprinkle with cinnamon and sugar and a dollop of whipped cream, if desired.

SERVES 6 TO 8

At age four, A. J. went blind from a brain tumor syndrome. I wanted to perish. Watching my child suffer was the hardest thing I've ever had to do. Dr. Harvey Buchsbaum saved his little life and mine. After many painful spinal taps and a shunt, A. J.'s illness was arrested. But he saw the world differently from that time on. His blindness affected more than his sight. He became intensely shy and sensitive, yet stronger still with his other senses.

An "angel," our friend Parker Linekin, came to protect us and bring us hope at that difficult time. Parker, a teacher and practitioner of the martial arts, trained Adrian in karate and gave him a mastery over his own being. By age six, A. J. had earned a brown belt and had miraculously taught himself to see out of his left eye. With his severely damaged optic nerves we never knew how he did it. But while some things were getting clearer for us both, some were not.

Jim Croce's fame and its rewards were becoming publicized, and as his widow, I was a magnet for greedy, self-serving people who wanted to prosper from my newfound "wealth." Hardly prepared for the parasites that descended upon me during these years, I made terrible mistakes and suffered from them greatly.

At the same time, litigation was begging at our door, and I had to make serious spiritual and ethical decisions about opening it. Having had plenty of experience with attorneys and courts (with my parents' custody battles), I didn't want to have to fight in that arena. I hated it! But sometimes there are values you must honor, even though it can get you into a lot of trouble. In this case, I felt it was the right thing to do. Jim and I had worked too hard to let someone take it all away from us.

So I hired the first of what ended up being about ninety attorneys to get back what should have been ours from the start.

Like litigation, these ribs are messy, but definitely worth it.

KOREAN BARBECUE SHORT RIBS AND SAUCE WITH BASMATI RICE

≈ ≈

4 pounds beef short ribs
Korean Short-ribs Marinade
   (see directions below)
Korean Barbecue Sauce
   (see directions below)
3 cups mung bean sprouts
3 cups prepared Basmati Rice
   (see directions below)

6 cups baby salad greens
1/4 cup Japanese Vinaigrette
   (see page 255)
6 tablespoons Soy Mayonnaise
   (see directions below)
1 tablespoon white sesame seeds

MARINATE THE SHORT RIBS in the Korean marinade for 3 hours.

   Blanch the bean sprouts in boiling water for 1 minute. Drain, rinse, and chill. Prepare the Basmati Rice. While the rice cooks, broil or grill the short ribs for 4 to 5 minutes on each side, under the broiler. When the ribs are done, lightly brush them with Korean Barbecue Sauce. Cut the short ribs into bite-size pieces.

   In a large bowl, toss the baby salad greens with the Japanese Vinaigrette. Evenly distribute the salad mix, Basmati Rice, bean sprouts, and short ribs onto 6 plates. Top the bean sprouts with 1 tablespoon Soy Mayonnaise. Sprinkle the ribs with sesame seeds and serve.

KOREAN SHORT-RIBS MARINADE

1 cup soy sauce
1/3 cup mirin
   (Japanese sweet cooking wine)
3/4 cup plus 2 tablespoons honey
1/3 cup rice vinegar
1 teaspoon red pepper flakes

5 cloves garlic, chopped
1 tablespoon fresh ginger, grated
1/2 cup green onions, chopped
2 tablespoons cilantro, chopped
1/3 cup salad oil
4 teaspoons sesame oil

IN A MEDIUM-SIZE MIXING BOWL, combine the soy sauce, mirin, honey, rice vinegar, red pepper flakes, garlic, ginger, green onions, cilantro, and oils. Mix well with a wire whip. Put in a nonreactive container and refrigerate.

This recipe makes 3 cups of marinade.

KOREAN BARBECUE SAUCE

1 tablespoon vegetable oil
1 clove garlic, chopped
1 tablespoon shallots, chopped
1/2 cup ketchup
1 tablespoon rice vinegar
1 1/2 tablespoons soy sauce
1/4 cup brown sugar

1/2 tablespoon whole-grain mustard
1/4 teaspoon paprika
1/2 tablespoon lemon juice
2 tablespoons pineapple juice
1/2 cup water

HEAT THE OIL in a heavy saucepot over medium heat. Add the garlic and shallots. Reduce the heat and "sweat" for 3 to 4 minutes. Add the ketchup, rice vinegar, soy sauce, brown sugar, mustard, paprika, lemon juice, pineapple juice, and water. Stir well. Over medium heat bring the sauce to a boil, then reduce the heat and simmer for 30 minutes, stirring occasionally. Remove from the heat and cool. Put the unused sauce in a covered nonreactive container in the refrigerator.

This recipe makes 2 cups of barbecue sauce.

BASMATI RICE

1 cup basmati rice
2 cups cold water

2 tablespoons whole butter
1/2 teaspoon salt

IN A SMALL SAUCEPOT, combine the rice, cold water, butter, and salt. Stirring constantly, bring to a boil. Cook over high heat until the water and rice are at same level. Cover and continue cooking over low heat for 8 minutes.

This recipe makes 2 cups of rice.

Soy Mayonnaise (Bean Sprout Salad Dressing)

2 tablespoons mayonnaise

1 teaspoon soy sauce

1/2 teaspoon brown sugar

1 tablespoon sour cream

3/4 teaspoon mirin

IN A SMALL BOWL, combine all the ingredients. Mix well with a wire whip.
This recipe makes 1/4 cup of mayonnaise.

SERVES 6

Coming home from dropping A. J. off at school one morning in 1976, I found a stranger sitting at my kitchen table. He was a happy-faced Frenchman who called me "Sweetie" and offered me a cup of my own coffee in my own kitchen.

His name was Jean Tetrault, from Montreal, and he explained that he had met my friend Bernadine Hawthorne, who worked with our public school system, at an international education conference that week in San Diego. Bernie thought it would be a good idea for Jean and me to meet. He said our "matchmaker" would be returning in a little while.

Obviously Jean felt comfortable in my life from the start. Actually he seemed to feel comfortable wherever he went on our planet. He explained his job as an adventure: he worked in education in Canada and with the United Nations and UNICEF and traveled extensively. Adrian and I shared his joy from that day on, often meeting him during his travels. What would we have done without our Jean?

Unlike my magnificent friend Jean who enhanced my life and Adrian's too, there were "bad guys." People who should never have entered our lives and definitely don't belong in my cookbook. It's pretty wonderful to have this chance to rewrite my history, and just leave them out.

My interest in education was strongly aroused at this time, especially because of A. J.'s eyesight and my own uncertainty about how to deal with his loss. Rather than put him into "special" education, as the San Diego School Board suggested, I opened my own preschool elementary, The New School.

At the same time, in 1975, A. J. and I were traveling often between San Diego and San José, Costa Rica. While in the midst of litigation in the States, I was sharing my views on children's learning and on Headstart programs down in Central America. By 1977 I became Vice Consul for Costa Rica in San Diego.

Whenever the opportunity for travel was there, we were eating our way through Mexico, Guatemala, El Salvador, and down to Costa Rica. On these trips, I discovered many of the ingredients that we use today in our menu at Ingrid's Cantina & Sidewalk Cafe.

Besides verifying our earnings, I decided, as I was about to turn thirty, that it was time to do an audit on me too. Once I addressed my self-image, I was determined to get rid of all my "excuses" and get a life.

Smoking was at the top of my list of things to delete from my existence, along with bell-bottoms and flabby thighs. I loved these beautifully packaged green-and-gold Dunhills, and though my addiction was not excessive (eight or so cigarettes a day), I decided it was serious enough to require professional assistance. Before I could change my mind, I enrolled at a clinic. After one week of negative reinforcement and being nearly "shocked" to death, I was up to a whole pack. The following week and three treatments later, I was up to two packs. This wasn't working. Negative reinforcement was not my way.

A. J., on the other hand, got the picture. "Mom, I only have one parent, please don't smoke" were the words that convinced me to quit. "I know you can do it," he said. I worked best with positivity. Or was it guilt?

Guilt has been a great navigator in my life, but it doesn't allow me to resist this Veal Picatta with Lemon, Basil, and Caper Sauce. The calories are worth it.

VEAL PICATTA
WITH LEMON, BASIL, AND CAPER SAUCE

જી ૪૭

1 1/2 pounds veal rump roast,
    cut into 3-inch round scallops
1 cup all-purpose flour
3 tablespoons butter or extra virgin olive oil

2 cloves garlic, finely minced
Salt and pepper, to taste
Lemon, Basil, and Caper Sauce
    (see directions below)

POUND THE VEAL very thin and dredge in flour on both sides. Melt the butter in a large skillet over medium-high heat and add the garlic. Add the meat and brown on each side. Cover the skillet and cook over low heat for 20 minutes, adding water as needed to keep the veal moist.

    Put the veal on plates and spoon the sauce evenly over the medallions. Serve with fettuccine and Broccoli Rabe with Olive Oil and Garlic (see page 34).

LEMON, BASIL, AND CAPER SAUCE

1 1/2 cups dry white wine
2 small shallots, minced
1/2 cup whole fresh basil leaves
4 tablespoons butter
1/4 cup capers

2 teaspoons lemon juice,
    freshly squeezed
Salt and freshly ground pepper,
    to taste

IN A MEDIUM SAUCEPAN, reduce the wine with the shallots and basil to 3/4 cup. Strain through a sieve lined with cheesecloth and return to the saucepan. Over low heat, whisk in the butter a teaspoon at a time. Then stir in the capers and lemon juice and season with salt and pepper.

SERVES 4

As athletic as I thought I was as a youngster, with gymnastics, field hockey, softball, and swimming, I had had asthma and allergies most of my life and was sure I could never run. If my son could teach himself to see without optic nerves, however, asthma was a mighty wimpy excuse for not running. So after practicing with my friend Parker Linekin, sprinting a block or two at first, I was up to six miles in under a month and eighteen before the year was up. Then my first race synched it. I had no idea people actually ran in public as a sport—with an audience, no less. I was thrilled to cross the finish line with crowds cheering, so thrilled I wanted to go back and do it again. Truthfully, the best part of any run is always the end. And then, the next best part is eating.

I found that by running far and often, I could eat whatever I wanted. And I ate oodles of noodles.

Ricotta Gnocchi with Wild Mushrooms and Sage

1 pound whole-milk ricotta cheese
    that has been hanging for at least
    2 days in cheesecloth
2 eggs
1 tablespoon butter, melted
1/4 cup Parmesan cheese, freshly grated

Kosher salt, to taste
Optional: 2 scant teaspoons flour
    (if the cheese is wet)
Sautéed Mushrooms
    (see directions below)

WHEN KATHLEEN DAELEMANS prepares gnocchi, she says it is very important that you only use cheese that has been hanging in cheesecloth and is "dry"—this usually takes 2 days to accomplish. In a large stainless-steel bowl, begin by whisking air into the ricotta cheese. If the cheese is extremely firm you might have to soften it with the back of a wooden or stainless-steel spoon and then whip it up a bit. The cheese should be light and fluffy before you add any ingredients. When you have achieved this, add the eggs, butter, and Parmesan cheese and incorporate completely. Season generously with kosher salt. If the dough is extremely wet, you may add a scant few teaspoons of flour barely mixed: Do not overmix or the glutens in the flour will create a sticky, inedible dough. You can roll the dough immediately into individual gnocchi. If the dough has become at all warm, refrigerate before rolling.

Roll the dough using a soup spoon. Spoon the dough into a pie tin filled with all-purpose flour. Working quickly, shape the dough into rough ovals. Each gnocchi will look different, but they must all be approximately the same weight and length. Do not let the gnocchi sit in the flour for any length of time. Put the rolled gnocchi onto cookie sheets lined with parchment paper. Lay them 9 across by 11. Be careful not to coat the gnocchi with too much flour. Do not overwork the gnocchi as you are shaping them.

SAUTÉED MUSHROOMS

1 tablespoon olive oil
2 tablespoons butter
1 pound mushrooms, sliced
Pinch salt and freshly cracked black pepper
3 sage leaves, torn

Salt, to taste
Optional: 1 1/2 cups arugula
Parmesan cheese, freshly grated,
  for garnish

PUT THE OLIVE OIL in the pan with 1 tablespoon of butter and melt over medium-high heat. When the butter has just melted, add the mushrooms and cook for at least 5 minutes, stirring often. Be sure all of the mushrooms are coated with the butter and oil. Salt the mushrooms and continue cooking. Add the sage leaves. Cook until the mushrooms are soft, about 5 minutes, then set aside. In the meantime, put a pot of water on the stove to boil.

When the water is at a fast simmer, gently drop in the gnocchi. While the gnocchi gently simmer (they will be cooked in 3 to 5 minutes), melt the remaining butter in a Teflon-like pan over a low flame. Do not allow the butter to break at any time. Add the mushrooms and gently heat through. Add the gnocchi to the pan and season with salt and pepper. Place into bowl. Note: If the butter separates, add a little more cold butter. Serve with 1/2 cup arugula per serving and garnish with Parmesan cheese.

SERVES 6 TO 8

PENNE PASTA WITH CHICKEN IN GORGONZOLA CREAM

ஃ ௯ஃ

1/4 cup walnuts

1/4 pound pancetta
     (available at most Italian
     specialty stores)

16 ounces dry penne

2 tablespoons olive oil

2 cups broccoli florets

Four 1/2 chicken breasts, skinned
     and cut into julienne strips

1/4 cup shallots, sliced

1/2 cup white wine

2 cups heavy cream

1/2 cup chicken stock

1 cup Gorgonzola cheese

3 to 4 tablespoons Parmesan
     cheese, freshly grated

LIGHTLY TOAST THE WALNUTS in a 350°F oven for 10 to 15 minutes, then set aside. Cook the pancetta in a skillet until crisp and most of the fat is removed; drain on paper towels and set aside. Cook the pasta in boiling salted water until al dente; rinse and stir in 1 tablespoon olive oil. Set aside. Blanch the broccoli in boiling water for 1 to 2 minutes; rinse and set aside.

To prepare the Gorgonzola cream: In a large pan heat the remaining olive oil. Add the chicken and shallots. Sauté over medium-high heat for 3 minutes. Add the white wine, cream, and chicken stock. Reduce for 5 minutes or until creamy. Stir in the Gorgonzola. Add the pasta to the pan and continue reducing until the desired consistency is achieved. Stir in the broccoli. Garnish with Parmesan cheese and the toasted walnuts.

Note: Pancetta is the same cut of pork used for bacon. It is cured in salt and spices, but is not smoked. There is no substitute for pancetta, but prosciutto or un-smoked ham could be used if it's unavailable.

SERVES 4

When I first came to San Diego from our little farmhouse in Pennsylvania, I'd had very limited experience with banks. When ASCAP royalties started coming in and I went to a savings and loan to get my first California checking account, they said they couldn't give me one. "Regulations," they explained. I was so embarrassed. It was very confusing having money to put into an account for the first time ever, and not being sure how to go about it.

I'd thought about taking the money I got from insurance and from our royalties and stacking it up in my living room, end on end. At least then I could see how much I had, instead of imagining it. It was no surprise to me that the women of the Woman's Bank thought my money would look much better in their new bank than on my living room floor. So when I gave it to them, they put me on their board.

Did you ever have a dream and you kinda remember you were in it but it's hard to place yourself? That's how I felt about sitting on that bank board across the table from all those women at the Woman's Bank. I had no right to be there and I'm sure everyone, including myself, knew it. But there I was in the mid to late seventies, out of my faded Levi's and into a suit.

These women of stature and means knew how to run things—meetings, banks, and even our country. One became our mayor, another a congresswoman, and another a thief. There's no accounting for character. But you can count on the fact that money does buy attention and a very expensive wardrobe. I'm certain that board members of this bank helped keep Saks and Gucci open, and they probably still do.

In between being a mom, litigating, serving as a vice consul, and being a "bored" member of the Woman's Bank, I threw in some music too. I wrote songs, put together a band, and persuaded my friend Gwinevere Hooker to become my unofficial promoter and road manager. Mike Douglas invited me to be a guest on his show, and Gwin and I went to Philadelphia so I could perform.

Since I couldn't take my band, I sent my music arrangements ahead with a letter explaining *exactly* how I wanted their band to play my songs. When I got to the TV studio, a tall, handsome gentleman was waiting for me with a big smile. He looked so welcoming and comfortable. *What a nice surprise,* I thought. I hadn't expected romance on this trip, but I was single and I wouldn't have said no if he had asked me to dinner.

He surprised me, "I knew it had to be you, Ingrid, when I got your letter and lead sheets with everything perfectly written out and explained. I just knew it had to be you."

I stared at him and he did look a little familiar. Then Ernie said he remembered how meticulous my school desk used to be at Friend's Select School with all the paper clips, pencils, and erasers separated by dividers and not a single piece of paper out of place. How funny. My third-grade infatuation was now producing *The Mike Douglas Show.*

I remembered what a nice young man Ernie DeMassa was. So personable and kind. I had always thought he was cute, but obviously he had been more impressed by my meticulous desk than by me.

"How's Phyllis?" he asked. "I had a crush on her, remember? Is she still single?"

Some things never change. I was still compulsive and he was still interested in my sister!

I performed a song I'd written called "Did You Have to Go Then" and then I had to go.

One afternoon in 1977 I got a phone call from Jonathan Moore, a British comedian friend of Jim Croce's who had worked with Jim throughout 1972 and 1973. Jonathan had been scheduled to do Jim's final tour with him of the Southern Baptist colleges. But the college authorities wouldn't allow Jonathan to perform his bawdy humor to the young "impressionable" coeds, so when the plane went down in Natchitoches, Louisiana, Jonathan's life was safe in L.A. Comedian George Stevens had taken Jonathan's place on the plane.

Though I had never met him, I'd known of Jonathan Moore through Jim and had heard Jonathan and Jim's outrageously funny taped cassettes and those of their friends Cheech and Chong. When Jonathan called, he was visiting San Diego and I invited him to come over to our home so we could finally meet in person.

In spite of himself, Jonathan was a very good pal to me too. Like many hyper comedians, he was a nonstop talker, and even I, champion talker that I am, couldn't find a break to jump into his conversation. I made my hottest Chile Rellenos (see page 205) for lunch and the heat distracted his English palate, at least momentarily. I quickly played him a cassette of my new music. At once, Jonathan insisted that I meet his English friend Jimmy Horowitz, a producer now living in L.A. He was sure we would work together well.

Jimmy Horowitz, a piano player and songwriter, was a producer for his own record company, Riva Records. Along with his partner, Billy Gaff, they had produced Rod Stewart and Jimmy's former wife, Leslie Duncan, in England. Air Supply and a young American named John Cougar Mellencamp were just coming aboard when I did. Their roster was getting very full for a small independent label, but Jimmy encouraged me to sign with them.

Jimmy's first visit to our home was magical. We sat down at my piano and he asked me to put lyrics to his melody. He had started writing the words to a new tune and called the song "Learning to Fly Again." As I listened to him play, new lyrics just came to me. Effortlessly, I completed his song and it was the first one we recorded on my solo album with Riva.

Shortly after I met Jimmy Horowitz, he invited me to his home on Doheny Drive in West Hollywood for what I thought was an intimate dinner for two. When I rang, Jimmy came to the door with his apron on and gave me a big hug. As I looked around the antique-filled house I noticed that the table had been set beautifully for five. There were freshly cut roses and counters with refreshments of every kind. The evening felt like it was going to be filled with surprises—the first came then.

The bell rang and when the door was flung open three British drag queens appeared, just going on and on about "Miss Horowitz dear," "Excuse me dear?" "Is this one (meaning me, of course!) staying for dinner, dear?" But after drinks the three queens lightened up on me and their extraordinary vocabulary and hilarious conversation were topped only by Jimmy's delicious English trifle. I call it the Queen's English Trifle, Dear.

THE QUEEN'S ENGLISH TRIFLE

One 12- to 14-ounce pound cake
Raspberry jam
1/2 cup medium dry sherry
1/4 cup brandy
5 egg yolks
6 tablespoons sugar
1 teaspoon cornstarch

Pinch salt
2 cups milk
2 teaspoons vanilla extract
1 1/2 cups heavy cream
1 tablespoon powdered sugar
Fresh raspberries, strawberries,
    or cherries, for garnish

TRIM THE POUND CAKE and cut into 1-inch slices. Lightly brush both sides of the slices with the raspberry jam. Line the bottom of a glass serving bowl with the slices (make 2 layers). Pour the sherry and brandy on the raspberry pound cake and allow the liquid to penetrate for at least 1 hour at room temperature.

Whisk together the egg yolks, sugar, cornstarch, and salt. Heat the milk, stirring until almost boiling. Very slowly pour the milk into the egg mixture. Transfer to a heavy saucepan and cook over medium heat, stirring constantly until the custard coats the spoon. Remove from the heat and blend in the vanilla. Set aside and allow to cool.

Whip the cream with powdered sugar until firm, reserving 1/2 cup for serving time. Cover the trifle with the custard first. Top with the whipped cream. Arrange the berries for decoration.

SERVES 8

C all her," he said. "You'll like her." What a crazy thing to have happen. I was in the depths of litigation in both Los Angeles and New York City, fighting estate battles as well as litigating the "system" of perpetuity for musicians' rights, and I was in need of a good friend. I had hired an investigator to find Pat Picardo and he had finally reached her on the same phone number I had used, unsuccessfully, for years.

If you've ever been in litigation, you know how paranoid you can get and how paranoid your friends get too. I was afraid to ask Pat for her help after being turned away by so many. But Pat had always been a champion, and I desperately wanted and needed her there. Bravely I dialed and it rang through.

"Pat Picardo?" I said, when someone answered.

"No, Pat Rosalia," she said. "Who's this?"

"Uhh, Ingrid," I responded reticently.

"I don't believe it," she told me. "I was just going to call you. Gene [Pistilli] and I were just speaking about you and wondering how to get Jim's old school desk to Adrian."

I was speechless.

"It's his sixth birthday this week, isn't it?" she asked.

I didn't know how to be thankful enough. Beside being a wonderful singer-songwriter of the original Manhattan Transfer and other colorful groups, she had been married to one of the defendants in my lawsuits, Tommy Picardo, now known as Tommy West. When Jim and I first moved to New York City in 1968, we had lived with Tommy and Pat. A year later they were divorced. Now, after all these years, Pat and I were reunited.

Pat came out to live with us in San Diego. She taught Adrian James to play the piano and he played her his first self-penned song. Pat was the most wonderful thing that had happened to our lives in a long, long time. While A. J. and Pat played, I made dinner.

OLD RUSSIAN PROVERB

Once upon a time, two little birds were flying safe and high over a great big delicious field when suddenly they were caught in a snowstorm. To get out of the blustering wind, they flew up high and dove down deep, right into a big mound of warm caca covered with snow. At once, a hungry wolf came sniffing by. The wolf heard the song of one bird singing for her happiness and warmth. Immediately the wolf devoured her, in one big bite.

The moral of this story is that it's okay to be in trouble. It's even okay to fall in caca. But if you do, don't sing about it! After all these years, I'm still learning this lesson.

With one record still unreleased on Riva Records and litigation still howling at my door, I was a silly bird to be singing. But in spite of the impossibility of being free enough from litigation to promote my music, I couldn't help myself. I loved to sing that much.

In 1980 I was reunited with veteran producer Nik Venet, who had coproduced the first album Jim Croce and I did for Capitol Records in 1969. Nik produced my second solo album, *In an Unfamiliar Way,* and as with the first one for

Riva Records, when the time came to mix it and to go out on the road to promote it, I was too busy in court to pursue my own career. I should have heeded that old Russian proverb, but back then, like Jim Croce's song says, "I Learned the Hard Way Every Time."

⊷

When I dove into the pool during the fall of 1980 and smashed my nose bone right up inside my head, not only did it hurt like hell, but I looked like a cranky raccoon. So when I learned that same afternoon that Jim Croce and I had won an ASCAP award for our country song "Age," I was feeling absolutely awful and didn't want to go anywhere.

My invitation to the awards show said that I was going to have to leave for Nashville in a couple of days if I wanted to be there in time to pick up our prize. Realizing that I was actually included in an award for a song Jim and I co-wrote, I couldn't pass up the opportunity to collect it personally. Besides, the words to the song still rang true and I was wondering just how long it would take me to get back up again.

AGE

> I've been up and down and round and round and back again,
> Been so many places I can't remember where or when,
> And my only boss was the clock on the wall and my only friend,
> never really was a friend at all.
> I've traded for pennies, sold my soul for less.
> Lost my ideals in that long tunnel of time.
> I've turned inside out and round about and back again.
> Found myself right back where I started again.

After examining my nose, my good friend Dr. Jim Grant assured me it was definitely broken. He said he could wait to fix it until I returned from Nashville, and gave me the medicine I needed to survive the flights. A. J. and I were on our way south.

After we had settled into a hotel in Nashville and were all gussied up and headed for the Convention Hall, I realized I had forgotten my little diamond engagement ring that Jim had saved so long to buy me. Along with a keepsake ring of my mom's and a baby ring with James Joseph Croce's initials on it, I had left it on the sink after washing my hands. I ran back to the room as fast as I could to get them, but there in the doorway, so big I could not pass by, was this woman in a maid's uniform swearing up and down that she had never, ever seen my rings, acting indignant that I would even ask. I was horrified. These rings were my most precious keepsakes, my good-luck charms, and they were gone. On top of that, the awards show I'd flown all the way down south to attend was about to begin without me.

A. J. picked up our award, and it was kind and generous of them to give it to us. But if anyone down there in Nashville has any knowledge as to the "wear-abouts" of my most prized possessions, I'd gladly trade the trophy for my lost rings.

All of us have quirks. One of mine was this fear that because my mother died at age thirty-six, I might too. But I didn't, and the party we had to celebrate my thirty-sixth birthday was a celebration of life. I decided it was time to leave the past behind and to set the gigantic goal of running a marathon. I looked in my friend Mark's running magazine and decided the race in Stockholm would be a great one. A. J. would be out of school and we could make a vacation of it. My son was very supportive of my running. He rode his Hutch and timed me every day while I trained.

In the late spring of 1983, we took off on one of our best trips ever. I was going to run my first marathon and A. J. and Jean Tetrault planned to visit every café along the way, eating éclairs and cream puffs while they watched me run.

Jean, A. J., and I had been rendezvousing for eight years now, ever since we'd met at my kitchen table in 1975. With all his experience traveling for the United Nations Jean always knew wonderful places to stay, terrific people to meet, and delicious meals to enjoy.

In May we met in Rome. We stayed at San Anselmo and pigged out on pizza by the piazza. I was serious about this race, and in every city we went to, from Rome to Venice, Paris to Geneva, Interlaken to Copenhagen, I ran my buns off. It was an interesting way to see the countries and to work up a great appetite. All this time, I vacillated between believing that I could win the race and doubting whether I could even finish it.

Finally, the night of the marathon arrived. At 11:00 P.M., it was still daylight in Stockholm. A little strange—but oh well! I was pumped up, scared, and as ready as I could be. To top it off, it rained like crazy that night. Yet people lined up all along the course with big smiles to cheer us on. Excited, but in pain, I started out with six-minute miles. To my grave disappointment, something happened in my twenty-fifth mile. My foot cut out and I ended up

Training for the Stockholm Marathon with A. J., 1983.

Photograph by Patrick Downs

limping my way over the finish line, wanting to laugh and cry at the same time. Jean and A. J. were there to catch me. And I was so glad it was done.

Completing the race was an extraordinary high—a sensation of great closure and joy. But like right after giving birth, I wasn't so sure I ever wanted to try it again.

That night I treated myself to anything I wanted. After the pizza, pasta, fries, and crème brûlée, I fell into bed.

CHOCOLATE-KAHLUA CRÈME BRÛLÉE

2 1/2 cups heavy cream
4 ounces unsweetened chocolate
6 egg yolks
2 whole eggs
1/4 cup granulated sugar
1/2 teaspoon vanilla extract

1 tablespoon instant espresso powder
4 tablespoons Kahlua
1 1/4 cups milk
3/4 cup superfine sugar

IN A HEAVY SAUCEPAN, heat 1/2 cup cream over moderate heat until it comes to a boil. Add the chocolate and stir gently while it melts. In a medium-size stainless-steel bowl whisk together the eggs, granulated sugar, vanilla, instant espresso powder, and Kahlua. Heat the remaining cream and milk in a heavy-bottomed saucepan until almost boiling. Gradually whisk in the chocolate cream mixture. Transfer the chocolate custard into the egg mixture in the stainless-steel bowl and whisk together slowly. Return the mixture to the saucepan and cook over moderate heat, stirring constantly with a wooden spoon until the chocolate custard coats the spoon (3 to 4 minutes). Cool the custard and strain it through a fine mesh strainer or cheesecloth.

Preheat the oven to 350°F. Place 8 flameproof 6-ounce ramekins into a large, high-sided pan, and fill them with the custard. Place the pan on a rack in the center of the oven and pour water into the pan halfway up the level of the custard. Bake 40 to 50 minutes covered lightly by foil. Remove the ramekins from the pan and cool. Chill for at least 4 hours, or overnight.

A few hours before serving, preheat the broiler. Sift superfine sugar evenly over the top of the custard. Set the custard under the broiler 3 inches from the heat. Broil until the sugar is browned and caramelized, about 1 1/2 minutes. Remove and chill.

SERVES 8

Though litigation was still awaiting me in San Diego, I felt bolstered by running my first marathon and rejuvenated by the times A. J., Jean, and I had spent together. Enjoying a vacation from our travels, A. J. and I went to the Isle of Elba. Good things were about to happen; the "second circle" was about to turn. I could feel it!

When I returned home to San Diego, doctors found a cyst on my vocal chord. I had it removed but I couldn't sing anymore. Out of boredom and in response to a last-minute request from my friends Marty Lee and Robin Helmer, I helped them cater a party for 250 guests that turned into 400 at the last minute.

For years, my homemade food had been complimented. The owner of a famous spa in California had eaten at our home on several occasions and offered, "If you ever decide to pursue your cooking, we'd love to have you as our chef at the Golden Door."

I didn't take her seriously, of course, but after the rush of feeding hundreds and making them happy, I recognized what a thrill throwing a great party and serving people could be. And I wondered, for just a moment, should I consider catering?

THE BLINTZ QUEEN

Russian, Jewish, and European Cuisine

Max and Ida Jacobson, my paternal grandparents, 1947.

My father's immigrant parents, Max and Ida Jacobson, came from Russia in the early 1900s. Grandpop Max was a gentle carpenter, a wonderfully uncomplicated man. A saint. In contrast, my Grandmother Ida was a shrew. No matter how you tried, you could never make this woman happy.

One time my grandparents came to visit us for dinner. We had worked all day preparing a delicious meal, and as the food was brought to the table Grandmom Ida ran out the back door, demanding that my father take her home immediately. "I can't stay here one minute longer, Sid," she complained. "Your floors are too hard!"

If Ida didn't get her way, she'd bitch and moan until there was no choice but to kill her or satisfy her demand. If food saves lives, I am convinced it saved hers. Many of the meals in this chapter are derived from Ida's "lifesaving" recipes.

Colorful magenta borscht is a reminder of Ida's feisty temperament. My Grandmom prepared our "Traditional Rossel," or "Ida's Beet Brew," at Passover. She learned how to make it in Kiev. Rossel is naturally fermented beet root. It takes about a month for the beets to ferment, so, as with Ida, you must be patient.

IDA'S BEEF BORSCHT

3 cloves garlic
2 large yellow onions
2 tablespoons vegetable oil
4 pounds lean beef brisket
1 quart Rossel (see directions below)
1 cup beets, peeled and slivered
6 cups water

3 whole beets, peeled
1/2 pound small round potatoes
Lemon juice, to taste
Sugar, to taste
Salt and pepper, to taste
2 teaspoons fresh dill, chopped
Sour cream

I LIKE TO BEGIN my soups by sautéing chopped garlic and onions in a saucepan for about 7 minutes in a couple tablespoons of vegetable oil over medium heat. Add a pinch of salt to bring out the flavors and to speed the cooking process. When the onions are translucent and golden, add the brisket to this pan and brown on all sides.

Heat the Rossel, slivered beets, whole beets, and water in a large, heavy nonreactive soup pot. Bring the liquid to a boil and reduce to medium-low heat.

Once the meat is browned, transfer the brisket, garlic, and onions to the soup pot and cook, partially covered, over medium-low heat for about 3 hours, skimming off the white foam as it rises. Add potatoes in the last 30 minutes of cooking.

Separate the brisket, whole beets, and potatoes from the liquid. Taste the liquid and add lemon juice, sugar, and salt and pepper to taste. Slice the beef for another course or remove the fat and put in the soup bowls at serving time. Refrigerate the borscht and remove the fat.

Heat and serve in individual bowls with a sprig of dill, a small potato cut in half, and a dollop of sour cream. Diced cucumbers and diced hard-boiled eggs may also be used as a traditional accompaniment.

Rossel

2 quarts water
6 pounds red beets, peeled and shredded

Boil the water and let it cool to room temperature. Put the beets in a large crock or glass jar with at least 2 inches of water to cover them. The beets must always be immersed, so add parboiled, lukewarm water when necessary. Keep the lid half on, covered with a kitchen towel.

In 24 hours, a white veil will cover the surface. Remove it, and every other day remove it again, stirring the beets each time and covering as before. In 1 month the Rossel is ready to be refrigerated and used for borscht.

Serves 10 to 12

Chilled California Beet Soup

This beet soup is Croce's California version of borscht. It's quick and uncomplicated.

3 pounds red beets
3 cloves garlic, finely chopped
1 cup yellow onion, chopped
2 tablespoons extra virgin olive oil
4 to 5 cups water

1 cup fresh orange juice
3 tablespoons lemon juice
2 teaspoons rice wine vinegar
Salt and pepper, to taste
2 teaspoons fresh dill, chopped

Bring a large pot of water to a boil and reduce the heat. Put the beets (without their greens) in the pot and cook about 40 minutes until tender. Drain and cool under cold water. Peel and quarter the beets and set aside.

Sauté the garlic and onions in the olive oil for about 7 minutes, until translucent. Add a pinch of salt. Combine the beets, onions, and garlic in a food processor and pulse until smooth. Add the orange juice, lemon juice, vinegar, and salt and pepper to taste. Add water (up to an extra cup if needed to reach desired consistency).

Chill, and serve accompanied by a sprig of fresh dill and a dollop of sour cream or plain yogurt.

SERVES 8 TO 10

After a second unsuccessful vocal chord operation, I discussed with friends all kinds of work possibilities, but nothing fun or rewarding came to mind. I invited my friend Joanne Kerr to our home one night to help me write a résumé. After twenty years in the entertainment business, performing, writing, publishing, and singing my music, I needed a new career. And after ten years of litigation, I needed a new life. It was late and I was hungry, so I offered Joanne some of my homemade blintzes. I used to freeze them by the hundreds as a handy offering for friends. They were quick, easy, and delicious, and after one scrumptious bite of my Mama's Cheese Blintzes with fresh blueberries and sour cream, Joanne turned to me and said, "Ingrid, this is what you should do." I laughed at her and with a tinge of sarcasm said, "What, open a restaurant?"

The next day I was in business. Blinchiki International, Inc., was born.

Initially, in March 1984, my one-thousand-square-foot rented kitchen on the corner of Fifth and University with a window out to the parking lot worked perfectly for packaged goods and takeout. But as soon as I began cooking and the aromas hit the street, people outside asked to come in.

I bought three little tables and a dozen chairs and set them in the kitchen, out of the way of the stove. Before I knew it, I wasn't just making blintzes, I had a restaurant.

I started with Grandmom Ida's Chicken Soup. It's not only a meal in a bowl, the stock is a wonderful base for many other dishes.

CHICKEN SOUP AND MATZO BALLS

֍ ֍

My friend Cheech Marin used a chicken stock like this for his California–Mexican-style soup-meal. Instead of carrots, he added sliced chicken, tomatoes, avocado, chopped red onions, and cilantro to his chicken soup. It was yummy.

6 quarts cold water
1 whole chicken, cleaned
Kosher salt and pepper, to season
5 carrots, cleaned and cut
*   into 2-inch slices*
4 celery stalks with tops,
*   cut into 3-inch pieces*

2 large yellow onions, peeled
1 parsnip, peeled
Matzo Balls (see directions below)
Parsley sprigs

IN A LARGE SOUP POT bring the water to a boil and reduce the heat. Rub the chicken inside and out with kosher salt and pepper. Put the chicken, carrots, celery, onions, and parsnip into the pot. Slowly bring the stock to a boil and skim off the foam as it appears on the surface. Simmer for 2 hours.

Remove the chicken and reserve for another use or as a condiment for the soup. Strain the vegetables and set aside, saving only the carrots for garnish. Refrigerate the soup to remove the fat, which, if desired, can be used for your Matzo Balls.

Have soup at room temperature, or warmer, and remove Matzo Balls from water and place in soup. To serve, place a matzo ball and soup in a bowl and garnish with a few sliced carrots and a sprig of parsley. Add chicken if desired.

MATZO BALLS

The recipe on the side of the Manischewitz matzo meal box has served me well. For fluffier balls, the less you handle them the softer they'll be.

6 tablespoons melted chicken fat
   or vegetable oil
4 large eggs

6 tablespoons chicken stock
   or seltzer water
1 1/2 cups matzo meal
Salt and pepper, to taste

BLEND THE CHICKEN FAT OR OIL, eggs, and stock or water together in a large bowl. Gradually add the matzo meal and salt and pepper, stirring as little as possible.

Cover the mixing bowl and place in the refrigerator for 1 hour. Remove from the refrigerator and shape into spoon-size balls (they will double in size).

Bring 8 quarts of water to a boil. Add salt if desired. Reduce water to a slight boil and gently add Matzo Balls. Cover, and boil gently for 20 minutes, until firm.

SERVES 8

It didn't take long for the health department, the Alcoholic Beverage Control people, the building department, the fire department, and more agencies than I knew existed to pay me a visit. You name the rule maker or regulator and they were at my door, and they weren't coming for my blintzes. Making my Potato Pancakes was a whole lot easier than dealing with their red tape.

POTATO PANCAKES

֍ ֎

4 medium russet potatoes

3 tablespoons dry bread crumbs or matzo meal

2 tablespoons heavy cream or mocha mix

3 eggs, beaten

1 medium yellow onion, grated

1/2 teaspoon salt

Pepper, to taste

1 teaspoon vegetable or canola oil

Clarified Butter (see page 174)

Plain yogurt, sour cream, or
    applesauce

PREHEAT THE OVEN TO 325°F. Grate the raw potatoes. Drain the excess moisture from the potatoes and put them in a bowl. Add 3 tablespoons bread crumbs or matzo meal, the cream or mocha mix, eggs, onion, salt, and a sprinkle of pepper. Heat the vegetable oil in a pan and cook by the spoonful, turning once. Transfer the pancakes to a platter, and put in a warm oven. Serve hot with a dollop of sour cream, plain yogurt, or applesauce.

For zucchini-potato, sweet potato, or pumpkin pancakes, substitute 1 pound grated zucchini, sweet potatoes, or pumpkin for 1 pound of russet potatoes and prepare the same way.

SERVES 5 TO 6

My reason for finding a job was more spiritual than financial. From the time I was little and helping the alteration ladies in my Grandmother Mary's dress shop or making blintzes in my Grandmom Ida's kitchen, work had been good to me. It gave me a feeling of accomplishment and self-esteem. It gave me an expression for my soul.

Starting out with my new agenda and one employee, the good thing was, I was doing what I knew best and what felt right, preparing and serving my Mama's Cheese Blintzes with cherries or blueberries and lots of sour cream.

BLINTZ CRÊPES

Because blintzes make it easy to change leftovers into fancy snacks, I like to make a large batch of batter and create a variety of "blinchiki." I sauté and brown them in butter and then freeze them by the dozen so when company comes I can simply defrost them in the microwave, and with a pint of sour cream or yogurt, I'm armed for guests at any time.

1 tablespoon butter
2 eggs, beaten lightly until blended
1 cup milk

1 cup all-purpose flour
Pam cooking spray
or other food release

MELT THE BUTTER and set aside. Using a blender, mix the eggs and milk at low speed. Add the melted butter. Add the flour slowly while the blender is still running at low speed. Once the batter is well mixed and coats the spoon with a thin film, refrigerate, covered, for 1 hour in a pitcher or bowl.

Stir the batter thoroughly and before making the crêpes, test the liquid by dunking a spoon in the mixture; again, it should coat the spoon with a thin film. Adjust by adding milk.

Using at least two and up to four 7- to 8-inch nonstick pans, spray with Pam, and heat the pans over medium-high heat. Pour about one cup of batter to coat one pan. Once covered, pour the batter out and into the next heated pan, pouring the remainder back into the pitcher or bowl. The thin layer of batter that remains on the pans will make a smooth, flexible crêpe. When the crêpes pull away from the edge of the pan (10 to 30 seconds), remove from the heat, tap them lightly or run a knife across the edge of the pan to release, and invert the crêpes on a dry towel to cool. Stir the batter at brief intervals to re-suspend the ingredients.

Note: For 100 crêpes, use 1 cup butter, 18 eggs, 2 quarts milk, 8 to 9 cups all-purpose flour, and Pam cooking spray or some other food release.

MAKES 18 TO 20 CRÊPES

MAMA'S CHEESE BLINTZ FILLING

1 large lemon
One 11-ounce can mandarin oranges,
drained and chopped
2 pounds large-curd cottage cheese,
or farmer's cheese
2 pounds ricotta cheese

2 eggs
1/2 teaspoon vanilla extract
1/2 teaspoon orange blossom
extract
Honey and cinnamon, to taste

REMOVE THE ZEST from the lemon. Strain the mandarin oranges well. Cut the oranges into tiny pieces and strain again, releasing as much liquid as possible to avoid soggy blintzes.

In a food processor or bowl, mix the cottage cheese and ricotta with the eggs, vanilla, orange blossom extract, lemon zest, and mandarin oranges. Add honey and cinnamon to taste.

Refrigerate for 30 minutes before stuffing the crêpes—the mixture should be creamy but firm.

With the cooked-side in, place the "tail" of your crêpe toward you and spoon about 1/4 to 1/3 cup of ingredients inside the center of your wrapper. Fold and hold the two opposite sides of the crêpe over the filling until they almost meet and then fold the "tail" over the ingredients, pulling the stuffing toward you. Fold the crêpe over until you form a seam on your blintz. Set the finished 3 x 2-inch flat eggroll-shaped blintz on a dry towel with the seam-side down.

To cook the blintzes, melt butter or margarine in a skillet over medium-high heat, beginning with the seam-side down. Sauté each blintz until golden brown and then flip onto the other side. To warm the ingredients in your blintz, lower the flame, and cook slowly to avoid burning the crêpe, about 5 minutes.

Blintzes may also be baked in the oven in a nonstick pan. Preheat the oven to 400°F. Coat the blintzes and the pan lightly with melted butter, margarine, or vegetable oil and bake for 20 to 25 minutes. If you are using frozen blintzes, double the cooking time.

FILLS ABOUT 25 BLINTZES

In 1977 my twin sister, Phyllis, flew west to San Diego ready to take her chance on California. Educated as an elementary and preschool teacher, Phyllis had worked in her profession for several years. But she needed a job to support her two sons, so she opted for working as a hostess in a family-owned bakery and café. Though they told her she was doing a "great job" on the door, she couldn't raise her family on compliments, so she learned to wait tables.

This blintz is dedicated to Phyllis and all the other wonderful waitpeople I know. The "experience" that hosts, hostesses, and waitpersons offer can make or break any meal. Please tip them well, because good service truly deserves it!

INGRID'S SPINACH AND CHEESE BLINTZ

4 cups frozen spinach
3 tablespoons butter
or extra virgin olive oil

1 cup sharp cheddar cheese, grated
1 cup mozzarella, grated

2 cups scallions, chopped   **Salt and black pepper, to taste**
1 tablespoon sesame oil

COMPLETELY DEFROST the spinach and squeeze out any excess liquid. Add the butter or olive oil to a large skillet and sauté the scallions about 2 minutes. Add the spinach and continue to cook about 5 minutes longer. Add the sesame oil, cheddar, and mozzarella, folding the spinach over the cheese until it melts. Season with salt and pepper. Remove the filling from the pan and cool before stuffing your Blintz Crêpes (see page 116).

If you refrigerate the mixture, it is best to bring the spinach to room temperature, and drain again before stuffing or your blintzes will be soggy.

Sauté or bake frozen blintzes, as above, and serve hot and golden brown with sour cream.

MAKES ABOUT 12 BLINTZES

The biggest difference between other restaurateurs and me is that when they started out in business they planned and prepared to open a restaurant. I simply went out to find a good place to work and it ended up being Croce's. When I jumped in and made blintzes, it never occurred to me that I needed a business and marketing strategy—and venture capital too. I had the purpose, but not yet the plan.

The love between my twin sister and me is so bonded that we can tell each other anything. Well, almost anything. In the spring of 1984 Phyllis agreed to come work with me, as long as I promised to stay in the kitchen while she ran the front of the house. What a team: a general in the front, a general in the back. And the fight was on to make a "real" restaurant out of my little blintz joint.

Did I say front and back of the house? We had to build one first. So as soon as Phyllis accepted the position, and after only a couple of months in business, I expanded out from my little kitchen into the front of the building. With great support from the health department and more generosity from my landlords (we had a month-to-month lease at only eighteen cents a square foot), we were really growing.

Phyllis opened the "bistro" for our blinchiki breakfasts and lunches while I cooked, marketed, hired, and cut red tape.

The twins were together again at long last, and to celebrate, Phyllis made her Sweet Noodle Kugel. We served it on our menu for a long time. (Phyllis always did love rich food that is white to beige.)

PHYLLIS'S SWEET NOODLE KUGEL

12 ounces dried curly egg noodles

4 tablespoons butter

4 eggs

4 cups half-and-half

1 small can condensed milk

3 tablespoons sour cream

8 ounces cream cheese

2 cups cottage cheese

2 tablespoons vanilla extract

1/2 cup sugar

1 teaspoon cinnamon

3 tablespoons sugar

Pinch nutmeg

Crumbs from 1 1/2 graham crackers

PREHEAT THE OVEN TO 350°F. Bring a large pot of salted water to a boil, cook the noodles, and drain. Melt the butter in the bottom of a 9 x 13-inch pan. In a large bowl, blend the eggs, half-and-half, condensed milk, sour cream, cream cheese, cottage cheese, vanilla, and sugar. Pour the creamy mixture into the buttered pan.

Rinse the noodles under running water, separate them with your hands, and add them to the egg and cheese mixture. Mix together the cinnamon, sugar, nutmeg, and graham cracker crumbs and sprinkle it over the top. Bake for 1 hour.

SERVES 8 TO 10

Some of our first customers were street people. They weren't paying customers, but they were faithfully waiting on our doorstep every morning when Phyllis came to work. At that time the Hillcrest community was a magnet for transients, and my twin sister was so kind, she couldn't turn them down. But it was soon clear that paying customers wouldn't sit with "Reagan's kids." While Phyllis's sweet generosity had encouraged them to tarry, it was tricky coaxing them to leave.

My landlord came up with a suggestion and Phyllis got the new opening duty. After all, what are sisters for? "Take the Polaroid and aim. They don't want the police to have their picture." Fortunately, it worked, and we never needed film. She just pointed her camera and they disappeared.

These Hot Potato Blintzes have a way of disappearing too.

HOT POTATO BLINTZES

12 medium potatoes
4 carrots
3 tablespoons extra virgin olive oil
2 cups yellow onions, chopped
1 cup scallions, chopped
3 cloves garlic, minced
1 can Ortega green chile strips, chopped

1/2 cup butter
1/2 cup sour cream
Salt and pepper, to taste
Milk, half-and-half,
*   or mocha mix, as needed*
Optional: serrano chiles,
*   finely chopped, to taste*

PEEL THE POTATOES and carrots and cut into large chunks. Bring a large pot of water to a boil, add the potatoes and carrots, and cook until they are easy to pierce with a fork, about 10 minutes. When the potatoes and carrots are ready, drain, and put them in a food processor or large mixing bowl.

Heat the olive oil in a large sauté pan, add the onions and cook until tender, about 7 minutes. Add the scallions, garlic, and chiles and cook 3 minutes longer.

Mix the cooked ingredients into the potatoes and carrots, and add the butter and sour cream. Blend well until the hot potato mixture is creamy but firm. Use milk, half-and-half, or mocha mix to reach a thick and creamy consistency.

For spicier potatoes add serrano chiles to taste.

MAKES 32 TO 36 BLINTZES

A short time after we opened our little restaurant, I expanded the menu from just blintzes to include Russian, Jewish, and European specialties. We served breakfast, lunch, and dinner daily. When a customer called to request that we cater a party for him, I opened Blinchiki Catering Company too. I couldn't turn him down.

I guess my talent for catering came from my mom. She never missed an opportunity to celebrate. When it was time to party, she'd set up a gorgeous buffet, then sit down at the piano and sing Rodgers and Hart tunes. Our dining room table would be piled high with hors d'oeuvres and elaborate platters of food.

Chopped chicken liver with onions was one of my favorite things on her table. It was rich, creamy, and crunchy. I have used this recipe often to please our guests.

CREAMY, CRUNCHY CHICKEN LIVER PÂTÉ

1 pound chicken livers, cleaned and halved
1 cup milk
2 eggs

1 1/2 cups white onions, chopped
1 clove garlic, peeled and chopped
1/2 teaspoon dried thyme

1 cup walnuts, chopped

3 tablespoons butter

1/2 teaspoon fresh sage, chopped

1/2 cup Madeira wine or brandy

PUT THE CHICKEN LIVERS in a bowl with the milk. Cover and refrigerate overnight.

Boil the eggs, peel, and refrigerate. Roast the walnuts in a pan over medium-high heat for about 5 minutes and set aside. Drain the chicken livers. In a medium saucepan heat the butter and sauté the livers, 1 cup of the onions, and the garlic until the livers are lightly browned and the onions are golden.

Cool the mixture and put in a food processor with a metal blade. Add the rest of the raw onion, thyme, sage, Madeira or brandy, and the two hard-boiled eggs and blend until creamy. Add the roasted walnuts and pulse quickly to maintain their crunchiness. Serve chilled with crunchy bruschetta (see page 45).

MAKES ABOUT 2 CUPS

Yes, we would love to cater your party," I assured a customer who called and wanted me to serve a traditional Passover dinner for himself and eighty-five guests—the next day.

By one o'clock on the afternoon of Pesach, I had pulled out my son's books from Hebrew school and read about the seder. I assembled a book of prayers, included my menu, and made souvenir copies for all the guests.

Then I went over to check out the party site. When I rang the bell, my newly divorced client answered the door barefoot, naked, and with only a towel to cover his erection. His large black Doberman was at his feet, staring at me like I was something good to eat. *Go home, Ingrid,* I screamed silently to myself, *right now!* But I couldn't quit.

Avoiding the obvious, I walked the property. It stretched a full block from the kitchen to the patio on the other end of the house where he wanted his appetizers served. The "ample" plates, utensils, and glassware that he had assured me were available for eighty-five were in matching sets of two.

The kitchen was the next sign of what a terrible mess I was in. A teeny-weeny electric stove, a microwave, a toaster oven without a plug, and a refrigerator that looked like it had been ripped out of a VW camper were the only equipment I had to work with for the party. Not a pretty sight.

But then my customer handed me my very first catering check. I was so proud, all I could say was, "I'll be back in an hour!"

As we unloaded, I put the brisket down in the kitchen to return to the car for more stuff. From the corner of my eye I saw that vicious Doberman leap onto the counter and swallow half the beef in one gulp. Fearful as I am of dogs, I was even more frightened of not having enough food for the party, and I moved quickly to rescue the remaining brisket.

Unbelievably, the customer scolded me for frightening his pup, then petted and consoled the dog while he proceeded to reassure me that his guest list had shrunk from eighty-five to sixteen, so there would be plenty of food for his pet. Then he reverently told me, as if to set the record straight and make things right, "I want you to know I was a great fan of your late husband."

Only two and a half of the four burners worked on the electric stove, and after less than an hour of cooking the capon, unbeknownst to me the oven turned off. At the last minute, I improvised: with only sixteen guests, I was able to cook individual portions on one burner and use the microwave for the rest.

I went back into the kitchen to clean up a bit and found a flooded kitchen floor. There I was standing in three inches of water, dishes and pots piled up high, when the first seder prayer was about to be recited. I wanted to cry. But all the food was cooked and ready to serve, the guests were waiting, and there was no time to feel sorry for myself. I swallowed my tears, waded through the kitchen to the dining room, threw open the door with a big smile, and, a platter of brisket tzimmes in my hands, acted as if everything was going just as planned.

Friday Night Brisket and Tzimmes

୪ ୨

1 lean 4-pound beef brisket
6 cloves garlic, crushed
Paprika, to taste
Salt and pepper, to taste
5 tablespoons vegetable oil
2 large onions, chopped
6 carrots, chopped

4 to 5 stalks celery, with leaves,
   chopped
2 cups water
Optional: 1 envelope
   dried onion soup
Tzimmes (see directions below)

PREHEAT THE OVEN TO 325°F. Rinse the meat with water and pat it dry. Mix the garlic, paprika, and salt and pepper with 2 tablespoons of the oil to form a paste. Rub the paste on all sides of the meat and let it stand for 30 minutes. Heat the remaining 3 tablespoons of oil in a heavy-bottomed casserole and brown the meat on all sides. Coat with dried onion soup if desired. Add the fresh onions, carrots, celery, and 2 cups of water. Cover the pot and place in the oven. While the brisket cooks, prepare the Tzimmes.

After the brisket has cooked for 2 1/2 hours, remove the lid and set aside the carrots and celery. Spoon half the Tzimmes from the pan, covering the brisket. Return both the brisket and Tzimmes to the oven and cook, uncovered, for 1 more hour, or until the beef is tender. Cook the rest of the Tzimmes for 30 minutes more and set aside for vegetarians.

Tzimmes

3 large carrots, peeled
   and cut into chunks

1 teaspoon salt
1 teaspoon honey

5 medium white potatoes,
    peeled and cut into chunks
3 medium sweet potatoes, peeled and
    cut into 1-inch-thick rounds

4 cups chicken broth or water
1 cup prunes, pitted
1 cup dried apricots
1 cup orange juice

PUT THE CARROTS, white and sweet potatoes, salt, and honey in a large pot. Add the chicken broth or water to about 1 inch above the ingredients. Cover and bring to a boil, then reduce the heat to medium low. Add the orange juice, prunes, and apricots. Continue to add chicken broth or water to prevent sticking. Cook about 30 minutes. Do not stir.

SERVES 8

KASHA AND VARNISHKAS
(BUCKWHEAT GROATS AND BOW-TIE NOODLES)

1 large onion, finely chopped
3 tablespoons vegetable oil
1 cup kasha (buckwheat groats), toasted
1 large egg, beaten lightly
2 cups boiling chicken stock or water

Salt and pepper, to taste
1/2 pound dried bow-tie noodles
2 tablespoons butter
Optional: 1 to 1 1/2 cups brisket
    gravy

IN A SMALL SKILLET, cook the onion in the oil over moderate heat, stirring until golden, and then set aside. In a bowl mix together the kasha and the egg until the kasha is well coated. Cook the kasha mixture in a skillet over moderate heat, stirring for 3 to 5 minutes until the groats are separated and toasted. Stir in the boiling water or chicken stock and simmer the kasha, covered, for 8 to 10 minutes, or until it is tender and all the liquid is absorbed. Season the kasha with salt and pepper and keep covered.

While the kasha is cooking, boil the bow-tie noodles in a large pot, stirring occasionally, for 8 to 10 minutes, or until they are al dente. Drain them well and return them to the large saucepan, and mix with the butter and salt and pepper. Add the kasha, the onion, and the brisket gravy. Salt and pepper to taste, and toss until the mixture is combined.

SERVES 8

I have my stepmother, Florence, to thank for her special holiday religious instruction and the feasts she prepared when I was a child. She is a wonderful cook and inspired me to prepare my homemade meals.

In addition to running my business and raising my son, I helped organize the Hillcrest Street Fair. I had a big, personal triumph when we sold twenty-six hundred blintzes on just one day of the event. The line to our booth wrapped around the block, and I got this towering feeling that blintzes were going to be the next fast food of the eighties.

I was the Blintz Queen! And after creating thirty-one varieties, I decided it was time to do some research and development to find out if there was a market for my product.

I packed up some samples and headed north to Los Angeles. I'd made an appointment to meet the man my research had identified as the Wizard of Blintzes. He sold more frozen blintzes on the West Coast then anyone else around.

When I arrived I found a big fancy office with gigantic movie bills on every wall. The star on all the posters was Debra Winger, and when I was introduced to the Wizard himself, Mr. Winger, I knew why. He was so proud of his little girl, he had to show her off!

"The Blintz Queen," at home on Pennsylvania Avenue, 1985.

Photograph by Harvey Wong

I showed off my delicious blintzes. Mr. Winger tried the Mama's Cheese, Chicken Pesto, and Apple Pie–Raisin-Nut. He liked them. He thought they should go in the gourmet frozen-food section in supermarkets across the country. I was so happy. Then he told me what he was willing to pay for them, and I was so sad.

Mr. Winger gave me my first reality check in the food business.

While I was off to a successful start in the catering business, I was still wondering, was San Diego ready for blintzes? Prospective customers were passing me by, and I realized that my personal quest to introduce every Californian to the blintz was ahead of its time. Perhaps, I thought, Kamish Broit might be a fast-food winner.

AUNT RUTH'S KAMISH BROIT
(ALMOND BISCOTTI)

3 large eggs
1 1/4 cups sugar
1 cup vegetable oil
2 teaspoons lemon zest
1 teaspoon vanilla extract
4 cups all-purpose flour
1 1/2 teaspoons baking powder

1/4 teaspoon salt
1 cup slivered almonds, chopped
Cinnamon sugar (1/2 cup sugar
   mixed with 1/2 teaspoon
   ground cinnamon),
   for sprinkling

GREASE A BAKING SHEET. In a bowl, mix the eggs, sugar, and oil until blended. Stir in the lemon zest and vanilla. In a separate bowl, sift the flour with the baking powder and salt. Add to the egg mixture. Mix until blended. Stir in the almonds evenly and refrigerate for 30 minutes.

Preheat the oven to 350°F. Shape the dough into 4 logs about 2 inches in diameter and place them on a baking sheet. Sprinkle the top and sides with half the cinnamon sugar (save the remainder for the second baking). Bake for 30 minutes. Transfer the logs carefully to a rack to cool for 30 minutes.

On a wooden board with a sharp knife, carefully cut the logs in diagonal slices about 1/4 inch thick—you will need 2 or 3 baking sheets. Bake about 7 minutes per side or until lightly toasted so they are beige and dotted in places with golden brown; the side of the cookie touching the baking sheet will brown first. Watch carefully so the cookies don't brown throughout. Cool on a rack. Keep in airtight containers (they keep for about 2 weeks).

MAKES 5 TO 6 DOZEN COOKIES

Years of litigation had taught me patience and how to spend money to achieve my goals. So the restaurant business was a natural progression. Now that I was in it, I just needed to find a familiar product that would sell easily . . . something you could carry and eat without a fork, knife, or spoon . . . something quick and easy.

"Poppers, a meal not just a muffin" became my next brainchild. Mrs. Fields did it with her cookies, why not Mrs. Croce with her poppers? My first was a banana bran nut popper, fashioned after my banana bread.

Once I developed my popper recipes, I needed a baker to make them. I put my first employment ad in the paper and asked for résumés to be sent to our business address.

I got a letter, not a résumé, from a gentleman named Stan Richards, and from the day we met, Blinchiki and my life were better for it. I didn't ask about his past employment. All I wanted to know was, could he do this job? His letter was so touching, he instilled trust in me, and on the spot, I offered him the baking position. The first and most naturally delicious muffin Stan made for us was our Blueberry Muffin.

BLUEBERRY MUFFINS

ॐ ॐ

2 cups all-purpose flour, unsifted
1 teaspoon baking powder
1/2 teaspoon salt
1/2 cup sugar
2 eggs, lightly beaten
1/2 cup condensed milk

1 teaspoon vanilla extract
4 tablespoons butter, melted,
   or vegetable oil
1 1/2 cups fresh blueberries
Vegetable cooking spray

PREHEAT THE OVEN TO 375°F. Sift together the flour, baking powder, salt, and sugar into a mixing bowl. In a separate bowl, combine the eggs, milk, and vanilla and then add the butter or vegetable oil. Make a well in the center of the dry ingredients and pour in the milk mixture, stirring with a fork just until the dry ingredients are moistened. Fold in the blueberries.

Spray the popover pans or muffin tins well with vegetable spray. Ladle the batter into twelve 3-inch muffin tins, filling each tin approximately 3/4 full. Bake for 20 to 25 minutes or until a straw inserted in the center of the muffin comes out clean. Cool in tins about 5 minutes, then remove. Serve immediately or allow to cool.

MAKES 12 MUFFINS OR 6 POPPERS

While the legal case I had paid dearly to bring to court was presented greatly below my expectations, I was what my attorneys called victorious in my litigation with the music producers, publishers, record company, and lawyers—if that's what you can call the waste of time and money I spent fighting to get back what was mine.

Healthy and dense, this wonderful muffin will make you feel "victorious" even if you're living in difficult and inconvenient times. Corn is one of my comfort foods and I sure needed consolation when I finished my lawsuit.

HOT CORN POPPER

1 1/2 cups yellow cornmeal
1 cup all-purpose flour
2 teaspoons granulated sugar
2 tablespoons double-acting
    baking powder
1/2 teaspoon salt
1 to 2 teaspoons chili powder, to taste
1 to 2 teaspoons jalapeño chiles,
    crushed, to taste

2 medium green chiles,
    chopped
One 15-ounce can creamed corn
    or 1 cup sweet corn kernels
1 cup condensed milk
    or mocha milk
2 eggs, slightly beaten
4 tablespoons butter, melted,
    or vegetable oil

PREHEAT THE OVEN TO 425°F. In a large bowl, sift together the cornmeal, flour, sugar, baking powder, salt, chili powder, jalapeño chiles, and green chiles. In a medium bowl, whisk together corn, condensed milk or mocha milk, eggs, and butter or vegetable oil. Make a well in the flour mixture and pour the liquid ingredients in the center. Stir and combine, mixing all the ingredients evenly.

Spray the popover pans or muffin tins well with vegetable spray. Spread the batter evenly into the pan or tin. Bake until the poppers are golden brown on top and a straw inserted in the center of the popper/muffin comes out clean, about 20 minutes in a standard muffin tin and 40 to 45 minutes in a popover pan.

MAKES 16 MUFFINS OR 8 POPPERS

Right before A. J.'s thirteenth birthday, we were walking in Balboa Park when our eyes fell upon a litter of pups for sale. If a boy doesn't have a dad, I thought, he should at least have a dog. Then all of a sudden I had three kids. A. J., Blinchiki, and now Jenny, a wonderful black-and-tan mutt. Before I knew it, I needed a time-management class and had no time to take one. I was working hard at scheduling my time, but how could I find enough hours to build a business, pick up after Jenny, and raise a teenage son? Somehow, you just do.

At close to thirteen, A. J. was a lot like his dad. He was either self-motivated or not at all. To my son, school was merely an interruption in his education. When he wasn't playing his piano, listening to his 78s, studying for his bar mitzvah, or entering a science fair with a project on how different styles of music affect different age groups, he was busy with his "mod Society," scooters, and secondhand stores. His days were full, and I felt caught between yielding too much independence and not giving him enough.

CRANBERRY PUMPKIN WALNUT POPPER

❧ ❧

1 orange, cut in half
3/4 cup water
1 cup fresh cranberries
1 1/2 cups condensed milk
1 egg
1 1/2 16-ounce cans pumpkin pie filling
3 tablespoons brown sugar
1 teaspoon vanilla extract

1/4 teaspoon nutmeg
1/4 teaspoon cinnamon
2 cups all-purpose flour
1 cup cornflakes or granola
1 teaspoon baking soda
1 cup walnuts, chopped
Cooking spray

PREHEAT THE OVEN TO 375°F. Squeeze the juice from 1/2 orange and place the juice and orange in a small saucepan with the water and cranberries. Cook for 2 minutes or until the cranberries pop open. Remove from the heat.

In a large bowl, put the milk, egg, pumpkin, brown sugar, vanilla, nutmeg, and cinnamon. Remove the orange from the saucepan and add the cranberry-orange mixture with all liquid to the bowl with the pumpkin mixture and stir gently.

In another large bowl, combine the flour, cornflakes or granola, and baking soda. Add the wet mixture to the dry ingredients and stir in the walnuts. Spray the popover pans or muffin tins well with vegetable spray. Bake poppers for 40 minutes and muffins for 20 minutes, or until a straw inserted in the center of the popper/muffin comes out dry.

MAKES 16 MUFFINS OR 8 POPPERS

Time was only one of the challenges with my son. Wisdom and care were others, and there was no road map or clear answer as to how to be a good mom. As I strove for balance, A. J. was helpful and sympathetic. And though not necessarily obedient, he was always kind.

Blinchiki, on the other hand, was a baby that demanded my attention all the time. In the beginning I had done most of the jobs myself and simply verbalized my needs to others. I struggled with simple concepts like "here's the recipe; now how do I get someone to follow it?" This was a sure sign of Blinchiki's "infancy" stage.

I needed a trained staff, guidelines, policies, and regulations, and our dog Jenny needed a bath! After work I would make and then join A. J. at our kitchen table for dinner; then it was off to yoga to reflect and relax. A cup of tea with our Original Popover served with orange marmalade is delightful after stretching. Ommm. Om mani padme hum. Back to the source.

THE ORIGINAL "POPOVER" POPPER

2 cups all-purpose flour
1/2 teaspoon salt
2 cups milk (extra milk as needed
   to reach creamy consistency)

6 tablespoons unsalted butter,
   melted
6 jumbo or extra large eggs

PREHEAT THE OVEN TO 450°F. Begin with the hot oven and then lower the heat to 375°F after 20 minutes of baking. Generously butter 6 popover pans. In a mixing bowl, whisk together the flour, salt, milk, and butter. Slowly whisk in the eggs until blended. Do not overmix. The batter should be the consistency of thick cream (add extra milk if needed).

Place the buttered tins or pans in the oven until heated, about 2 minutes—do not allow the butter to burn. Pour the batter into the greased popover cups and bake for 40 to 50 minutes (20 minutes at 450°F and 20 to 30 minutes at 375°F). Do not open the oven while cooking. Serve immediately, puffed up and hot with butter, honey, and jam.

SERVES 6

After paying for advice from an accountant and attorney who, I later learned, knew no more than I did about running a business, or for that matter negotiating my ten-year "nonnegotiable" lease, I was the proud owner of Croce's Coffeehouse at Horton Plaza, scheduled to open in October 1985.

But before we moved Blinchiki International downtown, it was time for my son to be bar mitzvahed at the Wailing Wall. Our good friends Tziona and Tzvicha Axelrod and their three handsome sons were kind enough to have A. J. stay with them for the summer in Israel and to visit Egypt and Jordan too. Tziona was A. J.'s teacher at Beth Israel School. I had never joined a synagogue and was more involved culturally than religiously with being a Jew, so A. J.'s interest in Judaism was very much his own.

A little old traditional rabbi officiated at the ceremony at the Wailing Wall in Jerusalem. They put these little boxes on A. J.'s arms, a prayer shawl around his shoulders, and a yarmulke on his head. A. J. was all decked out for the initiation, and afterward we partied at a park in Haifa and ate falafel and hummus.

This was an important spiritual respite. While A. J. was exploring his belief in God through his rite of passage, his questions were inspiring me. Although I had never been drawn to "group" religions, my spiritual philosophies were always serious considerations in my life and my business. And I was serious about my Cinnamon Apple Nut Poppers too. We had a standing order for these poppers from customers in Connecticut. They ordered dozens daily.

Cinnamon Apple Nut Popper

2 cups sweet seasonal apples,
   peeled and diced
1 teaspoon butter or vegetable oil
1/2 cup sugar
1/2 cup brown sugar
2 eggs, beaten lightly
1/2 cup vegetable oil
1 teaspoon vanilla extract
2 cups all-purpose flour

1 cup bran flakes
1 cup Quaker quick oats
1 teaspoon baking soda
1 teaspoon cinnamon
1/2 teaspoon nutmeg
1 teaspoon salt
1 cup walnuts, chopped
Cooking spray
Walnut halves, for garnish

PREHEAT THE OVEN TO 350°F. Dice the apples and sauté in the butter or vegetable oil in a medium saucepan over medium heat for 2 minutes. Stir in the sugar and brown sugar and remove from the heat. Transfer the apples and sugar to a large bowl and stir gently.

Put the eggs, oil, and vanilla in a second bowl and stir with a fork.

In a third bowl, combine the flour, bran flakes, oats, baking soda, cinnamon, nutmeg, and salt and stir with a fork until blended. Stir the egg mixture into the apples and sugar and mix thoroughly. Sprinkle the flour mixture over the apple mixture and mix well. Sprinkle the walnuts over the batter and stir until they are evenly distributed.

Spray the popover pans or muffin tins well with vegetable spray. Spoon the batter into the popover/muffin tins. Place half of an unchopped walnut on top of each muffin. Bake for about 40 minutes, or until a straw comes out clean when inserted into the center of the popper/muffin. (For regular muffins, bake for 20 to 25 minutes.) Serve warm with apple butter.

MAKES 16 MUFFINS OR 8 POPPERS

The George Keating Building, built by James and Merrit Reid in 1890 for the San Diego Savings Bank, had been occupied by numerous businesses, from the Humane Society to the Globe Locker Club for servicemen. After that, a couple of small businesses and cafés took over sporadically, but my new rental space had been vacant for some time. When I met my landlords, Bill and Ethel Drell, the Gaslamp district was just short of being a ghost town. Our location had no kitchen, and the floors, walls, and ceilings were all in disrepair. Outside were transients and crime. Only an optimist or a crazy person would have entertained the possibility of success at this location. But I had a vision of the enormous possibilities for San Diego's downtown.

Croce's Jazz Bar, 1987.

THYME IN A BOTTLE

My idea was that while the Gaslamp was still wild and woolly, Horton Plaza would be a "fortress" in the middle of redevelopment. With thousands of San Diegans and tourists hungry from their shopping frenzies and safely parked at Horton Plaza, I could promote my new restaurant from my mall location, escorting my customers right to the restaurant's front door only one block away. I just jumped in with all my heart and started selling Croce's every way I could.

To put the restaurant in shape, we took advantage of the wonderful Romanesque style of the Keating Building. Our baker and new kitchen manager, Stan Richards, and I teetered on scary tall ladders, trying to mix gold paint to embellish the modillions. Andy Martinez painted the walls white. Phyllis used a deep burgundy to trim and add color to the capitals.

We ordered traditional black-and-white tiles for the floor to give a true bistro feel, and got tables and chairs from a restaurant company that was going out of business.

I was hoping to bring in a bar and music to accompany our meals. But after waiting for our liquor license for over a year and a half, I was about to give up. I soon realized that without wine and a bar, our little restaurant couldn't make it. Then, just in time, my conditional Alcoholic Beverage Control license was finally issued and I was up and going again.

A friend helped me design the new space. We installed an antique bar and cabinets and ordered the glassware and spirits. Then we had this great idea of putting Jim Croce's face across the whole back wall of the club, as a tribute to the man and his music.

A friend introduced me to Janet Fenwick, an artist from England who had never heard of Jim Croce but was a great mural painter. From a photo, she drew his features, bigger than life. But her drawing lacked his presence. I gave Janet a couple of Jim Croce albums to take home with her and told her to listen and get to know him. After hearing Jim's songs, she redid the painting, and just as we were ready to open, the magic was there.

CROCE UNIVERSITY

Soups and Salads

In 1986 litigation was over. Basically, the diversity action—a portion of which was tried in court and a whole lot of which was not—sought to obtain damages from the defendants arising out of alleged breach of contracts as well as recision of the contracts on breach of fraud, conflict of interest, unconscionable practices, and breach of fiduciary duty.

I won back our writer and artist royalties. But the copyrights and master recordings of Jim's and my songs were purchased from the defendants by Lefrak Entertainment Company and Herb Moelis. The defendants' damages went toward paying the remaining legal fees and back taxes, and they all went away with their tails between their legs.

This exhausting, litigious battle had lasted for over a decade. While it set precedent for other artists who end up in court over conflict-of-interest issues, it basically got us what was already ours, a very, very small piece of the big pie. So much for greedy attorneys and our legal system!

In 1987, while I was glad our royalties were finally coming to the right address, the money couldn't buy back my self-esteem. I had been constantly at the mercy of the attorneys' whims for many years.

The legal arena had stomped all over my dignity, and I felt yucky when the battle was done.

Fortunately, I had found the right job. Every day I went to the restaurant to make my minestrone and learn the art of business and hospitality alongside my staff.

When the waiter walked by a piece of paper on the floor and didn't pick it up, I did. If the dining room assistant needed help to clear a table quickly, I got a tray. Or if the line cook needed a break, I jumped behind the stove and practiced the recipes until I got them right.

In time, my hard work gave me confidence in myself again. No job was so small that it didn't require my attention or so menial that I didn't do it with pride.

Before our employee manual was completed, everything had to be communicated verbally or by example. This was my opportunity to set the standard for Croce's and to practice myself what I asked of others. Croce's mission statement and philosophy came out of my beliefs and discoveries back then. So did "Croce University."

I was our first student.

Soup sets the tone for the meal and sometimes is a meal. This "big soup" suggests the big job I had ahead of me when I founded Croce University. It reminds me to be flexible and not bureaucratic. I have found that it's the ingredients, consistency, and personal taste that count. Rigid rules will fail you every time.

MINESTRONE

∂ ℘

Croce's hearty "summer vegetable soup" is served with grated Parmesan cheese year-round in California. Hot and fresh, or served at room temperature the next day (when it becomes rich and thick), minestrone is a wonderful meal. Accompany with a fresh green salad and crusty Italian bread.

1/2 pound dried cannellini beans,
    soaked in cold water overnight
2 quarts chicken stock, or water
4 tablespoons olive oil
2 ounces prosciutto, or sliced ham,
    about 3 slices
2 medium onions, peeled and chopped
2 large cloves garlic, peeled and chopped
2 tablespoons fresh parsley, chopped
1 teaspoon fresh sage
1 rib celery, coarsely chopped
1 potato, diced

1 carrot, coarsely chopped
1 small savoy cabbage,
    cored and shredded
1 pound elbow macaroni
2 tomatoes, peeled
Optional: One 14-ounce jar
    tomato sauce
1/2 teaspoon salt, to taste
1/4 teaspoon pepper, to taste
3/4 cup Parmesan cheese, freshly
    grated

DRAIN THE BEANS and cook them over medium heat in a large heavy pot with the chicken stock or water for about 1 hour, until tender. When the beans are done, replace the water to reach 2 quarts and set aside.

Sauté the prosciutto in 2 tablespoons of the olive oil, in a large stockpot with the onion, garlic, parsley, sage, celery, potato, and carrot for 12 to 15 minutes over medium heat until the vegetables are lightly brown. Add 1 tablespoon of olive oil and the shredded cabbage to the pot. Toss until the cabbage has lost some volume, about 5 minutes.

Meanwhile, cook the elbow noodles, al dente, in a separate pot with 1 tablespoon of olive oil. Set aside until a few minutes before all the vegetables are finished cooking and the soup is thick.

Puree 2/3 of the cannellini beans in a food processor and then add them to the stockpot with the vegetables. Add the tomatoes and sauce and cook at a very slow boil for 5 minutes.

Gradually add the remaining beans and broth to the stockpot in which the vegetables are cooking. Taste for salt and pepper and cook for 3 hours, or until the soup is thick. Allow the soup to cool at least 20 minutes before serving with 1 teaspoon of Parmesan cheese.

For vegetarian minestrone, the omission of prosciutto or ham or chicken stock changes, but does not diminish, the flavor of the fresh vegetables and herbs.

SERVES 8 TO 10

When I was small, our neighbors, often new immigrants without much money, bartered for my dad's medical services. My father's generosity had patients lining up outside his door offering him plumbing, art, and delicious homemade casseroles, coulibiacs, and pots of soup in exchange for his medical care. No matter how little the patient had to trade, there was always an exchange, not free service.

Balance was the answer, I believed. My dad showed me what money is for and what it is not for. Whether in Philadelphia or in Gandhi's India, a mutual relationship between people is essential.

When I opened Croce's I was beginning to understand how important it was to give something for something. It was not only a good way to do business, it was a good way to do life.

Mulligatawny originated in southern India, where it was used as a remedy for indigestion. Doing the right thing and eating this soup really does make you feel better.

Mulligatawny Soup

≈ ≈

3 tablespoons butter

1/2 cup onions, small diced

1/2 cup celery, small diced

1/2 cup carrots, small diced

1 tablespoon garlic, finely chopped

3 pounds chicken meat
   (6 to 8 parts)

1/2 teaspoon turmeric

1/4 teaspoon ground ginger

1/4 teaspoon ground coriander

1/4 teaspoon cumin

1/2 teaspoon curry powder

2 1/2 cups chicken stock

1/2 cup flour

2 cups heavy cream

2 tablespoons lemon juice

1/2 cup instant rice

1/2 teaspoon Tabasco sauce

Salt, to taste

1 teaspoon black pepper

IN A LARGE SAUCEPAN melt the butter and brown the onions, celery, carrots, and garlic for 5 minutes. Add the chicken pieces. Stir in the seasonings and cook for about 5 minutes longer, being careful not to let the pan burn. Gradually add the chicken stock and bring to a boil. Reduce the heat and simmer the chicken for about 1 hour, until tender and ready to fall off the bone. Remove the chicken and debone. Slice the chicken and return it to the saucepan. Over medium heat, using a wire whip, gradually add the flour until it breaks down. Add the cream, lemon juice, raw rice, Tabasco, and salt and pepper. Cook for 10 to 15 minutes, checking consistency. The soup should be thick and creamy.

Remove from the heat and serve.

MAKES 3 QUARTS

Nineteen eighty-seven was a pivotal year in the life of our restaurant, and in my life too. Everything we are today started here.

For years I had made my blintzes exactly three and one-half ounces in weight. Their skins had been folded just so and they were baked or sautéed to an ideal, unblemished golden brown. If they weren't perfect, they weren't served. And that was that.

Some cooks, and some days, were better than others in helping me reach my objective. But more items than we could afford were becoming "employee meals." I was admittedly giving away perfectly good blintzes rather than serving anything short of perfection.

My old method was not working. While my attention to detail and my attempt at regulation had helped build excellence in my business, these controls were losing profits and taking away what fun we had. I was stressed and realized that something had to give. I had to learn what compromise is for.

I can't remember the moment or even the day that I was ready to let go of my perfectionism. But in 1987 I accepted organized chaos as a phenomenon of nature, as our managerial profile, and as a way of life. I realized how hard I had

Croce's, on the corner of Fifth and F streets in the Gaslamp district of San Diego, 1991.

Photograph by Mary Kristen

worked at making things perfect and how they almost never were. If it wasn't the stove, or the cook, or the health department, or the produce order that didn't come in on time, it was something totally unforeseen that got me crazy. I knew I had to bend before I went broke.

Somehow I recognized the absurdity of even considering that I was really in control and that there was such a thing as perfection. All of a sudden I was totally embarrassed just considering my attempt at power and command, and I started to laugh until I cried.

Today "flexibility" is my intent and my challenge. But once I learned to smile at my little imperfect blintzes going out on the tray, I started to trust in other ways too. And I'm still learning.

On St. Patrick's Day, the evening before I was to open Croce's Jazz Bar, I went out to a club to do research and returned home about 10:00 P.M. My son and I were in the process of refurbishing our house, so that night A. J. was sleeping in my room. Exhausted from all the work involved in opening our new bar, I fell asleep immediately, only to be awakened moments later by the blaring of our smoke alarm.

I popped up like toast, ran to the landing, and discovered that the stairs were too hot to walk down. Adrian James, snoozing right under the blasted bell, never heard a thing.

Dressed in our flannels, we each grabbed our personal essentials—I, my alarm clock and running shoes; A. J., his black silk suit—and we jumped from the second-story balcony to safety. I ran to our neighbors' home and called the fire trucks. The news and TV reporters arrived along with the firemen, and while I stood there in my nightgown, anguished by our fire, a journalist asked if I could tell him how it felt to watch our house burn to the ground.

Being kind, I answered, "No comment, please." But he wouldn't take no for an answer, insisting that if the media covered my good news, they were entitled to the bad. I never spoke to him, and in response the reporter wrote, "The mementos had been placed above a floor furnace, and when Croce turned the heat on, the belongings were ignited." He falsely reported that all the Jim Croce memorabilia were gone—and implied that it was my fault.

The fact was, a week before the fire, I had taken most of the Croce memorabilia downtown to display at our new bar. And the fire started because the furnace had been improperly welded. When it blew and our freshly painted house burst into flames, most of Jim's photos and trophies were safe. All but the gold albums, which perished in the fire, had made the move safely. In a way, Croce's Restaurant & Jazz Bar saved the day.

Our Green Chile Stew seems appropriate for this account. It includes the color of St. Patrick's Day, the heat of fire, and the stew we were in.

GREEN CHILE STEW

࿊ ࿊

4 cups prepared Posole (see directions below)
6 cups Pork Broth (see directions below)
1 cup Green Chile Chicken Sauce
    (see directions below)

1 tablespoon red onion, diced
2 tablespoons tomato, diced
2 tablespoons lettuce, shredded
2 tablespoons fresh cilantro

MIX THE GREEN CHILE CHICKEN SAUCE with the Pork Broth and simmer with the Posole for 1 hour. Ladle the soup into 8 bowls and garnish with the red onion, tomato, lettuce, and cilantro.

POSOLE

4 cups posole
2 pounds pork butt, cut into 2-inch cubes
1 yellow onion, sliced

1 teaspoon oregano
2 cloves garlic, cut in half
4 gallons water

SOAK THE POSOLE OVERNIGHT in a glass bowl or a nonreactive container.

In a large stockpot, simmer the pork butt, yellow onion, oregano, and garlic in the water for 2 hours. Add the posole and simmer for 2 to 3 more hours, or until the posole "blossoms." Skim the pot of excess fat, keeping the broth clear. Strain and reserve the broth and posole for the Green Chile Stew.

PORK BROTH

2 tablespoons corn oil
2 pounds pork butt, cut into 1-inch cubes
8 cloves garlic, diced and roasted
1 1/2 cups red onion, chopped
1 yellow onion, chopped
3 quarts water

15 Anaheim chiles, roasted,
    peeled, seeded, and chopped
1 teaspoon oregano
1 teaspoon salt
4 serrano chiles, roasted, peeled,
    and chopped

Heat the corn oil over medium heat and brown the pork butt. Add the roasted garlic and red and yellow onion and sauté until golden. Add 1 cup of water and scrape the bottom of the pot to release the pork scraps. Pour in the remaining water and simmer for 30 minutes. Add the Anaheim chiles, oregano, and salt. Simmer for 40 minutes. Add the serrano chiles and simmer for 10 minutes.

Green Chile Chicken Sauce

1 tablespoon olive oil	*2 cups chicken stock*
1/2 medium onion, finely diced	*6 tablespoons roux*
1/2 cup garlic, chopped	*Salt, to taste*
1/2 pound green chiles, chopped	*1 1/2 pounds chicken, shredded*

Heat the olive oil in a large saucepot. Add the onion and garlic and sauté until soft—do not burn or color this mixture. Add the green chilies and chicken stock and bring to a boil, stirring frequently. Add the roux and mix well until fully incorporated, stirring frequently so as to prevent scorching. Bring the sauce back to a boil. Season with salt. Add the shredded chicken and simmer for 15 minutes more. Add more roux if needed. Remove from the heat and cool.

This recipe makes 2 1/2 cups of chile sauce.

Serves 8

The day after the fire, I proceeded with a catering job we had contracted to do, found a place for A. J. and me to stay, filed an insurance claim, and opened Croce's Restaurant & Jazz Bar.

For our "soft" opening, Daniel Jackson played with his quartet. Between sets, Jim Croce's music permeated the club and restaurant. On a break, I went to the kitchen to check on the next day's orders and when I returned to the bar, I saw that fourteen Japanese businessmen had arrived. They were toasting with beer mugs and singing along with Jim Croce, loud and clear, "Bad, Bad Wewoy Bwon."

The lighthearted image of these men and the hefty tab they rang up that night were wonderfully encouraging on the heels of our tragedy. In a strange way, after the fire I felt that my life was starting over. Like the phoenix "wising"!

ROASTED EGGPLANT BISQUE

1 medium eggplant

1/2 medium onion

Salt, to taste

1 teaspoon olive oil

5 cups chicken stock

6 cloves garlic, peeled

1 1/2 cups heavy cream

1 teaspoon white pepper

1/4 teaspoon Tabasco sauce

2 tablespoons chives, finely
chopped, for garnish

PREHEAT THE OVEN TO 300°F. Cut off the stem end of the eggplant. Cut the eggplant in half, then into thirds. Place on a large sheet pan. Quarter the onion and put the sections with the eggplant. Lightly salt the eggplant, then drizzle with olive oil. Roast in the oven until golden brown, about 15 minutes.

Put the chicken stock into the soup pot along with the garlic and roasted eggplant and onion. Boil until tender, about 15 minutes, then puree. Add the cream, white pepper, and Tabasco. Cook over medium heat for 10 more minutes.

Serve in individual bowls and garnish with a sprinkle of chives.

SERVES 6 TO 8

To attract customers, at A. J.'s suggestion we developed a traditional jazz venue at Croce's Jazz Bar. But San Diegans were not ready to pay a cover charge for local talent, so I paid for the music myself.

I booked local bands three times a day, seven days a week, for brunch, for happy hour, and for our dinner customers from eight until midnight. In addition to A. J. Croce, friends like Shep Meyers, Hollis Gentry, Joe Marillo, Daniel Jackson, and Peter Sprague were our first performers. In no time, if you wanted to hear jazz in San Diego, you came to Croce's.

My Grandmom Mary was a successful businesswoman. I knew she adored my twin sister and me, but with her busy schedule she had little time to show it. Every day after school, we girls took a cab to her dress store at Seventh and South streets, shed our schoolbooks, and found work for ourselves. Phyllis loved to put on makeup, paint her nails, and try on the dresses so she could look like a grown-up salesperson. I went to the register to help my grandmother count the cash and to the alteration department, where Frances, our head seamstress, would teach me to sew and to use the big steam machines.

South Street was colorful and interesting. I was thrilled by the commotion, all the things to see and do. There were pawnshops, numbers writers, all kinds of wheelers and dealers, and best of all, there were "jillions" of restaurants and delis. The minute you hit South Street you could smell the ethnicity.

When I moved to San Diego, I wanted to re-create the excitement of the melting-pot community I had experienced on Philadelphia's South Street. I also wanted to bring the class and quality I enjoyed while living on Rittenhouse Square to San Diego's downtown. Croce's was going to be my upscale "South Philly West." Though no one else could see it at the time, I believed it was a plan that just needed time and hard work to make it happen.

Food was the reason I was in the restaurant business, but once we had jazz in our bar, it kind of backfired on us. Guests connected Croce's with great music but were hesitant to accept that we had great food too.

Still challenged to entice patrons to dine, in 1987 I began a seven-year ad campaign on KIFM radio. Using Jim's songs behind my voice, I told personal stories about our food and good times, and how Croce's Restaurant offered breakfast, lunch, and dinner in a welcoming setting. "When you're not home, be here" closed every commercial, and in time, listeners took me up on my invitation.

Our Curried Pumpkin Soup and Hot Corn Chowder with Chile Poblanos were welcoming additions.

Curried Pumpkin Soup

%⅄ ℣⅄

1/4 cup butter

1 large onion, chopped

3/4 cup scallions, sliced

4 cups pumpkin puree (see directions for
how to cook a pumpkin below),
fresh or canned

4 cups chicken broth

1 bay leaf

1 teaspoon brown sugar

1/2 teaspoon curry powder

1/8 teaspoon nutmeg

1 teaspoon parsley, finely chopped

2 cups half-and-half

Salt and pepper, to taste

Roasted pumpkin seeds or 2 table-
spoons finely chopped chives

Optional: 1 cup sour cream

In a medium-large saucepan, sauté the onions and scallions in butter until golden brown. Stir in the pumpkin. Add the chicken broth, bay leaf, brown sugar, curry powder, nutmeg, and parsley and simmer, uncovered, for 15 minutes.

Transfer the soup to a food processor and puree with the half-and-half. Return the soup to the saucepan and simmer 5 minutes, adding additional half-and-half or chicken stock to reach the desired consistency, creamy with medium density. Add salt and pepper to taste. Serve with a handful of roasted pumpkin seeds or chopped chives. A small dollop of sour cream or crème fraîche may also be used to garnish.

How to Cook Your Pumpkin

One 3-pound pumpkin

Preheat the oven to 350°F. Cut the pumpkin in half vertically and discard the seeds and stringy pulp. Place the pumpkin, cut-sides down, in a shallow baking dish and add water about a 1/2 inch high. Bake for about 1 hour or until tender. The pumpkin is ready when it is easily pierced with a fork. Cut each half into wedges and peel. A 3-pound pumpkin yields about 3 pounds cooked.

SERVES 6 TO 8

HOT CORN CHOWDER WITH CHILE POBLANOS

2& 8&

1/4 cup unsalted butter

1 large onion, chopped

2 stalks celery, chopped

Pinch cayenne pepper

2 cloves garlic, chopped

6 cups chicken stock

1/2 teaspoon fresh thyme, minced

1 teaspoon salt

2 red potatoes, peeled and diced

4 cups corn kernels

2 cups half-and-half

6 small poblano chiles, charred, peeled, and chopped

Salt and pepper, to taste

2 tablespoons cilantro, finely chopped

IN A LARGE STOCKPOT, melt the butter and add the onions, celery, and cayenne pepper over moderate heat. Sauté 5 minutes, add the garlic, and stir for 1 to 2 minutes until the onions are translucent. Add the stock, thyme, salt, potatoes, and 3 cups of the corn and simmer the mixture for 15 minutes.

Transfer the solids with a slotted spoon to the food processor and puree with the half-and-half. Add the puree back to the pot, and add the chopped chiles and the remaining cup of corn. Cook 5 minutes, stirring occasionally. Season to taste with salt and pepper. Garnish with chopped cilantro. Serve with Crab and Avocado Quesadillas (see page 223).

SERVES 8

Though our customer comment cards didn't directly indicate the benefit of the radio spots, I found that when I greeted guests at the front door many of them recognized my voice immediately from my KIFM commercials. Folks were thrilled that I was actually there working the floor. Many wanted to hear me tell more Jim Croce stories or talk about the sixties. Often, I found myself joining tables of folks who came in as strangers and left as friends.

Our advertising was working as naturally as our Cream of Tomato Soup with Fresh Herbs. Our patrons kept coming back for more.

CREAM OF TOMATO SOUP WITH FRESH HERBS

3 to 4 medium tomatoes, diced
1/2 can tomato paste
1/2 stalk celery
1/4 large onion
1 or 2 cloves garlic, peeled
5 cups chicken stock
1 1/2 cups heavy cream
2 teaspoons dill

2 teaspoons basil
1 teaspoon oregano
1 teaspoon tarragon
3/4 teaspoon rosemary
1 1/4 teaspoons black pepper
Salt, to taste
Fresh parsley sprigs, for garnish

IN A LARGE SOUP POT combine the tomatoes, tomato paste, celery, onion, garlic, and chicken stock. Bring to a boil on medium heat and cook for 15 minutes. Remove from the heat and puree in a food processor.

Return to the heat, add the cream, herbs, and pepper. Cook over medium heat for 10 to 15 minutes. Season with salt and pepper.

Garnish with fresh parsley sprigs.

SERVES 6 TO 8

Slowly but surely our customer base developed. Along with our radio spots, billboards, and print ads for our music lineup, Croce's was getting some great press.

Carroll and Barbara Armstrong, who had just moved to San Diego from New Orleans, heard the news about Croce's and came to hear our jazz. Talking to them on their first visit to Croce's, I learned that Barbara and I had been on the same gymnastics team back in Philadelphia at Girl's High School and that Carroll was the new director of sales at the San Diego Convention Center.

Carroll's conviction and talent gave me confidence that the convention center would be a success and that before long conventioneers would flood the Gaslamp quarter. That summer, tourists were beginning to fill our coffeehouse at Horton Plaza, giving us hope that with tourism and conventioneers, Croce's was going to become a great "destination."

Though they weren't lining up to get in yet, we needed to prepare for the crowds. Internal controls required my immediate attention, and Croce's demanded air-conditioning, new dishware, chairs, and soupspoons for our Cream of Broccoli Soup.

Cream of Broccoli Soup

1 onion, chopped
4 cloves garlic, minced
1 tablespoon Clarified Butter (see page 174)
5 cups chicken stock
1 pound broccoli

2 cups heavy cream
Pinch salt
1/4 teaspoon white pepper
1/4 teaspoon ground nutmeg

In a large pot sauté the onions and garlic in the clarified butter until tender, 5 to 7 minutes. Add the chicken stock and heat to a boil. Add the broccoli and cook for 2 to 3 minutes until the color is very green. Remove from the heat and puree the soup in a food processor until very smooth.

Put the pureed mixture in a pot and add the cream. Bring to a slow boil and reduce for 30 minutes. Season the soup with salt, white pepper, and nutmeg.

SERVES 6 TO 8

In 1987 I attended numerous wine-tasting dinners and seminars in preparation for a series of black-tie wine-tasting dinners at Croce's. While I had noble ideas, I found I was too busy to do the catering myself. I was seriously in need of a chef.

On October 13, 1987, chef Fay Nakanishi walked in the door. When Fay accepted the position, I requested that she use my recipes initially so we could get our controls up to par before we attempted a new menu.

The first soup Fay developed at Croce's was our French onion, and the moment I tasted it, Chef Fay got her way. Croce's onion soup is a temptress, a great favorite not only in our restaurant but in our clubs too. It's very jazzy, French, and sexy, with croutons and Gruyère. Now we were talking gourmet!

FRENCH ONION SOUP

1 tablespoon Clarified Butter (see page 174)
2 pounds yellow onions, sliced
2 tablespoons all-purpose flour
1/2 cup red wine
1/2 gallon veal, beef, chicken or
  vegetable stock
2 tablespoons brown sugar

1/2 teaspoon kosher salt
1/2 teaspoon black pepper
1/2 teaspoon thyme
1/4 teaspoon Herb de Provence
6 to 8 seasoned croutons
6 to 8 slices Gruyère cheese
6 to 8 tablespoons Parmesan cheese,
  grated

IN A LARGE SAUTÉ PAN heat the butter until it's very hot. Add the onions and cook slowly until the onions are caramelized, stir in the flour, and mix well. Deglaze the onions from the pan with the red wine and add the veal, beef, chicken, or vegetable stock, scraping the bottom of the pan to free any stock particles. Add the sugar, salt and pepper. Wrap the herbs in cheesecloth and add to the soup. Simmer for 30 minutes. For best results, allow soup to sit overnight before re-heating for service.

At time of service, ladle onion soup into deep bowls. Top each portion with a crusty crouton, a slice of Gruyère cheese, and a tablespoon of Parmesan cheese. Place bowls under a medium-high broiler for 2 minutes or until the cheese melts and turns a golden brown.

Serves 6 to 8

My Grandmother Ida's kitchen stance and demanding personality prepared me for the difficult cooks who worked at Croce's over the years. Sister Phyllis learned how temperamental some cooks can be firsthand when our new Chef Fay threw her first tantrum and her first and last plate in Croce's kitchen, missing my sister's head by an inch. After the flying dish, we talked. Our plates stayed on the racks until plating, and Chef Fay stayed with us in our kitchen for over seven years.

Respect is earned, not demanded. As I explained to Fay, chefs are not God in Croce's kitchen—I am.

With Phyllis as our daytime manager, we hired a second restaurant and bar manager for evenings. We developed programs to acknowledge the good work people were doing, started our Jim Croce's Music Awards for local musicians, and offered Croce scholarships for employees who wanted to further their education. Julie Gelfat, who became Croce's most outspoken cheerleader, came on board that year as my personal assistant to help with music and public relations.

We started to hold "town meetings" at which everyone was challenged to find solutions to our problems. Together we came up with ideas to improve "our" business. And we prospered by the good ones and learned from the bad. Acknowledged on the spot with "Croce bucks" or on the floor by higher check averages and better tips, employees were getting the big picture.

Many of these good folks who joined our extended family back then stayed with us for many years, matriculating and learning at Croce University. In the kitchen we had Otis Hitt, Bill Bloomhuff, and Jeff Hurlbut. On the floor were Michael "Hawk" Harrelson, Kitty Rice, Rita Rafalski, Mark Grahl, and Paul Osborne, who came and went as the Bali wind blew. In the bar were cocktail waitress Marisa Chavez, our outrageous bartender, Larry Lowy, and our beautiful Southern belle, Sharon Fordham. These wonderful people are part of our original Croce's family, and I'm thankful for them all. They weathered the changes, as did our Cream of Chicken Soup with Dill.

CREAM OF CHICKEN SOUP WITH DILL

2 tablespoons olive oil

8 ounces chicken breast meat

5 tablespoons butter

1/2 cup celery, diced

1/2 cup onion, diced

1/2 cup zucchini, diced

1/2 cup carrots, diced

1/2 tablespoon garlic, chopped

1/3 cup flour

3 cups chicken stock

1 cup raw potatoes, cubed

1 1/2 cups heavy cream

6 tablespoons lemon juice

1/2 teaspoon black pepper

2 tablespoons dill

Salt and pepper, to taste

IN A LARGE SOUP POT add the olive oil and chicken breast. Roast the chicken, then remove the skin, dice the meat, and set it aside. Heat the butter in the same pot. Add the celery, onion, zucchini, carrots, and garlic and cook 5 minutes. Add the flour and mix well. Add the stock and bring to a boil. Add the potatoes and cook 20 minutes.

Add the cream, lemon juice, pepper, and dill. Adjust taste with salt and pepper.

SERVES 6 TO 8

Persuading employees to seize the initiative, to be resourceful, effective, and sensitive to the bottom line isn't easy. But while other companies fail, I believe we succeed more than not. We do our best to revitalize our staff, to educate people about controls and accountability and how much they matter.

I believe in transferring decision-making to individuals. Asking each employee to be responsible for his or her own job is vital to our agenda. Right up front, I explain that Croce's is not just about making a living—it's a commitment, a way of life.

Our employee manual really spells this out to our staff. It's one of our greatest inspirational tools, right below paychecks and just above job descriptions. Many refer to it as our bible. Not only does the employee manual tell our history and purpose, it is an up-to-date guide to our current policies and the laws we need to follow to succeed at Croce's and within the community at large.

We've been pleased at how much employees appreciate being clearly shown what is expected of them. Such instructions are not often available in the restaurant industry, or in life for that matter.

Follow each step and you will succeed with our Chilled Avocado Soup, just as many have succeeded at Croce's with our manual.

CHILLED AVOCADO SOUP

ॐ ॐ

2 large ripe avocados
2 teaspoons fresh lemon juice
1/2 cup dry white wine
1 1/2 cups chicken stock, heated to the
　　boiling point
Salt, white pepper, cayenne pepper,
　　to taste

1 cup half-and-half
Fresh tomatoes, chopped
Fresh dill, to season
Cilantro or parsley sprigs, for
　　garnish

Slice each avocado into quarters and starting at the stem end, peel off the skin. Slice the peeled avocado into a large bowl. Generously sprinkle with fresh lemon juice to prevent discoloration and to add flavor. Mash the avocado flesh with a fork to make a rough puree. Stir the wine and chicken broth into the puree (enough broth to permit easy pouring). Add the salt, white pepper, and cayenne pepper to taste; enrich the soup with the half-and-half. Pour the soup into a tureen, cover, and refrigerate. When you are ready to serve, garnish with the fresh chopped tomatoes, sprinkle with fresh dill, and a cilantro or parsley sprig.

For an unusual presentation, serve the soup inside a ripe papaya that's been cut in half and scooped out.

SERVES 6

After my final interview with each new employee, Kristen Fullerton, our trusty human resources manager, goes over our philosophy, our expectations, and all the rules and regulations we need to follow to achieve excellence. We also provide a list of principles for success and describe our awards and other ways of recognizing employees. Our structure and our communication network teams are diagrammed, and a flowchart of our organization is given to each new person to show where he or she fits on the team.

We're not a very big company. It's just that if you ask for excellence and professionalism, I believe you need to offer it too. And having a clear plan helps all of us reach our goals.

When we give an orientation and training package to new employees, we mark off on our "First Day Checklist" what they have received in order to document that the proper information has been given. Orienting a new member of our team is no easy task, but it's important that we do it well.

Another thing we do well is our Thai Chicken Salad with Fire Peanuts. We jokingly called this Fay-Ray's Thai Chicken Pasta, and it stuck.

Thai Chicken Salad

꘎ ꕤ

Six 6-ounce chicken breasts
Thai Marinade (see directions below)
1/2 cup celery, cut into julienne strips
1/2 cup carrots, cut into julienne strips
1/2 cup onion, cut into julienne strips
1 1/2 cups Japanese Vinaigrette
(see page 255)
1 pound dry angel-hair pasta
3/4 cup shiitake mushrooms

1 tablespoon plus 2 tablespoons
olive oil
6 tablespoons green onion,
chopped
6 tablespoons cilantro leaves,
rinsed well
3/4 cup Fire Peanuts (see directions below)
Sprinkle of sesame seeds

MARINATE THE CHICKEN BREASTS in the Thai Marinade for 2 to 3 hours.

Marinate the celery, carrots, and onions in the Japanese Vinaigrette for 1 hour.

Cook the pasta in salted boiling water until al dente. Drain, rinse, and stir in 1 tablespoon olive oil. Chill in the refrigerator for 1 hour.

Sauté the mushrooms in 2 tablespoons olive oil until done. Set aside.

Cook the chicken breasts on the grill or under the broiler for 10 minutes or until done.

Arrange the chilled pasta on 6 plates to form a bed. Arrange in the following order for each salad: marinated vegetables, mushrooms, Japanese Vinaigrette, green onions, and cilantro. Warm the chicken breasts and arrange in a circular fashion on top of each salad. Garnish each salad with 2 tablespoons of Fire Peanuts. Sprinkle with sesame seeds.

Thai Marinade

6 tablespoons jalapeño jelly
5 tablespoons Pickapeppa sauce

1/2 cup honey

MIX ALL THE INGREDIENTS in a food processor for 30 seconds.

FIRE PEANUTS

3/4 cup unsalted shelled peanuts
1 1/2 teaspoons sesame oil

3 drops chile oil

PREHEAT THE OVEN TO 300°F. Put all the ingredients in a large bowl and mix well. Spread the peanuts on a sheet pan and bake for 10 to 12 minutes, or until they are a dark mahogany brown.

SERVES 6

Our expectations and principles have been selected from experts in business and in life and from a lot of the mistakes I myself have made. Some may seem obvious, but they're always a wonderful reminder. While we don't require employees to carry their manuals with them, we do suggest that they read them regularly to refresh their memories—I do.

For example, I remind myself all the time that excellence is never an accident. We all need to work at it constantly—plan for it and keep our standards of performance high. We have found that excellence is contagious at Croce's. But to perpetuate our high standards takes mighty hard work and lots of energy. It also means we need to keep our vision strong so that everyone keeps heading for the same goal.

Many guests and employees head for our New Mexican Cobb Salad with Lime Yogurt Dressing.

NEW MEXICAN COBB SALAD WITH LIME YOGURT DRESSING

1 head romaine lettuce
1 head iceberg lettuce

1 ripe avocado, diced
2 medium tomatoes, diced

*2 cups Lime Yogurt Dressing (see directions
below)*
*1/2 teaspoon Fire Fry Seasoning (see
directions below)*
1/2 cup Monterey Jack cheese, grated
2 tablespoons corn kernels
*One 8-ounce chicken breast, grilled,
marinated, and cut into julienne strips*

1/2 cup cheddar cheese, grated
12 red tortilla chips
12 blue tortilla chips
4 tablespoons cilantro leaves
8 tablespoons pumpkin seeds

ARRANGE THE GREENS in a mound in a large glass salad bowl. Toss with the Lime
Yogurt Dressing and sprinkle with the Fire Fry Seasoning. From left to right, top the
salad as follows: Jack cheese, corn, grilled chicken breast placed on an angle down
the center, avocado, tomatoes, and cheddar cheese. Arrange the chips close together.
Toward the back of the salad, garnish with the cilantro and pumpkin seeds.

LIME YOGURT DRESSING

1/2 cup lime juice
1 cup rice vinegar
1 tablespoon soy sauce
1 teaspoon garlic, chopped

2 teaspoons black pepper
Salt, to taste
2 cups peanut oil
1 1/2 cups yogurt

COMBINE THE LIME JUICE, rice vinegar, soy sauce, garlic, black pepper, and salt
in the bowl of a food processor. Process until well blended. While the machine is
running, slowly add the peanut oil. Add the yogurt next and process until just
mixed.

This recipe makes 7 cups of dressing. Keep refrigerated for up to one week. It
can be used generously on fresh greens and vegetables.

FIRE FRY SEASONING

2 cups Lawry's seasoning salt
1 cup granulated garlic
1 cup black pepper

1 cup cayenne
1 cup rosemary
1 cup cumin

Mix the above ingredients. This mixture will keep for a long time; simply use to season anything hot.

I can remember working without our employee manual and job descriptions, but today it would be like working without a net. Our town meetings are just as important; without them we would lose touch with family and what we are all doing here.

These fun and enlightening gatherings are usually accompanied by a tasting of new seasonal menu items and the wines that are paired with them by our excellent wine director, Mary Sullivan. It's also our opportunity to introduce new policies and new laws that keep us interdependently healthy. At these rallies we give prizes for excellence, award dollars for comment-card winners, and honor our employee of the month.

Sometimes it takes a lot of work to make these meetings inspirational. But this open forum is our best way to educate, praise, and recognize our peers. It's a chance for a "family" reunion, and at the same time it gives us all an opportunity to pause and say thank-you for the great job we're doing.

Appreciate someone you love with our Crimson Red Pear Salad with Blue Cheese, Fennel, and Arugula. It's a wonderful way to give thanks.

Crimson Red Pear Salad with Blue Cheese, Fennel, and Arugula

2 pears, sliced
1 medium head of fennel, cored and
cut into slivers

4 tablespoons Champagne Vinai-
grette (see directions below)
Salt, to taste

4 cups arugula salad
8 walnuts, broken into small pieces

Pepper, to taste
1/2 cup blue cheese, crumbled

IF THE SKIN OF THE PEAR is tough or fibrous, peel it off. Arrange 5 slices of pear on each plate. Toss the fennel, arugula, and walnuts with salt, pepper, and the vinaigrette in a stainless-steel bowl. Place in the center of the plate. Crumble the blue cheese over the salad and make sure some hits the pear slices. Be careful not to overdress the salad. It should be very light and stand tall on the plate—it should not be heavy and oily.

CHAMPAGNE VINAIGRETTE

1/4 cup Champagne vinegar
Pinch of kosher salt

1/2 cup olive oil
1/8 cup walnut oil

PLACE THE VINEGAR in a bowl, add the salt, olive oil, and walnut oil and whisk together. Taste and adjust the seasonings as desired.

SERVES 4 TO 6

Some employees at Croce's have never gotten all the way through school. So Croce University is about education for students at all levels, from grade-school dropouts to graduate students. Since we don't necessarily expect our staff to "retire" from our restaurants and bars, Croce University offers the wonderful gift of helping people to learn excellence while they are here on the job.

When we interview new employees, we look for "students" who will use our business as a training ground, who will take with them more than the money they earn when they go. And someday, when they come back to visit their alma mater, they too will join us for a great meal and some good hugs at Croce's.

As a full-time business student at San Diego State University, Eddie Perea started at Croce's as a security doorman. He asked more questions than almost anyone I remember. He was always friendly and welcoming, but as he advanced from doorman to bartender to supervisor, he had some trouble keeping up with the responsibilities and sticking to the rules. Though these were usually small issues, they were important nonetheless. Eddie seemed to take our advice to heart; he was always polite and respectful, but sometimes the advice didn't stick.

One Sunday, Eddie called to say he would be late getting to work from a baseball game. When he arrived, he was intoxicated—cause for immediate termination according to the manual. I asked him what he'd had to drink at the game, and he told me honestly: six beers, four shots, and a couple of margaritas (something like that anyway). Straight-faced, I asked him if he thought that might be too much before work. And straight-faced he said no. He was a big guy, he told me, and he could handle it.

Because Eddie truly loved his job and we loved having him with us at Croce's, I asked him to come back the next day and we'd talk. When he came into my office, bashfully, he said that after "thinking about it," maybe he had had too much to drink. In fact, he said, it was totally out of line and he wondered what he was thinking about to do such a thing.

I wasn't willing to give up on Eddie. His merits far outweighed his mistakes. I wrote him up, gave him his final notice, and offered him one more chance.

After Eddie got his last chance, he was a new man. Something clicked for him, and he was asking a lot of questions but still following our rules and becoming an excellent team player. Even with his studies at college, he came early, stayed late, and was generous with his time and knowledge for all employees and management alike. He was on top of it!

At Croce's we honor one another with our "Make My Day" contest and selection of an employee of the month. Everyone at Croce's is encouraged to recognize the exceptional actions and performance of his or her team members, and in 1994 Eddie Perea was our winner.

Our contest works like this: at the end of each month, the employee with the highest number of responses to our Make My Day/Haga Mi Día form is selected as employee of the month. At the end of the year, we select an employee of the year from these monthly winners and give him or her a one-week paid vacation anywhere in the world.

While Eddie headed off to London, we got to stay home and enjoy one of my favorite salads at Croce's, our Pacific Niçoise.

PACIFIC NIÇOISE

4 cups loosely packed mixed field greens

4 tablespoons Raviagote Vinaigrette
  (see directions below)

1/2 cup loosely packed feta, crumbled

1 tablespoon olive oil

Four 5-ounce portions swordfish, grilled

1 small red onion, sliced

4 white creamer potatoes,
  quartered

2 cups haricot vert, blanched

1 cup yellow wax beans, blanched

1 pint red pear tomatoes

1/4 cup chicken stock, as needed
  (may substitute water)

1/4 cup parsley, chopped, for
  garnish

Salt and pepper, to taste

ARRANGE THE FIELD GREENS at the top of a large round plate. Drizzle with 2 tablespoons of the vinaigrette and top with the feta. Salt and pepper the swordfish (for additional flavor, use Dijon Ginger Butter, see page 251) or sauté it in a Teflon pan over medium-high heat with the olive oil.

While the fish is cooking, heat an 8-inch sauté pan. Add 1 tablespoon of the vinaigrette, red onions, and potatoes and sauté lightly. Add the beans and tomatoes, then the remaining tablespoon of vinaigrette. Sauté lightly, then deglaze with a small amount of chicken stock or water. Season with salt and pepper and parsley.

To serve, put the fish on the center of the greens and arrange the vegetables around it; sprinkle with parsley.

Raviagote Vinaigrette

1 tablespoon capers, rinsed and chopped

2 shallots, minced

1/3 cup Champagne vinegar

Pinch salt

1 tablespoon Dijon mustard

2/3 cup salad oil

COMBINE THE CAPERS, shallots, Champagne vinegar, salt, and Dijon in a stainless-steel bowl. Whisk until incorporated. Add the oil and whisk until all the ingredients are combined.

This recipe makes 1 cup of dressing. It keeps well, tightly covered and refrigerated, for up to one week.

SERVES 4

Croce's has an awards picnic once a year. We close the restaurant for the day, party, and recognize our hard work, vision, and achievements. Before we head for the beach, we do our summer town meeting, at which we give out a bunch of awards, prizes, and dollars in recognition of excellence.

Past "graduates" as well as family members are invited too. We supply the staples and beer, and employees bring their potluck and compete with their recipes to win the prize.

Some folks are better guests than employees, better servees than servers. It's hard to recognize up front which position will stick. And sometimes it changes midstream.

If someone decides to move on from Croce's or if we feel that they should, we certainly try not to alienate a good friend. My buddy Joe Anderson has become just that. It doesn't always work out this well, but when Joe left our employment to become our guest, we both gained a new perspective and respect for our relationship, and for this concept. Joe served us well as a door host, and now we serve him well at our bar. I think we're both happy for that.

I've noticed that people are fickle. We like something one day and we're tired of it the next. Many of us have gotten so spoiled by all the wonderful restaurants out there, we've become difficult to please when we go out to dine, we critique the food, presentation, wine list, service, and even the critics themselves. Believe me, I know what an H.M.C. (high-maintenance customer) can be. I am one.

At Croce's we appreciate our H.M.C.s; they keep us good and getting better. And as we aspire to squelch the faultfinding side of human nature, we try doubly hard to make the dining experience at Croce's delicious, welcoming, and surpassing the expectations of our most demanding H.M.C.s. It's our hope that our greatest critics become our greatest friends.

With the business community beginning to recognize opportunities in the Gaslamp, I welcomed change and the support of competitors who wanted to invest and play a part in San Diego's future. Although for a while we were one of the only games in town, a flourishing city needed more than Croce's to succeed, and I was anxious for neighbors to join us. Fio's restaurant opened across the

Members of our roundtable and staff at Croce's Tenth Annual Awards Picnic, May 1994. *Left to right:* Kathy Miller, Caroline Joyner, Deborah Ogburn, Kristen Fullerton, Ingrid Croce, Suzanne Rogers, and Kim Kovacs.

Photograph by Jim Rock

street from us, and as a result of Jack Berkman's public relations, people I didn't know existed in San Diego showed up at their restaurant for lunch. Fio's overwhelming success was ours too. It forced us to keep redefining ourselves and checking to make sure we were the best we could be.

When has a restaurant arrived? A restaurant has arrived when the business can be sold for a profit. By the close of 1987, when I was complimented by a couple of lucrative offers to sell, I felt successful. Although we were not profitable yet, it seemed that others believed we would be and that prosperity was just a wait away.

I was thrilled by the bids, but I turned them down. I was invested in my community, and while their money looked mighty good, I couldn't walk away from my dream and my Croce's family.

Though it was still just a "vision" back then, Croce's was destined to be the cornerstone of the Gaslamp's dining and entertainment scene. To encourage us further, Croce's Restaurant & Jazz Bar won the Alonzo Horton Award for "redevelopment of the Gaslamp" that year. I was proud, but mostly happy that they knew we were there.

Growing up in a city is a strange way to see the world. It often segregates us from nature and hardly ever offers us a chance to personally explore physical and spiritual frontiers. That's what I was yearning to do. And more important, to find someone to do it with. The truth is, I was lonely.

To take a break, I often walked to Horton Plaza and browsed in a bookstore. One day I was looking for a self-help primer for women who love too much. But by surprise *Abandoned: A Nostalgic Look at Rural America* jumped into my hands.

Fate must have sent it my way. I bought it and studied the pictures of farmers and their families. And suddenly, out of the blue, though I had never been there, I had a longing for the heartland. The open plains of sunflowers were somehow nostalgic and the cornfields made me hungry as well.

Rockin' and Travelin'

Croce's Daily Specials

When I turned forty, something absolutely wonderful happened. The obstacles that had blocked my path moved out of my way, or maybe *I* did. As the new year smiled on me, the veils were lifting to a softer, kinder world and life seemed brand spankin' new. As much as I longed for a mate, I'd come to the conclusion that it just wasn't my turn.

I was content sharing life with my son, rebuilding our home, continuing my work, and enjoying our award-winning halibut.

Alaskan Halibut Nasi Goreng

⁂

2 eggs

1/4 cup water

1 cup all-purpose flour

4 cups panko crumbs

Six 5-ounce fillets of Alaskan halibut

Pinch salt and white pepper

3 tablespoons Clarified Butter
   (see page 174)

1/2 pound fresh mushrooms, sliced

1 teaspoon fresh garlic, chopped

6 large prawns, shelled and deveined

2/3 cup plus 1 tablespoon sherry

1/4 cup fresh lemon juice

2 1/2 cups heavy cream

3 tablespoons Nasi Goreng (an
   Indonesian hot chile sauce)

1 1/2 tablespoons Sambol Oleek
   (a tomato-based hot chile
   sauce)

1/4 cup green onions, chopped

PREPARE THE BREADING BY lightly beating the eggs and water in a stainless-steel bowl. Prepare 3 separate shallow bowls for the flour, egg, and panko crumb mixtures. Season the halibut fillets on both sides with salt and pepper. Lightly flour the fish, shaking off any excess. Dip in the egg and drain. Coat in the crumbs. In a nonstick skillet over medium heat, warm the Clarified Butter until hot. Put the fish in the skillet and brown on one side. Turn the fish over and put the pan in a 400°F oven for 10 minutes, or until the fish is done.

Remove the pan with the fish from the oven and place it on the stovetop over medium-high heat. In the pan juices sauté the mushrooms until golden brown. Add the garlic and prawns, then deglaze with the sherry and lemon juice. Let reduce slightly, about 1 minute, then add the heavy cream, Nasi Goreng, and Sambol Oleek. Adjust the seasoning. Let the sauce reduce until thickened. Add the green onions last. Remove the fillets from the pan and set on a plate. Place a prawn on top of each fillet and pour the sauce over the fish.

SERVES 6

One afternoon at lunch, a cowboy hat and boots attracted my attention. Phyllis, who was managing at the time, knew him as a regular, a generous tipper, and a gentleman.

Shortly after I noticed the "cowboy," one of my favorite employees was arrested. I called Randy Whaley, a Croce customer and local attorney, to ask if he could help. He said he'd send his law partner to the jail, and the next day he successfully returned my cook.

A week or so later when Randy came to lunch, I went to his table to thank him for his assistance; sitting next to him was his partner. The lawyer who had helped my friend turned out to be the stranger with the boots! Thankful for their counsel, and thinking they were both cute, I played cupid for my girlfriends and invited the guys to join us for our New Year's Eve party.

"You're inviting me to a party and you don't even know my name?" the cowboy teased. He was right. I felt like maybe I was being a bit presumptuous or pushy even, and just as I was about to back off, the stranger looked me in the eye and said, "It's a tough one." He paused. "It's Jim."

This Shelton Farms chicken breast with rosemary and lemon is anything but tough. It's straightforward and downright juicy.

Shelton Farms Chicken

6 to 8 boneless chicken breasts
Lemon Rosemary Marinade (see directions below)

Put the chicken breasts in the Lemon Rosemary Marinade for 2 hours, or overnight if possible.

Lightly salt the chicken and grill to perfection. To spice it up, serve with our Traditional Mexican Mole (see page 213).

Lemon Rosemary Marinade

2 lemons, sliced thin
3/4 cup olive oil
1 tablespoon fresh rosemary, coarsely chopped

1/2 teaspoon salt
1 tablespoon cracked black pepper

MIX ALL THE INGREDIENTS in a large bowl.

SERVES 6 TO 8

Jim never made it to our New Year's Eve party. When I saw him and Randy the following week at lunch, they apologized for missing it and guaranteed they wouldn't pass up the opportunity again. "Then come for Joanne's birthday party tonight," I suggested, holding them to their promise.

Jim came alone. After giving him a quick tour of Croce's, I invited him to join us at table twenty-one for a champagne toast. Jim was totally comfortable at a table of five strong women. His composure made me relax and his humor made serious me unusually silly.

Jim mentioned that he was piloting a small plane to Catalina the next day and whimsically asked if I'd like to go along. "I'd love to go," I told him. He responded daringly, "You'd have to stay the night." "Fine," I bantered, feeling amazingly safe.

The pause in conversation revealed his surprise, or maybe I just plain scared him. A couple of hours flew by too quickly and the night was over before I got the details of our flight.

The next morning I wondered if I'd misunderstood. I thought we'd had a date, but he never phoned. *I don't even know his last name,* I realized, but I wanted to.

You'll want this dish too! We served this dish at Blinchiki, before we opened Croce's and it has stayed with us over the years. Coulibiac is a traditional Russian dish that originally utilized leftover vegetables, kasha, and fish and was a dish for the poor. Today it has amassed the wealth of time and experience. Croce's Coulibiac is a valuable asset to our restaurant.

Salmon Coulibiac

ॐ ॐ

2 sheets puff pastry, cut into 12 squares
1 large bunch fresh spinach leaves
Kasha (see page 126)
Mushroom Duxelle (see directions below)
Six 2 1/2-ounce salmon portions

6 tablespoons lemon butter
1 egg, for egg wash
Lemon Hollandaise Sauce (see
    directions below)

PLACE THE PUFF PASTRY on a floured work surface. Cut each sheet into 6 squares, approximately 4 x 4 inches. Place the 6 pastry squares on the work surface. Put 6 spinach leaves in the center of each pastry. Spoon 1 tablespoon each of Kasha and Mushroom Duxelle on the spinach. Place the salmon portion on top. Spoon 1 tablespoon of the lemon butter on top of each salmon.

Preheat the oven to 350°F. Place the top pieces of the pastry on each coulibiac. Press down the edges to seal securely, then crimp the edges decoratively. Using a pastry brush, lightly egg wash the edges of the pastry. Bake for 15 to 20 minutes. Serve with Lemon Hollandaise Sauce.

Mushroom Duxelle

1/2 pound whole mushrooms
2 teaspoons Clarified Butter (see page 174)
2 tablespoons shallots, chopped

1/4 cup white wine
Salt, to taste
White pepper, to taste

USING A FOOD PROCESSOR and chopping blade, finely chop the mushrooms or slice them thinly by hand. Heat a 10-inch sauté pan with butter. Add the mushrooms and shallots. Cook for 3 minutes. Deglaze with white wine. Let the mushrooms reach a boiling stage, then reduce to medium low. Let the mushrooms cook down until all the liquid has evaporated. Adjust the seasoning with salt and white pepper. Remove from the heat and cool.

LEMON HOLLANDAISE SAUCE

6 egg yolks
6 tablespoons white wine
1 cup plus 5 tablespoons Clarified Butter
     (see directions below), warm

Pinch salt
Pinch white pepper
Pinch cayenne
1/4 cup lemon juice

SET A MEDIUM POT of water on medium-high heat and bring to a boil. In a medium stainless-steel bowl whisk together the egg yolks and white wine for a few seconds until light and frothy. Place the stainless-steel bowl on top of the boiling water. Continue to whisk the mixture over the saucepan—do not put the bowl directly on the water or you will risk overcooking the eggs.

Whisk rapidly over the heat until the mixture becomes thick and has tripled in volume. Remove the bowl from the heat and continue to whisk 30 seconds more to ensure the eggs do not overcook. Add the Clarified Butter with a ladle while gently whisking until the sauce stiffens.

Finish the sauce with salt, white pepper, cayenne, and lemon juice to taste.

CLARIFIED BUTTER

1 cup unsalted butter

PLACE THE BUTTER in a medium stockpot over low heat until fully melted. Remove from the stove and skim the foam from the top. Ladle the Clarified Butter from the pot without disturbing the milk solids in the bottom.

One pound of butter makes 3/4 pound Clarified Butter (volume decreases by one-fourth).

SERVES 6

All weekend long I thought about this thirty-seven-year-old, never-married, available man—an Iowan crop duster, Beatles lover, and a radical of the sixties who'd left behind a rock and roll band and the family farm to study law.

The next day I went to see *The Last Emperor* with a friend from work. After the show, as the lights went up, I felt a hand on my shoulder. I turned and, to my surprise, it was Jim. "I've been trying to reach you all weekend," I blurted out.

"That's funny, he was with me," retorted Jim's young friend as she grabbed him by the arm and pulled him closer. It never occurred to me she was more than a younger sister, so I was comfortable, not covetous.

Jim, too, was totally at ease, and in front of God and his twenty-two-year-old date asked, "Would you like to meet tomorrow night to discuss your cook?" We had some details to go over about his client, my recently incarcerated employee, and he was taking the opportunity to rendezvous. "I'll meet you at Croce's about 6:30, if that's okay?"

It's better than okay, I thought, and said, "Sure."

This New Zealand Rack of Lamb with Passionfruit Demi Glaze is also better than okay; it's daring and provocative and will stay "Gentle on Your Mind."

New Zealand Rack of Lamb with Passionfruit Demi Glaze

☙ ❧

6 to 8 lamb racks (8 or 9 ounces each)
Salt and pepper, to taste
3/4 cup chile paste

Passionfruit Demi Glaze (see
directions below)

PREHEAT THE OVEN TO 450°F. Season the lamb racks with salt and pepper. Rub with chile paste and cook to the desired degree of doneness, 20 to 35 minutes.

Remove from the oven. Cut the lamb racks in thirds. Drizzle the Passionfruit Demi Glaze over the lamb.

Passionfruit Demi Glaze

1/4 cup sugar

1/4 cup cognac

4 cups Veal Stock (see directions below)

3 tablespoons passionfruit compound

1 tablespoon white vinegar

Salt and white pepper,

    to taste

In a medium pot over medium heat, caramelize the sugar, then deglaze with the cognac. Add the Veal Stock, passionfruit compound, and vinegar. Bring to a boil, then reduce to low heat. Reduce the sauce by half. Season with salt and white pepper.

Veal Stock

2 onions

2 large carrots

1 stalk celery

5 pounds veal bones

1/4 cup olive oil

One 6-ounce can tomato paste

1 head garlic

1 pint mushrooms, cleaned

3 bay leaves

1 teaspoon black peppercorns

4 stems fresh thyme

3 stems fresh oregano

5 stems curly parsley

Preheat the oven to 350°F. Peel and quarter the onions. Peel and cut the carrots into thirds. Break the celery stalk in half. Toss the veal bones, onion, celery, and carrots with the olive oil. Lay on a cookie sheet and brown in the oven. The vegetables will cook about 20 minutes faster than the bones, so remove when done, turning once when cooking. Cook the veal bones until brown on all sides; it should take approximately 40 minutes.

Put the veal bones and vegetables in a pot and cover with cold water. Bring to a boil and skim any foam or impurities. Reduce the heat and add the tomato paste, garlic, mushrooms, bay leaves, peppercorns, thyme, oregano, and parsley and simmer approximately 2 1/2 hours. The stock is done when it tastes full-flavored.

Serves 6 to 8

Thyme in a Bottle

Our last weekend together, Jim Croce and I had visited a tattoo parlor on Broadway in San Diego. I remembered laughing to myself about how my anguish over our relationship had me wanting to tattoo *Jim* on my hip, cross it out, and write it all over again.

Then I had a more recent memory of the book that had jumped into my hands right before the new year, the one about old farms, midwestern farmers, and the heartland.

Just when I'd given up on finding a mate, Jim from Pickle City, Iowa, came into my heart as if he'd always been there. Granted there were some basic questions to be answered, like "What's your last name and where's Iowa?" But these were mere details. The important thing was, after our meeting at table twenty-one he felt like an old friend, and we just had some catching up to do.

When you taste our Lemon Chicken, it too will seem like an old friend, or a new one you'll want to enjoy often.

LEMON CHICKEN

&⁍ ⁌&

6 to 8 boneless chicken breasts
1/2 cup flour
3/4 cup Clarified Butter (see page 174)
3 tablespoons shallots, chopped
2 cups mushrooms, sliced
3/4 cup white wine
1/2 lemon

3/4 cup Veloute (see directions below)
4 1/2 cups heavy cream
Kosher salt, to taste
White pepper, to taste
Parsley, chopped, or arugula, for garnish

PREHEAT THE OVEN TO 350°F. Dredge the chicken in the flour seasoned with salt and pepper. Heat a saucepan over a medium-high flame until hot. Add the Clarified Butter and sauté the chicken breasts until golden brown on both sides. Add the shallots and mushrooms, then deglaze with white wine. Squeeze in the juice from 1/2 lemon.

Put the pan with the chicken in the oven and cook until done, 10 to 12 minutes. Remove from the oven, place on the stovetop. Add the Veloute, heavy cream, salt, and white pepper. Bring to a boil and reduce the sauce until thickened. Put the chicken breasts on plates. Pour the creamy lemon sauce on top and garnish with parsley or arugula.

VELOUTE

2 tablespoons butter
3 tablespoons flour

2 cups milk, heated to a boil
Pinch salt and white pepper

IN A SAUCEPAN, prepare a roux by melting the butter over a low flame. When the butter is melted add the flour, stirring constantly. Cook slowly about 2 minutes until the butter and flour are combined—do not color. The roux will froth at this point— turn off the heat and whisk in the boiling milk all at once. Set the pan over medium-high heat and stir constantly until the sauce boils (about 1 minute). Season with salt and white pepper.

SERVES 6 TO 8

From the start, I was charmed by Jim. He was secure and adventurous, not pompous at all. Since our first date, he had pursued me with courageous gentility, always calling when he said he would, always arriving on time. Although he was often outspoken, Jim's strong ethics and his midwestern manners tempered his delivery. I was extremely lucky to find a combination of strong convictions and intelligence in such a kind and gentle man.

Surprisingly, he was even more verbal than I with his thoughts and feelings. He loved conversation, and his intelligence and candidness assured me I could be my strongest self and he'd be stronger still.

After a romantic dinner one evening, we debated whether to take a safari to Africa or just camp out in Borrego Springs for the night. Ready for adventure, we

Jimmy Rock and Ingrid, 1988.

Photograph by Mary Sullivan

opted to go back to my house. When Jimmy Rock hung his tie on the handle of my bedroom door, he promised he wouldn't go as long as it was there. The next morning I superglued it to the doorknob and Jim never left again.

Now since we're talking monogamy here, this Cabernet Madeira works great with lots of things, but we do it with just one.

TOURNEDOS OF BEEF WITH CABERNET MADEIRA SAUCE

Eight 3 1/2-ounce tenderloins
Cabernet Madeira Sauce (see directions below)

CHARBROIL THE BEEF FILLETS to the desired doneness. Top each fillet with an equal amount of Cabernet Madeira Sauce.

CABERNET MADEIRA SAUCE

1/2 large onion

1 stalk celery

1 carrot

1 tablespoon butter or olive oil

1 cup mushrooms

1/3 cup garlic cloves

3 thick strips raw bacon

1 tablespoon tomato paste

1/2 cup Madeira wine

1/2 cup Cabernet

6 cups Veal Stock (see page 176)

1 tablespoon roux (see page 20),
   as needed

COARSELY CHOP THE ONION, celery, and carrot. In a large pot, heat the butter or olive oil. Cook the vegetables, mushrooms, garlic, and bacon over medium heat, stirring frequently. When the onions become translucent, add the tomato paste. After about 5 minutes, add the wines and let it cook down by half. Add the Veal Stock and bring to a boil. Reduce the heat to a simmer and cook the sauce down by half. Salt and pepper to taste. Thicken with a small amount of roux if needed. Strain the sauce if preferred (personally, I like it chunky).

SERVES 4

Jim Rock never fought to take me away from my history, only my neuroses. He just walked into my life, gave me all his love, and his peace and comfort became mine too. At least, most of the time.

I still had my peculiarities, and fear of abandonment was at the top of my list. As I was getting comfortable in our relationship, I also got scared.

One morning before leaving for work, I wrote a love note to Jim and left it on the kitchen counter. Sitting at my desk downtown, I looked at my watch at 5:05 P.M. and suddenly panicked.

I realized Jim would return to the house before I could get there and I'd have no time to retrieve the card I'd left for him. Somehow, since writing it, I'd gotten insecure and paranoid. I was sure I'd written something inappropriate or stupid.

I was convinced that what I'd "confessed" would make him go away, and I desperately wanted him to stay.

My fear of desertion was out of control, so I called Jim from work immediately and begged him, "Please don't open your card."

When I got home, after Jim told me he'd already read my letter and he was still there, he called me into the kitchen and lifted me onto the counter as if I were a little girl. Then one of the best things ever happened. He told me he wanted the right to "screw up."

"Of course," I assured him.

"Well," he said, seizing my complete attention, "you have that right too!"

My heart stood still, and I heard him.

"I do?" I asked innocently. And for absolute, positive, consummate security, "I have the right to screw up?"

"Yes, you do," he said.

The fact is, I've been screwing up ever since. And Jim's still here.

LAMB CHOP WITH SPICY PEANUT SAUCE

Eight 6- to 8-ounce portions lamb chops
3/4 cup red wine vinegar
1/2 cup plus 2 tablespoons olive oil
1 bunch cilantro, chopped
1 cup green onions, chopped
3 cloves garlic, minced
1 teaspoon curry powder

1 teaspoon oregano
1 teaspoon black pepper
1/2 cup brown sugar
1 tablespoon salt
Spicy Peanut Sauce (see directions
 below)

To MARINATE THE LAMB CHOPS, place them in a nonreactive flat-bottomed dish. Pour the red wine vinegar over the meat and rub the chops with 1/2 cup olive oil.

Add the cilantro leaves, green onions, garlic, curry powder, oregano, black pepper, brown sugar, and salt. Coat the lamb evenly with marinade and refrigerate, covered. This can be done up to 24 hours in advance.

Grill or sauté the lamb chops. Put 1 tablespoon of the olive oil in a Teflon pan. Heat, but do not burn, the oil over a medium flame. Add the lamb chops to the pan. Cook until medium rare, approximately 2 minutes per side. Set aside the first batch and cook the remaining 4 lamb chops.

Heat the Spicy Peanut Sauce over a medium flame and ladle over the lamb chops before serving.

SPICY PEANUT SAUCE

2 cups roasted peanuts
1/2 cup green onions
1/2 cup cilantro leaves
2 tablespoons hoison sauce (available at most Asian specialty stores)

1/2 cup plum sauce
1 tablespoon Sambol Oleek (available at most Asian specialty stores)
1/2 cup chicken stock

PUREE THE PEANUTS in a food processor using the steel blade. Then add the remaining ingredients except for the chicken stock. Continue running the machine until the peanut sauce is smooth and the green onions are chopped small. Add the chicken stock while running the machine for about 30 seconds. The sauce can be made up to 2 days in advance, and kept in the refrigerator.

SERVES 8

Escrow came through on the new house we had found to replace the one that got scorched. For several months after the fire, we'd been renting, but A. J. and I were anxious to settle down. When Jim moved in with us I was happier than I can remember. But Adrian James was less eager to accept a new family member.

A. J. was very protective and slow to trust. He was also justifiably concerned because, unfortunately, my past emotional relationships had been with inappropriate "drama mates." Since his dad had died, I had never met a man like Jim Rock, a man who enhanced me in every way and made me proud to be with him always. So while the man in boots and a cowboy hat had taken up residence in my heart and in my life in a very short time, my son wasn't as sure. When I told A. J. that Jim had asked me to marry him, he responded with, "What's the rush?"

In March 1988 Jim Croce won the Philadelphia Music Foundation Hall of Fame Award and A. J. and I were going back east to visit family and pick up the prize together. After that, we had a vacation planned in Amsterdam, just the two of us.

At the show our son did a great job performing a medley of his father's songs executed in A. J.'s own style on a Steinway baby grand. David Bromberg then presented Jim's Hall of Fame Award to A. J. before an audience of appreciative Jim Croce fans.

A. J. was proud of his dad's success. But at sixteen he found Jim Croce a hard act to follow. Yet, with A. J.'s own music at the center of his life, there was no way around the continual comparison between him and his father. Never willing to ride on his father's accomplishments, our son was nonetheless appreciative of the audience's praise.

This was not a good time for A. J. Our house had burned down, school sucked, and my imminent marriage to Jim Rock was bringing in a stepfather where no father had been since he was two. While I was in love and feeling incredibly happy, A. J. was down.

Since I'd met Jimmy Rock, making sense of my cluttered, busy life had never been as easy or anywhere near as much fun. All the pieces were coming together, and I felt safe, secure, and more comfortable than ever to be there for my son.

While I was in Amsterdam watching the tulips bloom, I wrote Jim letters. It felt good trusting him at home, having good, uninterrupted times with A. J. and a vacation from work. Distance made my heart grow and grow, but there were still things I had to work through. Like my past.

I told Jimmy Rock that I'd been very lonely in my life. He smiled and quoted Kurt Vonnegut, "Lonesome no more."

I said I'd felt sad that so many people were around me because of my name. He looked at me seriously, and said, "Ingrid?"

The time was close when Ingrid Croce would become Ingrid Croce-Rock. And my life was changing beautifully. Ingrid means daughter, Croce means cross, and now Rock, my new name, was to be my salvation.

From the time A. J. had played and booked bands in the basement under our restaurant, I had explored the possibility of expanding Croce's into the "Jazz Cave" below. I wanted a space large enough to bring in big acts that couldn't be staged in our Jazz Bar. We invested in surveys and appraisals, but after all was said and done, the Jazz Cave was short-lived when a good friend, sound engineer Jim Jirovsky, discovered that the steel beams from the basement amplified the bass sounds into our restaurant above.

Then the Mercantile Building right next door to Croce's came up for rent. Jimmy Rock and I decided to open Croce's Top Hat Bar & Grille, named after Jim Croce's song.

At the same time, Jim left his law practice to help me. He says I made him "an honest man," confirming that we had similar sentiments about attorneys.

As if my schedule weren't busy enough, I was introduced to a friend of Jim's, literary agent Bill Gladstone, who suggested that I write a book. I thought, *Why not,* and I was excited by the idea of doing this cookbook. Bill's proposal, however, was the Jim Croce biography, which he assured me needed to be done first. I asked my fiancé if he would help me take on that project. Before you write a biography about your first husband with your future husband, think seriously about it!

Or just relax and enjoy these Prawns Wrapped in Basil and Prosciutto. They're a lot easier to swallow.

PRAWNS WRAPPED IN BASIL AND PROSCIUTTO

෯ ஜ

30 large shrimp
30 large basil leaves

10 ounces prosciutto, thinly sliced

WRAP EACH SHRIMP with 1 basil leaf and then 1 slice of prosciutto. Skewer the shrimp, 5 per skewer. Grill to perfection. Serve with polenta and Roasted Pepperonata Salad (see page 16).

SERVES 6

Jimmy Rock had been a drummer and guitarist and put himself through college playing in small auditoriums and clubs in the Midwest. He had a good ear for music, the one he could still hear with anyway. He loved the Beatles, Dylan, and me and when it was time to deal with musicians, he was right there to help.

I must credit A. J. alone with bringing traditional jazz to Croce's Jazz Bar. But when Jim and I opened Croce's Top Hat, we all agreed that this venue would showcase rhythm and blues and diverse entertainment, including national acts. While rhythm and blues was our mainstay, we did comedy, rock and roll, and everything else we could to bring in customers.

For a short while we offered an open-mike night. Robin Williams came to dinner, and took us up on it. He did a forty-five-minute set for free. But even with Mr. Williams, Top Hat was not an overnight success. Sometimes there were more folks in the band than in the audience. For me this was déjà vu. I had experienced this from "Both Sides Now"—in the sixties and seventies as a performer, in the eighties as an entrepreneur.

When I was a child, our surrogate mother and housekeeper, Lois, was like family from the time I was two. Lois Walker was a savvy, sexy "Tina Turner," my Tinker Bell. When my mother was working late or on a "hot" date, Lois took my sister and me home at dark to do our homework and then she tucked us into our beds. Lois told us all kinds of street lore about her son "Big Jim Walker" and her daughter "Peaches." Her tales were exciting, more along the line of "You Don't Mess Around with Jim" than "Father Knows Best."

Unbeknownst to her, Lois was my role model, my soul mate. She worked hard, played hard, and had this terrific way of making it all the same thing. People either loved her or feared her, but everybody knew her name.

South Street was her street, like Fifth Avenue in San Diego was becoming mine. Her favorite place to take us to eat was Jim's Philadelphia Cheese Steaks, and back then they were the best. Steak sliced paper-thin on a soft Italian roll with melted cheese and fried yellow onions. Yumm!

This item is dedicated to Lois Walker. When we opened Top Hat it was my first choice for our grille menu. If you're counting cholesterol, don't! Just give yourself a break and enjoy it. At Croce's Top Hat and Ingrid's Cantina, our Philadelphia Cheesesteak is a big-time star, and our Southwestern variation with New Mexican spicy fries is hot too.

Jim's Philly Cheesesteak (Southwest Style)

෯ ৡ

2 pounds beef sirloin, sliced thinly against
  the grain (Philly style)
1 tablespoon Clarified Butter (see page 174)
  or olive oil
1 clove garlic , minced
2 medium onions, sliced thin
1 cup green pepper, cut into julienne strips

1 cup green Ortega chiles, sliced
1 tablespoon jalapeño pepper,
  chopped
Salt and pepper
6 torpedo rolls, sliced and toasted
12 slices mozzarella or Monterey
  Jack cheese

SHRED OR CHOP THE RAW BEEF. In a large nonstick skillet heat the butter or olive oil with the garlic. Add the onions, green peppers, chiles, and jalapeños and season to taste with salt and pepper.

Preheat the oven to 350°F. Slice the torpedo rolls lengthwise and toast. Divide the cooked steak mixture into 6 equal portions and place on the toasted roll. Top with 2 slices of mozzarella or Jack and put in the oven for 5 to 7 minutes, until the cheese melts. Serve with spicy fries.

MAKES 6 SANDWICHES

Phyllis asked her ex-husband and good friend Mel Horowitz and his wife, Linda, who owned Point Loma Embroidery, if they could put our logo on jackets for Croce's. They had already provided us with T-shirts, hats, and bags, but we hadn't graduated to the big stuff yet and for our birthday Phyllis wanted to surprise me.

She had our first jackets manufactured, and they sold great. Another big seller was our Blueberry Peach Cobbler.

BLUEBERRY PEACH COBBLER

4 cups peaches, peeled and sliced

2 cups blueberries

1 teaspoon lemon juice

1/4 teaspoon almond extract

1/2 cup plus 5 tablespoons sugar

3 cups flour

1/4 teaspoon cinnamon

1/4 teaspoon nutmeg

2 tablespoons baking powder

1/2 teaspoon salt

8 tablespoons cold unsalted butter

2 eggs, slightly beaten

1/4 cup milk

PREHEAT THE OVEN TO 400°F and butter a 2-quart baking dish. Arrange the peaches in the bottom of the dish. Pour the berries over the peaches. Combine the lemon juice and almond extract and pour over the berries and peaches. Sprinkle 1/2 cup sugar over the fruit, and bake for 20 minutes.

While the fruit is cooking, mix the flour, 3 tablespoons sugar, cinnamon, nutmeg, baking powder, and salt together in a bowl. Cut the butter into the dry ingredients until the mixture resembles cornmeal. Combine the beaten eggs and milk, and add to the dry ingredients until just combined.

Remove the fruit from the oven. Quickly drop large spoonfuls of the dough to cover the surface. Sprinkle the remaining 2 tablespoons sugar over the dough. Return to the oven and bake until the top is firm and golden brown—about 15 minutes.

Serve hot with homemade vanilla ice cream or brandy-flavored whipped cream.

SERVES 6

W hen I met Jim's mom and dad, I wanted them to be my own. Vernon and Evelyn Rock represent the best in the American experience. With all my travels and familiarity with fame, their life together was all I ever wished for: secure, uncluttered, loving, and full.

I met them first, briefly, in San Diego. Vernon and Evelyn were very accepting of me and the craziness in my life. I'd never met such an adorable, nonjudgmental pair.

In July 1988 I went to Iowa for my first visit to the Rocks' hometown and to attend a celebration at Jim's old high school gym in Blencoe. The occasion was a party in honor of Jim's parents' fiftieth wedding anniversary. All of Vernon's and Evelyn's friends and family would be there to honor them and to meet me.

The night I arrived, I slept in Jim's childhood bed, across from the farm, the cornfields, and the sunflowers, which really did appear to grow up to the sky. In the morning I walked to the park where Jim had played baseball for years; the ball field is the true home he still claims. I walked down the road past the church and the community center to the grocery store, the bank, and the diner where the farmers meet to talk about feed, weather, and loans.

I was as anxious as a kid at Disneyland to see firsthand what Iowa was really like and where people bonded for life and made love stay. Among the 327 people in Jim's hometown were many couples who had been married for fifty years or more. This was just how I'd always imagined life could be, and it took me forty years to finally come home.

The neighbors and family who came to celebrate at the party set out food buffet style so everyone could help themselves. Being there was even better than Jim had described. The ordinary was extraordinary in every way, and I was so thankful my life hadn't ended before I'd gotten a benchmark on what "normal" could really be.

I wasn't just marrying Jim; now I was marrying his whole family. In just a couple of months we started what Jim's parents had been practicing for fifty years. A happy marriage!

In the Midwest, steak and potatoes are a happy marriage too.
Top Sirloin with Roasted Garlic Sauce fit the bill perfectly.

Top Sirloin with Roasted Garlic Sauce

ஃ ௐ

Six 6- to 8-ounce top sirloin steaks
Roasted Garlic Sauce (see directions below)

PREHEAT THE OVEN TO 350°F and place the steaks under the broiler for about 6 minutes per side.

Roasted Garlic Sauce

6 to 8 large cloves garlic, peeled
1 tablespoon olive oil
1 tablespoon butter
1 tablespoon onion, small diced
1 tablespoon celery, small diced
1 tablespoon carrot, diced

1 tablespoon tomato paste
3/4 cup port wine
4 cups Veal Stock (see page 176), heated
Salt and white pepper, to taste

PREHEAT THE OVEN TO 300°F. Toss the garlic in the olive oil and roast in the oven until golden brown, about 10 minutes.

In a saucepan heat the butter. Add the onion, celery, and carrots and cook over medium heat until the vegetables are brown and tender. Add the tomato paste and roasted garlic and cook for 5 minutes. Deglaze with port wine and reduce for 5 minutes. Add the veal stock to the pot. Reduce by half. Adjust the seasonings.

Serve with Garlic Mashed Potatoes and gravy.

SERVES 6

Let me share with you, as if it weren't obvious, that it's a good idea to get someone else to provide the meal if you're writing a book, opening a bar, incorporating a restaurant, and planning your own wedding. Find a good caterer or, if you have your own restaurant, ask your catering manager and chef to do it.

I conceded to relinquishing our wedding menu to our chef but insisted on preparing the turkeys and stuffing—for two hundred. Wrong move! It's hard to stuff a turkey in a wedding dress.

Our chef could easily have used my recipe and prepared the turkeys and stuffing without me, but Thanksgiving would have seemed like just any other day if I hadn't helped make the meal. And I really wanted it to be special.

My whole life, I'd put all my energy into action. I envisioned the perfect family, the perfect community, the perfect world, and I fought to make it happen. But then when I wasn't looking or trying at all, the perfect Jim walked into my lonely life. And after our wonderful wedding, our perfect honeymoon was about to begin—with Jim, A. J., and me.

In December 1988 all three of us began our travels to Bangkok, New Delhi, Agra, Varanasi, Kathmandu, and back to Bangkok. We started in Thailand with a ride in a Tuk-Tuk to Lumpini Park and Wat Aroon.

On our second day, when we stopped for lunch at an open market, A. J. watched with amazement as his new stepfather ate the hottest chile ever and just about died. The color drained completely from Jim's face. Sweat beads formed and fell from his forehead, and he turned a whiter shade of pale than we'd ever seen. Thankfully, it only took a couple of Kingfisher beers to save the day.

Build a fire with this spicy rendition of our delicious Thai cuisine, a creation of Bill Bloomhuff's.

SPICY THAI SALAD WITH CHICKEN AND THAI BIRD CHILES

1 1/2 pounds chicken breast or chicken
  tenderloins
1 head romaine lettuce
1 bunch mint
1 bunch cilantro
1 teaspoon gingerroot, grated
1/2 cup roasted peanuts, finely chopped

1 to 2 Thai "bird" chiles (or
  serrano chiles), finely diced
1 red onion, finely diced
1 lime
1 tablespoon rice wine vinegar
1 teaspoon fish sauce

BOIL THE CHICKEN fully for 20 to 30 minutes in a large pot with salted water.

While the chicken cools, wash the romaine, mint, and cilantro thoroughly. Mince the chicken either by hand or in a food processor. In a mixing bowl put the chicken, ginger, nuts, chiles, and red onion and toss. Squeeze the juice of the lime into the mixture and add the vinegar and fish sauce.

Serve this family style on a serving platter garnished with whole romaine leaves. Guests can make tortilla-like cups with the romaine. Spoon the chicken mixture into the leaves and add a sprig of mint and a sprig of cilantro.

This dish can be prepared up to 2 days in advance and kept, tightly covered, in the refrigerator.

SERVES 4

After a week in Bangkok, during which we visited more Buddhas and temples than I can remember, we caught a plane to Delhi, arriving just in time for A. J. to relieve his piano-playing withdrawal on the old "Steinway" at the Taj Mahal Hotel. I went to read and Jim took a walk. This is what happened next.

Excerpts from Jim's Travel Diary

While A. J. played in the bar and Ingrid read *Lonesome Dove,* I wandered into the streets of India. As I walked alone I watched scenes of human life unfold before me: barbers snipping nose hairs, camel riders disrupting traffic, and pedicab drivers begging to take you anywhere, just to make them happy.

There were taxis honking, dogs barking, burros nearly breaking under their heavy loads. Kids of goats dodging, kids of scrambling men. Veiled women balancing and Hindu women tending children. Amongst fruit stands, I saw an old truck going about thirty miles an hour and pulling a broken-down tractor.

At once, a child on a bike was struck. The boy, not more than eight, was pinned beneath the skidding wheels. Instantly, I ran for the truck, along with every able-bodied man in earshot of the boy's screams. The stare of the older man beside me pushing the truck was most surprising. He was shocked that an American was at his side.

The driver bolted from the truck and ran. The engine stalled, but the truck was in gear and the tractor wedged in behind it. We could not budge it and the child continued to scream.

Then we rocked it back, but the child was not free and we couldn't let the truck roll back again on top of him. So we held and gave it all our might. But it was not enough.

Thankfully, at that moment, an elephant happened by. This thirty-four-year-old pachyderm with its rider gently pushed the truck off the child. The boy was pulled to safety. He screamed and writhed and cried for his mama, his foot mangled, exposed to the bone.

Meanwhile, about thirty men broke and ran after the fleeing driver, who was quickly caught. A circle formed around him while several men took turns slapping him harshly with their hands, yelling loudly and calling him a "fool." When a policeman came riding by on his bicycle, explanations were given and the man was apprehended. Another child standing nearby told me that the driver would have to pay for the boy's wages while he recuperated. Then the policeman paraded the man away to jail and jeers were heard by everyone along the street.

While waiting for Jim to return from his walk, I put down my book, looked out the hotel window to the street, and saw this wonderful elephant with a rider on him. Jim returned shortly after and told me his story. How mystical his tale seemed to me, but it was just ordinary stuff in India.

Tandoori Chicken is ordinary in India too. It's especially delicious with raita and chutney.

TANDOORI CHICKEN WITH CUCUMBER RAITA AND CHUTNEY

2 teaspoons cumin seeds
1/2 teaspoon cardamom seeds
1/2 teaspoon mustard seeds
1/2 teaspoon whole cloves
1/2 teaspoon black peppercorns
1/2 teaspoon red chili powder
1/2 teaspoon ground turmeric

1 medium onion, chopped
3 cloves garlic, chopped
3 cups plain yogurt
6 to 8 chicken breasts
Cucumber Raita (see directions
below), for a side dish

PUT ALL THE SPICE SEEDS from the above list in a saucepan, dry. Brown them on medium heat until they start to pop. Let the spices cool and grind them until fine in a coffee grinder.

In a food processor mix all the spices together with the onion and garlic. Mix this into the yogurt. Marinate the chicken in this mixture in a nonreactive bowl for up to 12 hours before serving. Bake the chicken in a 9 x 11-inch baking dish in a 400°F oven for approximately 40 minutes.

Cucumber Raita

2 cucumbers, peeled, seeded, and cut
    lengthwise
1 teaspoon kosher salt
2 cups yogurt
1 small Thai chile, seeded, chopped small

1/4 teaspoon cumin powder
1/4 teaspoon coriander powder
Salt and pepper, to taste

Sprinkle salt on the cucumber slices. Drain the liquid from the cucumbers. Combine all the ingredients in a mixing bowl. Add salt and pepper to taste.

Serves 6 to 8

Exercise was my favorite means of ensuring that I could enjoy all the food I wanted to. So while A. J. played the piano and Jim explored, I took the treadmill route. Visiting a gym in any third-world country is a tremendous way to gauge progress. Not only are the age and sophistication of the equipment a good test, but the timeliness of the health magazines, and the condition of the women who use them, tells much too. India was no exception. Of all the gyms in all the countries I've visited, I had the most fun in New Delhi.

The equipment was puny, but the women were not. Their exercise machines looked like they came out of a revolution, with motors fastened to eight-inch cinches of heavy canvas. The women who squeezed into these contraptions looked admiringly at inspirational posters of Jane Fonda from the seventies that hung on the walls. But they ate little Famous Amos chocolate-chip cookies and Mars bars and joked and giggled while they rattled the fat.

The next day, our guide Manjit Singh took us on a tour of the Peugeot scooter factory (at A. J.'s request) and for a drive in his jeep to the country. There we saw villages that were essentially built of cow manure. Young girls carried cow patties on their heads and shoulders for fuel. Everywhere, even in the rural areas, there were sounds, people, and movement. My senses were exhausted, all of them being constantly stroked by the ethnicity of the country. Home seemed a long way off.

Just at that point, our guide asked where we were from. San Diego, we told him. "Oh, really," he said. "I just escorted some other visitors from Southern California." We told him we owned a restaurant there and he said, "It wouldn't be Croce's, would it?"

It took two endless days to get out of Agra for the fifty-five-minute flight to Varanasi. We were delayed by nature's fog, general incompetence, and a pilots' slowdown (Indian for "strike").

A. J. woke up sick to his stomach, and we all remembered the milkshake and muttonburger he'd gobbled the day before, not a suggested "daily special." At the airport, we were faced with a tour group of obnoxious Americans, dancing Lithuanians, a talkative Indian professor, a Japanese man doing a Jerry Lewis impression, and a cockpit crew who had just left their planeful of passengers sitting on the runway.

When we finally arrived in Varanasi and reached our hotel, the restaurant had closed, so we ate candy bars, watched a bad John Wayne movie, and I dreamed about our Muscovy Duck with Noodle Pillows.

Muscovy Duck Breast
with Szechuan Peppercorns in a Cabernet Demi Glaze (with Noodle Pillows)

෮ ෯

Six to eight 6-ounce duck breasts
Roast Duck Marinade (see directions below)
4 tablespoons butter
1 cup carrot, cut into julienne strips
1 cup onion, cut into julienne strips
1 cup celery, cut into julienne strips
1 cup bean sprouts
1 cup snow peas, cut into julienne strips
Salt and pepper, to taste
3 tablespoons chicken stock

4 Noodle Pillows (see directions below)
8 tablespoons chile oil
2 cups leeks, cut into julienne strips
1/4 cup vegetable oil
2 cups Cabernet Demi Glaze (see directions below)
1 bunch cilantro leaves
2 tablespoons white sesame seeds

MARINATE THE DUCK BREASTS in the Roast Duck Marinade for 2 to 3 hours, or overnight, in the refrigerator.

Place the marinated duck breasts on a grill fat side down, and continually turn to avoid grease flareups. Cook to desired doneness. Remove and set aside.

In a large sauté pan, heat the butter. Add the carrots, onions, celery, bean sprouts, snow peas, and salt and pepper. Cook over medium heat until al dente. Add the chicken stock. Place the Noodle Pillows on a large plate. Ladle the chile oil over the noodles. Slice the duck breast on a bias and set aside.

Fry the leeks in the vegetable oil and set aside.

Place the sautéed vegetables on the Noodle Pillows. Place the duck slices attractively around the vegetables. Ladle the Cabernet Demi Glaze at the base of the plate, slightly touching the slices of duck. Garnish with the leeks, cilantro, and sesame seeds.

Roast Duck Marinade

1 cup soy sauce

1 tablespoon cracked black pepper

1/2 cup Szechuan peppercorns, crushed

PLACE THE DUCK BREASTS on a cutting board skin side up. Using a knife, poke holes in the duck breasts. Put in a large bowl. Pour the soy sauce over the duck breasts. Lightly sprinkle with black pepper. Sprinkle the Szechuan peppercorns generously over the duck.

Noodle Pillows

2 packages Chinese noodles

2 egg whites

Salt, to taste

2 teaspoons black pepper

4 green onions, sliced thin or on a bias

Sesame wok oil, for frying

BRING A POT OF WATER to a boil. Add the noodles, stir gently, and cook for 10 seconds. Drain immediately and rinse with cold water. Let the noodles drain well. Beat the egg whites with salt and pepper until foamy. Add the chilled noodles and green onions. Mix gently with egg whites. To cook, fry gently in a nonstick pan with sesame wok oil. Each noodle pillow should be 2 to 3 inches in diameter.

Cabernet Demi glaze

1 tablespoon butter

3/4 cup onion, small diced

1/2 cup carrot, small diced

1/2 cup celery, small diced

1 tablespoon garlic, chopped

1 tablespoon tomato paste

1/2 cup Cabernet wine

2 cups Veal Stock (see page 176)

HEAT THE BUTTER in a saucepot, and add the vegetables and garlic. Cook over medium-high heat, stirring constantly, until tender and brown. Add the tomato paste and cook for 1 minute. Deglaze with the Cabernet wine, and reduce for 3 minutes. Add the veal stock, and bring to a boil. Reduce the heat to low and reduce by half. Strain through a cheesecloth.

SERVES 6 TO 8

The next day we welcomed Christmas with one of the most extraordinary experiences of our lives, a boat excursion on the holy river Ganges. At sunset we were gliding past the bathing ghats and cremation sites. Never have I been so taken by the panorama of life and death as it flows so naturally close on the river Ganges.

While Indians brushed their teeth in the blessed water, corpses' ashes settled on the waves. The customs and traditions of the people were steeped in everything around us and we became part of their scene.

Our next objective was to reach Sarnath, the buried Buddhist city where Lord Buddha gave his first sermon under the *bodhi* tree.

Jim came up with a wonderful idea for a short story about how the leaves from this revered tree could be boiled into a brew and bring wisdom to the world in the form of "Bodhi Beer." He'd built a sort of Indiana Jones adventure around it, and I was thinking how good it would be if we could offer "Bodhi Beer" at Croce's. More intelligent, spiritually strong customers and staff couldn't hurt. Besides, Bodhi Beer had a nice ring to it!

Before Jim and I were married an old friend, Helen Trembley, who had traveled the world many times over, gave us a gift of wisdom: of all the places she'd visited, her favorite experience was climbing the Himalayas with Sherpa guides. So when we planned our honeymoon we built it around this trek.

We were all in good shape for the climb. I was still running forty to fifty miles a week, Jim was fit, and A. J. was seventeen. We met Mani Grun, our guide, at the hotel, and our backpacks were added to the extensive trekking supplies already loaded onto his truck.

Four small, wiry men weighing under one hundred pounds each and wearing light clothing, hats, and gloves were waiting when we arrived at the bottom of the mountain. After welcoming us with smiles and "Namaste," they quickly took off ahead, hauling more on their little backs than I had imagined possible. Beds, linens, tables, chairs, and pounds of *mis en place* for our meals were wrapped in blankets and tied tightly inside their packs as they hauled up the steep trail and quickly out of sight. In no time we were trekking with Mani Grun behind them, winding our way up the Himalayas, carrying our own weight only.

The weather was clear, and after a few hours' ascent we rounded a bend for our first culinary surprise of the journey, a four-course lunch with freshly baked rolls, spiced fruit juice, and fresh flowers on the table. The campfire "chefs" were our servers too. So no problem between the front and the back of the house here.

It only got better from this meal on. And as spectacular as the scenery and the people were along the way, as a restaurateur I couldn't help imagining the elaborate job descriptions I'd have to write for these Sherpas! Not only was their climbing and carrying ability wondrous, but their expertise in preparing and serving cuisine was equally inspiring. In all capacities these men were excellent. Every job from managing to dishwashing was accomplished with pride. They were prepping, sautéing, and broiling their way effortlessly to the top, and they were thinking ahead every step of the way.

Before using a pot, they coated the outer bottom with mud to protect it against the direct flame. That way when they were done cooking, they could break away the claylike shield and clean the pot quickly, without damaging it.

I also noticed that they began their preparation of every meal by boiling water, for tea, for rice, for sauces, and finally for cleanup. The pot simmered till the end.

After prepping, they always began their campfire with one small flame, then another and another right next to each other, until every dish had its own burner. The sequence of courses—appetizer, bread, first course, main course, and dessert—was executed with personal care, attention, and ownership. Plate presentation was as important as the freshness and creativity of their products. Chefs all over the world could take lessons from these talented, good-natured Sherpas. As fast as they blazed the trails, their cooking never took a backseat to their climb. Every meal was memorable and always served with a smile.

From the river Ganges to the Buddhist temples in the Himalayas, our honeymoon was beyond belief. It was truly a spiritual encounter, and Jim, A. J., and I were sorry to leave.

On our final night in Nepal, when we returned to our hotel room, I opened my briefcase for the first time since leaving San Diego. There I found a letter that a fan, Tracy Bedell, had written to me about Jim Croce.

Her message was very touching. She had first heard Jim's music when she was a young girl and her parents were going through a divorce. Her mother had been greatly comforted by Jim's songs, and since that time she too had become a fan. Tracy attended Northwestern State University, where Jim had played his last concert before his plane crashed in the field in Natchitoches, Louisiana, just miles from the school. She wanted to build a memorial to Jim Croce at her alma mater and was kindly offering her time to help make it happen. Her letter asked for my involvement.

After I wrote her a thank-you note, I showed both our letters to Jim. In preparation for the Jim Croce biography I had asked my husband to write with me, he got the idea that maybe Tracy Bedell could help us locate the people who were with Jim before he died. Jim's death had always had some mystery around it, and A. J. and I were never comfortable with the story we'd gotten. When we returned, Jim intended to call Tracy himself. Even before he agreed to write the book with me, his wheels were turning and he was stirring his "Atman stew."

INGRID'S CANTINA & SIDEWALK CAFE

Southwestern Cuisine

For fifteen years I had been approached and lured by all sorts of biographers, moviemakers, publishers, and such wanting to buy the Jim Croce story and make it their own. I was happy they were so interested in my deceased husband, but flattery and money didn't move me to sell out. As keeper of his faith, I know that food, music, and friends were what Jim Croce and I were about, and opening Croce's restaurants and bars felt like a good way to keep that memory alive.

Still, over and over, fans wanted to know more, and now, with the loving support of my husband, Jim Rock, I was ready for closure. I had unsettling questions about Jim Croce's life and death. Finally, going out and finding answers made sense.

With our agent Bill Gladstone's insistence that Jim Rock and I write the biography of Jim Croce, we decided to take a trip to Santa Fe to seriously discuss the possibility of researching and writing "The Jim Croce Story."

Often overly zealous and optimistic about new projects, I luckily had Jim Rock's realistic perspective to balance me. While neither of us had ever written a book before, I naively didn't imagine it would be that hard.

I went on and on about why it was a good thing to do this biography. Jim, the rational thinker in our family, didn't say no; he just listened patiently and suggested we put the brakes on long enough to consider the gravity of the project.

"I owe it to them," I told him forcefully. "All those terrific people who have faithfully bought Jim's albums and CDs over the years. I know they want Jim's story and no one else can do it but me."

He didn't buy that, of course. But he was anxious to help me. "Not so fast, Ing. Let's have a margarita and fathom what all this means."

What an excellent idea! Especially at sunset in Santa Fe. So while I savored my margarita over salsa cruda and chips, we conferred, Jim Rock style.

Croce's Salsa Cruda is best with tortilla chips and maybe a couple of margaritas.

CROCE'S SALSA CRUDA

5 large tomatoes, cored and diced
1 onion, diced
1 serrano chile, seeds removed and diced
1/2 cup cilantro, chopped

Juice from 3 limes
3/4 teaspoon salt
1 tablespoon black pepper

IN A STAINLESS-STEEL BOWL, combine the tomatoes, onion, and serrano chile and mix. Add the cilantro and the lime juice. Season with salt and black pepper.

MAKES 4 TO 5 CUPS

Now if there's one thing a driven, ambitious lady needs, it's a thoughtful, strong-willed man, and I found me a wonderful one. But that doesn't mean I always take his advice.

While we went 'round and 'round on the pros and cons of writing this biography, one thing we immediately agreed upon was the great taste of our Christmas Chile Rellenos and the beautiful red and green chiles.

CHRISTMAS CHILE RELLENOS

*24 medium-size Anaheim chiles, roasted
    and peeled*
1 large onion, chopped
1 cup corn kernels
2 cups Monterey Jack cheese, grated
2 tablespoons cilantro, chopped
5 eggs, whisked
1/2 cup water

*2 cups panko crumbs or
    breadcrumbs*
1 cup fontina cheese, grated
*1 cup Red Chile Sauce
    (see directions below)*
*1 cup Green Chile Sauce
    (see directions below)*
1 cup green onion, chopped

LEAVING THE STEMS ON, make a slit in the side of each Anaheim chile and remove the seeds. Combine the onion, corn, Jack cheese, and cilantro in a bowl, then fill each chile with about 2 1/2 tablespoons of stuffing.

Whisk the eggs with water. Dip the chiles into the egg mixture. Roll in the breading, patting the chiles with your fingers to get complete coverage.

Preheat the oven to 375°F. Heat the oil in a skillet to 375°F (before the oil smokes). Deep-fry the chile rellenos 2 to 3 minutes each. Place the cooked rellenos on a baking pan. Top with fontina cheese and place in the oven for 5 minutes. Arrange 3 rellenos per person on each plate. Top the rellenos with 2 tablespoons of red chile next to 2 tablespoons of green chile. Sprinkle with the green onion. Serve with rice and beans.

For a lighter version, bake the stuffed chiles in the oven for 20 minutes.

Red Chile Sauce

6 dried California red chiles
3 cloves garlic, chopped
4 1/2 tablespoons olive oil
1/4 teaspoon cumin
1/4 teaspoon dried Mexican oregano

1/2 teaspoon salt
1 tablespoon white vinegar
2 teaspoons flour

Rinse the chiles and place them in a medium saucepan. Cover with water and bring to a boil. Remove from the heat and let stand until softened, about 30 minutes. Reserve the chile liquid. Place the chiles and 3 cups of the soaking liquid in a food processor. Puree until smooth.

In a medium saucepot over medium heat, sauté the garlic in the olive oil. Add the cumin, oregano, salt, vinegar, and flour to the pan. Bring to a boil and simmer for 2 to 3 minutes. Put in a food processor with the chiles and blend until smooth.

This recipe makes 2 cups of chile sauce.

Green Chile Sauce

6 to 8 fresh tomatillos, husks removed
2 green jalapeño peppers, roasted, peeled, and seeded
1/2 bunch cilantro
1 cup onion, chopped

2 cloves garlic, peeled and chopped
Pinch salt
Lettuce leaf, for color

Place the tomatillos in a pot, cover with cold water, and bring to a boil. Drain immediately. If the cores of the tomatillos are large, remove them with a knife. Otherwise, put the tomatillos, jalapeños, cilantro, onion, garlic, salt, and lettuce leaf in a food processor and blend until smooth and green.

This recipe makes 1 cup of chile sauce.

Serves 8

Thyme in a Bottle

Casamientos (Mexican-style Rice and Beans)

2 cups black beans, cooked and washed well
1 onion, chopped
2 cloves garlic, minced
1/2 teaspoon cumin
1/2 teaspoon salt
1/2 teaspoon pepper

1 tablespoon vegetable oil
1 1/2 cups long-grain rice, steamed
5 cups water
1 flour tortilla
Salt and pepper, to taste

COOK THE BEANS with the onion, garlic, cumin, and salt and pepper until they are tender, 30 to 40 minutes. Allow them to cool and wash in a colander under cold water. Place in a bowl and mix with the vegetable oil.

Put the rice in 3 cups of boiling water for 2 minutes then remove the rice and rinse with cold water. In a separate saucepan, place a flour tortilla in the bottom of the pot (a Mexican technique to prevent the rice from burning; discard the tortilla after using) and put the rice on top. Add 2 cups of cold water and heat on low for 10 to 15 minutes until the rice has absorbed all the water. Cool the rice in a large mixing bowl and mix with the beans. Season with salt and pepper.

SERVES 6

Green Chile Chicken Enchiladas

Twelve 6-inch-round blue corn tortillas
2 tablespoons vegetable oil
1 1/4 cups Green Chile Chicken Enchilada Sauce (see directions below)
1 chicken breast, cooked and shredded

4 tablespoons green onion, chopped
6 tablespoons fresh tomato, diced
1 cup Monterey Jack cheese, grated
6 tablespoons sour cream

Soften the blue tortillas in a pan with a little hot oil for 30 seconds on each side. On a baking sheet put 4 stacks of 2 tortillas each. Put 2 tablespoons of the Green Chile Chicken Enchilada Sauce on top of each stack of tortillas. Next, put half of each of the following: chicken, green onions, tomatoes, cheese, and sour cream. Place 1 tortilla on top of this mixture, followed by the rest of the chicken and cheese.

Bake in a 350°F oven for 8 to 10 minutes until the cheese is melted and bubbly. Remove from the oven. Garnish with the green onion, tomatoes, and dollop of sour cream.

Green Chile Chicken Enchilada Sauce

2 teaspoons olive oil

4 tablespoons onion, finely diced

2 green Anaheim chiles, seeded and chopped

1 cup chicken stock or water

1 teaspoon garlic, minced

Salt, to taste

1/2 chicken breast, cooked and
   shredded

1 teaspoon roux

Heat the olive oil in a large saucepan until hot but not smoking. Add the onion and sauté lightly. Add the green chiles, chicken stock or water, and garlic and bring to a boil, stirring frequently. Remove from the stove and puree in a food processor until smooth. Put the chile puree back in the saucepan and bring to a boil again. Season with salt and check the consistency, which should be smooth and creamy. Stir in the shredded chicken. Add roux if needed. Remove from the heat and cool.

This recipe makes 1 1/2 cups sauce.

Serves 4

Our decision to write the book was made over chicken enchiladas. Whether it was my convincing arguments or the delicious green chile that encouraged him, Jim began listing the people we needed to talk to about Jim Croce and started to develop a direction for the book.

When we returned to San Diego as "writers" Jim also came up with the idea that we should open our second restaurant, Ingrid's Cantina & Sidewalk Cafe.

The chile had gotten to our brains. As if we didn't have enough to do, we decided to offer Southwestern food with Top Hat's rhythm and blues, just as Croce's offered contemporary American cuisine with jazz. Truth is, we couldn't give up our chiles.

Though Southwestern food was a by-product of writing the biography, it became a partner in our adventure, a delicious sidekick.

After our field trip, before we actually rented the location and opened the Cantina, we invited a friend of ours, Southwestern food specialist Jeanné Wilson, to Croce's to educate our staff about the traditions and history of the cuisine. Jeanné brought along her extensive knowledge of traditional Southwestern recipes and customs and shortly after her visit, Chef Fay and sous-chef Cindy Race came up with their wonderful offshoot of the empanada and Italian pasta.

Testing chiles at Los Chileros in New Mexico, 1989.

Photograph by Jim Rock

They stuffed the traditional raisin and nut empanada filling inside our beef fillet, wrapped it in a delicate puff pastry, and served it with a jalapeño hollandaise.

SANTA FE WELLINGTON

꧁ ꧂

6 hot Italian sausages, poached,
    skin removed, and chopped
1/2 cup green Anaheim chiles, chopped
1/2 cup raisins, chopped
1 cup brown sugar
1 teaspoon allspice
Four 5-ounce beef fillets

1 tablespoon extra virgin olive oil
Eight 4 x 4-inch squares of puff
    pastry dough for each fillet
8 tablespoons Roasted Jalapeño
    Hollandaise Sauce (see
    directions below)

MIX THE SAUSAGES, chiles, raisins, brown sugar, and allspice to make the filling.

Sear the fillets in a sauté pan with the olive oil over medium-high heat for 2 minutes per side before preparing the Wellingtons. On a baking sheet place four 4 x 4-inch squares of the pastry dough, one for each fillet. Place the fillet on top of the pastry dough, and cover with 1 1/2 tablespoons of the filling. Put the remaining 4 x 4 squares of pastry dough on top of the stuffing. Brush the edges with the egg wash and pinch the edges to seal, rendering an oval-shaped Wellington. Bake in a 350°F oven for 15 to 20 minutes. Ladle 2 to 3 tablespoons of Roasted Jalapeño Hollandaise Sauce over each Santa Fe Wellington.

ROASTED JALAPEÑO HOLLANDAISE SAUCE

2 egg yolks
2 tablespoons white wine vinegar
1 jalapeño pepper, roasted, seeded,
    skinned, and diced
1 tablespoon lemon juice

1 cup Clarified Butter
    (see page 174)
Pinch salt
Pinch white pepper
Pinch cayenne

In a stainless-steel bowl whisk together the egg yolks, vinegar, jalapeño, and lemon juice for a few seconds until light and frothy. Continue to whisk the mixture over a saucepan of boiling water (do not place the bowl directly on the saucepan or you will risk overcooking the eggs). Whisk rapidly over the heat until the mixture becomes thick and has tripled in volume.

Remove the bowl from the heat and continue to whisk 30 seconds more to ensure the eggs do not overcook. Add the clarified butter very slowly with a ladle while gently whisking. When done adding the butter, the sauce should be stiff in texture. Finish the sauce with salt, white pepper, and cayenne to taste.

SERVES 4 TO 6

Semolina Linguine
with Prawns and Chicken
in Blackened Tomato Cream Sauce

1 pound dry linguine

1/4 cup Clarified Butter (see page 174)

2 chicken breasts

1 cup onion, sliced

1 small red pepper, cut into julienne strips

1 small yellow pepper, cut into julienne strips

1/2 cup white wine

3 cups Blackened Tomato Sauce
(see directions below)

2 cups heavy cream

24 large prawns,
cleaned and deveined

Salt and pepper, to taste

1 1/2 cups green onion, chopped

Boil the linguine until al dente and set aside.

In a large sauté pan heat the Clarified Butter. Add the chicken, onion, and peppers and sauté lightly. Deglaze the pan with the white wine. Remove the chicken; cut into julienne strips, and return to the pan. Add the Blackened Tomato Sauce, cream, and linguine. Bring to a boil and let the sauce thicken. Add the prawns and cook until they turn pink, 2 to 3 minutes. Season with salt and pepper. Top with the green onion and serve.

BLACKENED TOMATO SAUCE

1 large dried pasilla chile
1 cup boiling water
1 medium onion, cut into eighths
2 tomatoes
2 jalapeño peppers

1/3 cup tomato sauce
1 1/2 cloves fresh garlic
8 tablespoons red wine vinegar
1 teaspoon salt

PUT THE PASILLA CHILE in a bowl, cover with the boiling water, and soak for 30 minutes. Place the onion, tomatoes, and jalapeños on the broiler and roast, turning frequently until lightly blackened all over. Remove the tomatoes from the broiler and set aside to cool. Put the jalapeños in a sealed plastic bag to steam. After they have steamed for 10 minutes, peel and seed the jalapeños. When the tomatoes have cooled, remove the cores.

In a food processor, in two batches, puree together the soaked pasilla chiles (reserve the soaking water), roasted tomatoes, jalapeños, chopped onions, tomato sauce, and garlic. Pour the pureed mixture into a medium saucepot, add the reserved water from the pasilla chiles, red wine vinegar, and salt. Cook over medium heat for 30 minutes.

This recipe makes 4 cups of Blackened Tomato Sauce.

SERVES 8

Arlo Guthrie, an old friend of Jim Croce's and mine, happened to be playing one night in November 1989 at a club nearby. Jimmy Rock had listed Arlo high on the list of people to talk to about Jim Croce, so he suggested that we pay him a visit.

I didn't want to go up there and begin asking Arlo questions, but this time Jim insisted. He proposed not only that Arlo might have stories to tell us, but also that he might stimulate me to remember some of mine.

I was stubborn. Other than encouraging A. J.'s career and booking the club, I had been a recluse from the music scene for some time. Disillusioned by fighting years of legal battles with the music industry, I hated the business. I'll admit it, I was bitter.

That's a good word for the way I felt back then—and for my first response to this rich mole sauce. But Andy Martinez's Traditional Mexican Mole goes wonderfully on our Chile Rellenos and Shelton Farms Chicken Breasts. And today it happens to be one of my favorite flavors ever. I'll warn you it's not for the meek, and I can relate to that in a very personal way. It's outgoing, definitely intense, a bit complicated, and even caustic at times.

TRADITIONAL MEXICAN MOLE

Roasted Chile Peppers (see directions below)
2 tablespoons sesame seeds, roasted
2 tomatoes, peeled and roasted
1 tablespoon unsalted peanuts or peanut
   butter
1 tablespoon walnuts
Pinch salt
4 tablespoons sugar

1 clove garlic
1 slice onion
8 slices French bread, toasted
2 cups water
2 cups chicken stock
4 ounces unsweetened chocolate,
   melted

PUT THE ROASTED CHILES, sesame seeds, tomatoes, peanuts, walnuts, salt, sugar, garlic, onion, and bread in a food processor and very slowly add water and chicken stock to build until the mole is the consistency of a thick paste. Add the chocolate and cook on medium-low heat for 15 to 20 minutes, stirring constantly.

This is a terrific accompaniment to an uncomplicated grilled chicken breast, duck, turkey, or steak. It is also wonderful spread on a warm tortilla.

ROASTED CHILE PEPPERS

1 teaspoon lard or vegetable oil
8 black chiles, dried
8 red pasilla chiles, dried

4 cascabel chiles
8 mulato chiles

ROAST ALL THE CHILES in a small amount of lard. (Andy insists that you must use lard to keep the mole traditional. However, for vegetarian mole, substitute lard with vegetable oil.) Remove the seeds and insides and discard. Soak the chiles in water for 15 minutes until soft.

Wash the peppers thoroughly using rubber gloves; avoid touching your eyes. There are several methods to prepare chiles. Roast the whole fresh chiles over a barbecue grill, turning them with tongs every couple minutes until the peppers are charred. On the stovetop over an open flame, use a long-handled fork to char-grill the peppers, turning them to blister and blacken all over, about 5 minutes. Or broil the peppers, putting them in a large shallow roasting pan 2 to 3 inches under the broiler and blackening them evenly, turning them every 5 minutes to allow all sides to blister, about 20 minutes.

Place the roasted peppers in a bowl, cover with plastic wrap, and sweat the peppers to loosen the skin. When the peppers are cool, starting at the blossom end, peel the skins back with a knife, cut off the tops, and remove the seeds and ribs.

SERVES 10 TO 12

M y reluctance to see Arlo wasn't personal. I just hadn't been to a concert in years. In some ways it was too painful, and in others, I was being bullheaded and stubborn and I was scared. Fortunately, my husband persisted and we drove to San Juan Capistrano, bought our tickets, and passed a note to the manager of the club telling the headliner we were in the audience.

Once I was there, of course, I was glad we came. Because I hadn't seen my friend in almost twenty years, I feared he would not even remember me. But a few minutes later, Arlo was standing there. He gave me a big hug and invited us to his dressing room to talk. He was so kind and generous I felt enormously embarrassed about the bitter attitude I'd nursed for so long.

After Jim and I enjoyed both of his sets, Arlo told us we had to come visit the family for Thanksgiving ("Jackie would love your suede outfit, Ingrid"). All four of his kids, the dogs and cats, neighbors and friends would be there too. It would be a reunion. You know, like the one that "Alice's Restaurant" was about.

We bought our plane tickets, and a week later, A. J., Jim, and I celebrated our first wedding anniversary at the Guthries' in Massachusetts. Except for the golden curls that had turned to silver, Arlo was the same, only better. Jackie was as beautiful, warm, and wonderful as any earth mother can get. The queen of all earth mothers. She hugged me and welcomed us to what would be my favorite Thanksgiving ever. The next day we all drove to New York City, where Arlo does his annual Thanksgiving concert at Carnegie Hall. That night Arlo sang "Amazing Grace" and told a wonderful story that gave me goose bumps, the one about John Newton, who wrote the tune, and about the remorse he felt one night as his slave ship headed west. Somehow, while on deck that night, Newton was inspired and realized what a terrible, terrible thing he was doing.

But then Newton was brave. He turned that ship around and returned all those people to Africa. He did the right thing.

Arlo said we might think that only one person can't make a difference. But, he assured us, we do and we can. If each of us just stopped and did the "right thing," then together we could change the whole world. I started to cry, and so did just about everybody else in the audience.

Arlo always had a wonderful talent for totally entertaining you, melting your heart, and making you smarter—all at the same time. He still does.

The difficulties and sensitivities of writing a biography about my first husband with my present husband hadn't fully registered yet. From the time Jim Rock and I met, I had been totally up front with him.

But the process of rehashing my past took a lot more energy, time, and courage than just living it. It's also not half as much fun. Worse yet, it was often impossible to be in the present with Jim Rock while I was still "back there" with Jim Croce.

In retrospect, I was nuts to try this. The only nuts I should have incorporated were the ones in our piñon sage dressing stuffed warm and safe inside Shelton Farms game hens. I'm sure the delicious stuffing we shared had something to do with our progress. It certainly didn't hurt the Pilgrims and it fueled our fire and kept us together through it all.

SHELTON FARMS GAME HEN

෪ ৡ

Six 14- to 16-ounce game hens
8 to 10 cups Piñon Sage Stuffing (see
   directions below)
Salt and pepper, to taste
3 cups Green Chile Sauce (see page 206)

1 cup Cilantro Lime Butter
   (see directions below)
Optional: 6 dried red chile
   threads (available in gourmet
   food stores), for garnish

PREHEAT THE OVEN TO 425°F. Stuff the game hens with the Piñon Sage Stuffing. Season the outside of the hens with salt and pepper. Place the stuffed hens on a sheet pan and roast for 15 minutes. Reduce the heat to 350°F and continue roasting until an internal temperature of 150°F is reached, 20 to 30 minutes.

While the game hens roast, put the Green Chile Sauce in a large saucepan. Bring to a boil. Remove from the heat and stir in the Cilantro Lime Butter and set aside. Put the game hens on the plates and pour the sauce evenly over them.

Extra stuffing may be heated in a covered casserole dish and served with the game hens.

PIÑON SAGE STUFFING

1 loaf Kings Hawaiian Bread
3 tablespoons olive oil
3/4 cup onion, finely diced
2/3 cup celery, finely diced
6 tablespoons butter

1/2 teaspoon salt
2 1/2 tablespoons sage
1 1/2 tablespoons parsley,
   chopped
1/4 cup pine nuts, roasted

1/4 cup chicken stock

1/2 teaspoon black pepper

1/3 cup raisins, coarsely chopped

BREAK THE BREAD into walnut-size pieces and set aside.

Heat a large saucepan over low heat. Add the olive oil, onion, and celery and sauté until soft. Add the butter and cook over low heat until the butter melts. Add the bread, chicken stock, pepper, salt, sage, parsley, pine nuts, and raisins and mix until the bread becomes moistened. Spread the stuffing onto a sheet pan and let cool.

This recipe makes 8 to 10 cups of stuffing.

CILANTRO LIME BUTTER

1 pound unsalted butter, softened

2 tablespoons fresh lime juice

1 tablespoon lime zest

2 tablespoons cilantro leaves, coarsely chopped

1 teaspoon salt

1/2 teaspoon white pepper

1/2 teaspoon red chile flakes

1/2 teaspoon cumin

SOFTEN THE BUTTER to room temperature. In a large mixing bowl, combine all of the prepared ingredients. Mix thoroughly with a wire whip.

SERVES 6

Camping out was also an important ingredient in working on our book. It bonded us. And after our honeymoon trek in the Himalayas, I was gung ho on campfire cooking. Jim and I became almost religious about spending Thursdays, our one day a week off, in the mountains or the desert, depending on the season. I brought along foodstuff and cooked in between writing and enjoying nature's views.

When we met, Jim Rock had classified himself as a "Cro-Magnon camper," but when he and I went on our outings, we did it in style. Not only was I invested in making our time alone special, but the truth is, as a restaurateur, I hardly ever got to cook anymore. I looked forward to this time each week when I could practice my recipes, and there was no love spared in making Jim the best barbecue and tamales I could.

Jim's Barbecued Baby-back Ribs and Barbecue Sauce

4 baby-back ribs
1 cup water

Barbecue Sauce (see directions below)

Marinate the ribs for 1 hour, or overnight, in 1/3 of the Barbecue Sauce mixed with 1 cup of water. Place the ribs and juice in a large skillet and cook 10 minutes. If baking the ribs in the oven, bake for 20 minutes (add water, if necessary, to keep moist). Remove the ribs from the pan and baste them all over again with another 1/3 of the barbecue sauce. Bake meaty-side down, in a preheated oven at 350°F for 30 minutes. To grill on a barbecue, keep an eye on the ribs so as not to burn them and grill 5 to 8 minutes on each side. Baste again with the remainder of the Barbecue Sauce and serve with roasted corn on the cob and a green salad.

Barbecue Sauce

2 tablespoons butter
2 cloves garlic, minced
1/2 red onion, finely diced
6 medium tomatoes, coarsely diced
1/4 cup chile paste
1/4 cup ketchup
2 tablespoons Dijon mustard

1/2 cup light brown sugar
1 teaspoon cayenne pepper
1 teaspoon ancho chile powder
2 tablespoons Worcestershire sauce
1/4 cup soy sauce
1/2 cup rice vinegar

Heat the butter in a saucepan over moderate heat and add the garlic and red onion. Cook 5 minutes. Stir in the tomatoes and simmer for 10 minutes. Stir in the remaining ingredients and simmer 20 minutes more. Puree in a food processor and allow the sauce to cool.

Serves 4

Irma's Tamales

ॐ ॐ

1 1/4 cups water

3 dried pasilla chiles

2 cups instant masa

2/3 cup canola oil

1/2 teaspoon salt

1 teaspoon baking powder

Chicken Filling (see directions below)

16 corn husks

3 carrots, cut into julienne strips

2 large raw potatoes, cut into
*   julienne strips*

1 jalapeño pepper, seeded and cut
*   into julienne strips*

Croce's Salsa Cruda (see page 204)

Bring the water to a boil, pour it over the pasilla chiles, and let the mixture stand for 10 minutes, or until the chiles have softened. Pull the chiles from the liquid, and pour the liquid into a blender or food processor. Remove the stems and seeds from the chiles, and add them to the liquid in the blender or food processor. Blend until smooth.

Put the masa, oil, salt, and baking powder in a bowl and mix until thoroughly combined. Add 1 cup of the smooth "chile water" and mix until incorporated (the remaining 1/4 cup chile water will be used for the chicken filling). Set the masa dough aside.

Prepare the Chicken Filling per the recipe below.

Rinse the corn husks under warm water, removing and discarding any silken "threads." Put in separate containers, within easy reach, the masa dough, the Chicken Filling, the carrots, the potatoes, and the jalapeño pepper.

Begin making the tamales one at a time. Place one corn husk in front of you on a large clean counter. Put 1 1/2 tablespoons of the prepared masa dough in the center of the corn husk, and then 2 heaping teaspoons of the Chicken Filling on top of the dough. Top with 2 slices of carrot, 1 slice of potato, and 1 sliver of jalapeño. Fold the corn husk into thirds lengthwise and then into halves. Set aside. Prepare all of the tamales the same way.

Stack the tamales in a steamer filled two-thirds with water and steam over medium heat for 30 minutes. Serve with Salsa Cruda.

Chicken Filling

1 tablespoon olive oil
1/4 cup chile water (see directions above)
One 2 1/2-pound chicken, boiled, deboned, and shredded

Salt and pepper, to taste
1 teaspoon garlic powder
1/2 teaspoon Mexican oregano

Heat the olive oil in a large skillet until hot, but not burning. Add the chile water, chicken, salt and pepper, garlic powder, and Mexican oregano and cook for 5 minutes over medium-high heat.

Makes 16 tamales

In 1988, when we opened Croce's Top Hat, Rick Saxton of "Uncle Mother Productions" came to me asking if we might need a sound engineer. As a matter of fact, we did. My husband, who had virtually developed every aspect of the club, had been covering the sound since we opened. But he was anxious to relinquish the job and Rick seemed perfect for the position.

Rick was an experienced sound engineer, a musician in his own right, a veteran of Vietnam, an ex–telephone lineman, and a true longhaired hippie of the sixties. He had a wonderfully calm and compassionate disposition and I hired him on the spot.

The first night Rick did sound for us it just so happened that A. J. Croce and His Band were playing. Once the sound check was done and the band was on stage Jim became very protective of the club and exceptionally irritated about the feedback Rick was getting off of A. J.'s microphone. (He and Rick had not yet met.)

During the set, he went over to talk to Rick about the problem and I recognized some definite conflict happening. Our new sound man resolved the difficulty, but after the set was over I went to Rick to ask how he was doing. "Oh, I'm fine," he told me. "But who was that asshole that just came up to me." I told him calmly, "That asshole, Rick, was my husband."

You should have seen the look on Rick's face. I'll tell you I won't forget it. After eight years at Croce's, Rick has done a magnificent job with our sound, the musicians love him, and Jim and Rick are good buddies. To this day they both get a great kick out of this story.

Our "grail trail"—our search for the "truth" about the Jim Croce we knew and loved—was filled with surprises. The majority of the people we interviewed were still very much entrenched in Jim's memory. Old friends and family, who were as happy to meet Jim Rock as they were to see me, contributed greatly in helping my husband understand the strong effect Jim Croce had had on the people he touched, not only as a celebrity but more importantly as a man.

Overall, our journey offered us wonderful lessons and times. We went to see Jimmy Buffet on a couple of occasions, and his stories, though politely censored, were about their fun and games on the road. Cheech Marin was wonderful to us too, and along with his memories, he gave us his homemade chicken broth with fresh tomatoes, cilantro, avocados, and lemon. Yumm.

Still, there were holes in our story, and day-to-day information was harder to come by than we had expected. Fortunately, in Jim Croce's case, his music profiled the man best. His songs were the vehicle that most truly translated his essence. After a while we thought maybe a book wasn't necessary.

On May 28, 1990, Jim Croce received the Songwriters Hall of Fame Award. Above all other recognition, I think he would have been proudest of this one. A. J., Jim Rock, and I went back to New York for the celebration, where A. J. did another rendition of his father's songs; this time he accepted his father's prize from Sammy Cahn.

At the show, A. J. got to play some piano with B. B. King and I met Lena Horne, one of my favorite performers, who was singing Jim's hit "I've Got a Name" on her road show. Jim Rock got to watch Whitney Houston's cleavage as she leaned into the audience from the stage. It was a happy time for us all.

John Prine joins Jim Rock in the audience, while A. J. Croce performs at Winter Park, Colorado, summer 1993.

Photograph by Ingrid Croce

Leaving New York City, my husband and I worked our way home through Iowa while A. J. went to Nashville to visit Gene Pistilli and meet with John Prine and Al Bunetta, John's manager, to do some writing and performing.

After playing Croce's and other gigs professionally for over five years, A. J. was getting pretty good at the piano and at writing songs, and it wasn't just his mom who thought so. Record companies that had come down to scout A. J. at Croce's were offering deals to produce his first album, and he had recently written "Which Way Steinway" on his trip to Nashville, along with a couple dozen other tunes worthy of publishing and recording. When our friend Kenny Weissberg decided to manage A. J., he introduced him to his friend and agent Clint Mitchell, now at the William Morris Agency.

Private Records executive Ron Goldstein came to see A. J. at the club too. Ron took A. J. to his heart and was more patient and generous than I remember people ever being in the music business.

A. J. Croce's first album was coproduced by John Simon of The Band and singer-songwriter T-Bone Burnett, who was also producing Counting Crows in the next studio.

A. J.'s career was on track, but from this time on it was hard for Croce's to get him to do more than a couple of gigs a year. Happy to say, he was just too busy. (We're never too busy for a Crab and Avocado Quesadilla with Papaya Mint Salsa.)

CRAB AND AVOCADO QUESADILLA WITH PAPAYA MINT SALSA

1 cup shiitake mushrooms, sliced

1 tablespoon butter

Eight 12-inch-round flour tortillas

1 cup Pico Pica Sour Cream Sauce (see directions below)

6 teaspoons Croce's Salsa Cruda (see page 204)

1 pound Monterey Jack cheese, grated

8 ounces fresh crab

1 avocado, sliced

4 ounces green chiles, sliced

2 cups loosely packed green onion, chopped

2 cups tomatoes, chopped

1 cup cooked corn

Papaya Mint Salsa (see directions below), for garnish

Cilantro, for garnish

SAUTÉ THE MUSHROOMS in the butter for 5 to 7 minutes, or until softened, and set aside. On a flat surface, lay out the tortillas. Spread 1 tablespoon of the Pico Pica Sour Cream Sauce and 1 tablespoon of the Salsa Cruda lightly on the tortilla. Top the sauces with cheese, crab, avocado, chiles, green onion, tomatoes, mushrooms, and corn. Fold the tortillas in half and cook them on a flat griddle or a large sauté pan until the cheese melts and the inside ingredients are hot.

To serve the quesadillas, lay the tortilla crescents on a cutting board. Cut each quesadilla into 4 wedges and arrange on a plate with a dollop of the remaining Pico Pica Sour Cream Sauce, a healthy portion of Papaya Mint Salsa on the side, and a sprig of cilantro.

Pico Pica Sour Cream Sauce

1 cup sour cream
2 teaspoons Pico Pica or Tabasco sauce

COMBINE THE INGREDIENTS in a stainless-steel bowl and mix well with a wire whip. This recipe makes 1 cup of sauce.

Papaya Mint Salsa

2 ripe papayas
1/2 small red onion, diced
2 jalapeño peppers, seeded and minced
Juice of 1 orange
Juice of 2 limes

1 lemon, zest and juice
4 tablespoons mint leaves, finely
  chopped
2 tablespoons brown sugar

TAKE THE PAPAYAS and trim the outer skin off. Cut in half and remove the seeds. Chop the papayas into medium-size uniform chunks. Place all of the ingredients in a stainless-steel mixing bowl and toss gently.

This recipe makes 3 to 4 cups of salsa.

SERVES 4

Alot of pressure is put on celebrated people, who are only human. Just because they can sing, pen a tune, hit a ball, or "roller-skate in a buffalo herd," some people expect them to be better than us—or sometimes worse.

I bring this up because in going back and reviewing Jim's life, and wanting not to disappoint his fans, I have to say that for the most part the best thing about him was that he was pretty normal.

Smart, talented, and kinder than most, Jim's greatest problem was that he couldn't say no. He wanted to be loved so much, he didn't want to let anyone down. Being a hero was awkward for Jim. And the saddest part is that just as he was getting better at dealing with fame, he was becoming bigger than life to his fans. Then he had to go and disappear.

In getting information for Jim's biography, we had to talk to a lot of "stars." I get sweaty palms just thinking of the uncomfortable feeling produced by the "backstage syndrome," where everyone just stands there and stares at the celebrity, unable to act normal or even to have fun. It's so awkward for the hero, and until it's over, just as bad for the fan.

While I get almost claustrophobic about being in dressing rooms with stars and their entourages, two of my favorite people are practically professionals at it. In fact, they both know how to make it feel like there's a party going on, and whenever they're around, there usually is.

My sister-in-law Linda is an "enthusiast" who finds stars and their way of life so interesting and exciting, she could make them believe it too. Being around her is like being on an *I Love Lucy* episode. There's nothing mundane about the way she enjoys her stars. It's as much fun for her as our Spinach Fettuccine with Eggplant and Chicken is for me.

Spinach Fettuccine
with Grilled Eggplant and
Breast of Chicken with Roasted Garlic,
Sundried Tomatoes, and Peppers

1 1/2 pounds dry spinach fettuccine
1/4 cup Clarified Butter (see page 174)
1 small eggplant, grilled and cut into chunks

12 cloves garlic, roasted and
*   chopped*
1 teaspoon butter

1 small red pepper, grilled, seeded, and
    cut into julienne strips
1 small yellow pepper, grilled, seeded, and
    cut into julienne strips
1/2 cup loosely packed sundried tomatoes,
    cut into julienne strips
1/2 cup white wine
1/2 cup chicken stock

Salt and pepper, to taste
4 chicken breasts, grilled and
    thinly sliced
4 tablespoons Parmesan cheese,
    grated
Optional: 1/4 cup Croce's Pepper
    Fetishes™ (available at Croce's
    Restaurant)

BOIL THE SPINACH FETTUCCINE in water until al dente, drain, and set aside. Heat the clarified butter in a large sauté pan. Add the eggplant and sauté for 7 minutes over medium-high heat. Add the peppers and tomatoes and cook for 2 minutes longer. Pour the white wine to deglaze the pan. Add the chicken stock and the fettuccine. Mix together with Croce's pepper fetishes, garlic, and butter. Season with salt and pepper. Arrange on plates with the grilled chicken on top. Garnish with Parmesan.

SERVES 8

Now Connie, married for many years to Willie Nelson, is an "I Love Everybody" fan. Heck, she told me Ike Turner "was just the kindest man ever," and you've got to know Connie to know she meant it. Connie Nelson knows how to find the good in us all, and as far as I'm concerned, that can't be all bad.

It doesn't matter if you're famous or not, Connie's your fan and makes you feel important. There's no one I know who can narrate a better story, tell a bigger tale, or be a kinder or prettier outlaw than our Connie Nelson. This dish is dedicated to her, and to fans everywhere for all the goodness they bring to the world.

POLENTA DEL PUEBLO

1 box instant polenta
1 cup Blackened Tomato Sauce (see page 212)
1/2 cup corn kernels
1/2 cup green chiles, sliced
1 cup Monterey Jack cheese, grated
1 tablespoon olive oil

1/2 pound chorizo
1/2 cup green onion, chopped
1 large tomato, cored and diced
Cilantro, for garnish
1/2 cup sour cream

COOK THE POLENTA according to the instructions on the box and pour onto an 11 x 16-inch sheet pan. Pat the polenta with a moist hand to smooth the surface and refrigerate.

Preheat the oven to 350°F. Cut the cooled polenta into 8 squares and place the squares onto a sheet pan. Spread the Blackened Tomato Sauce evenly over each polenta square. Top each square with the corn, green chiles, and the Jack cheese, dividing all the ingredients equally among the 8 squares. Place in the oven for approximately 15 minutes, or until it is heated through and the cheese is bubbling and golden.

While the polenta bakes, heat the olive oil in the pan and sauté the chorizo until it is completely cooked and browned. Break the chorizo up with a spoon just before you remove it from the heat.

Place the cooked polenta squares on 8 serving plates. Sprinkle the cooked chorizo over the polenta equally. Garnish each plate with green onion, tomatoes, cilantro, and sour cream and serve immediately. This dish is delicious for breakfast, served with an egg over easy on top.

SERVES 8

Jim Croce lived a fairly happy, normal life until the mid-sixties. He had a traditional Italian Catholic upbringing, enjoyed lots of good Italian food, played the accordion at St. Dorothy's Church, and attended Villanova University. Then he watched Bob Dylan, Gordon Lightfoot, and Arlo Guthrie making a living at music, and fell in love with me. After that, things were never the same again.

When we met, he continued at Villanova until he graduated in 1965. Then something about the freedom in the air or the electricity he felt when we were together changed his plans for the future. Instead of getting a nine-to-five job as his family had hoped, music and making love became his existence. His parents, who loved "baby Jimmy," were having a lot of trouble accepting the man, and their disapproval hurt him badly.

But once Jim realized music could be his life, he had to follow his dream. What made him different from most good people was his sincere and memorable voice and a genius's talent for telling stories and writing and performing songs in a genuine way that touched us all. Other than that, he was normal.

When Jimmy Rock and I started our book, I wanted everyone to know what a good man Jim Croce was. How smart and generous, kind and giving, and how much we were in love. When we finished writing the book, I just wanted everyone to hear his songs. That's all.

THE LEGEND OF INGRID CROCE'S CANTINA & SIDEWALK CAFE

In 1969 Ingrid Croce received a student grant to study pottery in Mexico. Since Jim Croce was just another broke folksinger in Philadelphia, the young couple decided the time was right for traveling. They loaded up their International Travelall and headed south: Ingrid in search of an education, Jim in search of Pancho Villa.

They soon discovered that their money would only get them as far as the Mexican border. By the time the Croces reached the Rio Grande, they were flat broke again. In Laredo, they camped at the Three-legged Lucky Blind Dog Trailer Park and sadly considered returning to Pennsylvania. Jim sat strumming his guitar, thinking hard and singing softly in the moonlight. Ingrid harmonized while cooking a modest dinner. She was frying up a batch of blintzes and lentils from the back of the Travelall. Suddenly they noticed they'd attracted a big crowd of homesick, hungry campers.

With an eye for opportunity, Ingrid started selling Jim's beer and taking orders for dinner. She passed Jim's hat through the crowd, and before the evening was over they'd made enough money to fill the Travelall with gas.

They painted the side of the truck in big red letters that said CROCE'S ROLLING CANTINA and drove from campground to campground. Ingrid gathered recipes from the locals wherever they went, and the farther south they got the spicier her food became; blintzes became burritos; lentils, refritos.

Under the influence of Mexico, Jim was inspired to write new songs. In the dusty town of Sabinas Hidalgo, he penned a song titled "Malo, Malo Leroy Negro." In Tamaulipas he wrote "Embotellar el Tiempo"; in Guadalajara, "Rápido Roy"; and in Acapulco, "Nueva York No Es Mi Casa."

The traveling was so good, and the friends so many, that Ingrid completely forgot about school (and Jim decided not to remind her). Instead, the two continued to travel, making food and music wherever they parked the Rolling Cantina.

The Croces eventually reentered the Estados Unidos at San Diego, and immediately fell in love with the city. But it was time for them to return to their friends and family in Philadelphia. Ingrid was excited about her new "New Mexican–Southwest Philly" cuisine and Jim about the new songs he had written.

Unfortunately, record producers everywhere rejected Jim's songs. In a fit of desperation, he translated them into English. The rest is history.

Jim and Ingrid vowed one day to return to the land of mañana. Now you can experience the food, the music, and the magic of the days of Croce's Rolling Cantina right here at Ingrid's Cantina & Sidewalk Cafe. (Along with our Red Snapper Veracruz, created by our wonderful saucier and kitchen manager, Alfonso Morin.)

Red Snapper Veracruz

⚮

3 tablespoons olive oil

1 medium onion, chopped

5 cloves garlic, minced

3 whole dried cayenne chiles

6 medium tomatoes, diced

2 tablespoons capers, rinsed

3 bay leaves

Salt and pepper, to taste

3 red snapper fillets, deboned and
cut into 6-inch pieces

HEAT THE OLIVE OIL in a saucepan. Add the onion, garlic, and cayenne chiles. Cook until tender, 10 to 12 minutes. Add the tomatoes, capers, bay leaves, and salt and pepper. Bring to a boil, reduce, and simmer 10 minutes. Season the fish with salt and pepper and place in a pan with the sauce. Cover the fish with the sauce. Simmer until the fish is done, about 8 minutes, or until the fish is firm to the touch. Remove the fish from the pan first and place on serving dish. Serve the sauce from the pan over the fish.

SERVES 6

The original story of Ingrid's Cantina & Sidewalk Cafe came from a visit to Mexico I made with Jim Croce in the sixties. The tale grew over the decades, as did my love for flavorful Mexican and Southwestern cuisine.

Like all myths, the story was transformed over the years, and by the time we opened Ingrid's Cantina & Sidewalk Cafe in 1990, Jimmy Rock had reinvented, concocted, and penned it on our menu for all to see. Our painter friend John De-Marco took it in another direction and painted his version of the story in a Dali-esque canvas that fills the north wall of the cantina.

It's amazing how many customers and employees believe in "Malo, Malo Leroy Negro" and "Rápido Roy," even to this day, after reading the legend of Ingrid's on the back of our menu. Which goes to show how mighty the written word can be or how wonderfully trusting we all really are.

GAZPACHO

1/2 pound cucumbers, peeled, seeded, and
   diced into 1/4-inch pieces

2 avocados, diced into 1/2-inch pieces

1/2 cup jicama, diced into 1/4-inch pieces

2 tomatoes, diced into 1/2-inch pieces

4 cups tomato juice

4 cups V8 juice

1/4 teaspoon ground cumin

1/4 teaspoon kosher salt

1/2 teaspoon black pepper

3 pepperoncini, chopped (set the
   juice aside)

1/2 bunch cilantro, chopped

1 bunch green onion, chopped

6 tablespoons lemon juice

6 tablespoons water

PUT THE CUCUMBER, avocado, jicama, and tomato in a gallon container. Add the
tomato and V8 juices, cumin, salt, black pepper, pepperoncini, and pepperoncini
juice. Add the cilantro and green onion. Add the lemon juice and water. Mix well.
Chill 1 hour, or overnight if possible, and serve.

MAKES 2 1/2 QUARTS

When we advertised snake on Ingrid's menu we received an overwhelming response. "Only for the brave" is how we portrayed it, and there were many more daring customers than we had expected.

The challenge back then was not only finding enough snake to satisfy our customers' needs, but for Jimmy Rock to come up with enough "tales" about the daring ways to farm and charm the vipers and to steep our customers in his "snake" magic. Our Snake, Rattle, and Roll worked just like that—magic. We happily had difficulty keeping up with the demand.

Snake, Rattle, and Roll

❦ ❧

2 tablespoons Clarified Butter (see page 174)
1/2 pound chorizo, rendered and browned
12 ounces rattlesnake, braised and shredded
    (see directions below)
6 tablespoons green onion, chopped
2 serrano chiles, seeded and chopped
1/4 cup red onion, diced
2 cups tomatoes, diced

Juice from 3 limes
2 teaspoons cilantro leaves
2 tablespoons butter
12 eggs, beaten
1/2 cup cheddar cheese, grated
Twelve 9-inch-round flour
    tortillas

Heat a large sauté pan with 2 tablespoons Clarified Butter. Sauté the chorizo and snake until soft. Add the green onion, serrano chiles, red onion, and diced tomato and sauté for 2 to 3 minutes. Squeeze in the lime juice. Add the cilantro leaves and remove from the heat.

Heat a clean nonstick sauté pan with 2 tablespoons butter. Add the eggs and scramble. When the eggs are cooked, distribute evenly on 6 plates. Place the chorizo/snake mixture on top of the scrambled eggs. Garnish with the cheddar cheese and serve with warm flour tortillas.

Braised Rattlesnake

24 ounces rattlesnake, skinned and gutted
    (purchase as such)
8 cups chicken stock
1 cup tequila
1 carrot

2 stalks celery
1 large yellow onion
1 cup white wine
1 bay leaf

Preheat the oven to 425°F. Place the snake in a braising pan. Bring the chicken stock, tequila, and white wine to a boil on the stove with the carrot, celery, onion, and bay leaf and cook for 20 minutes. Cover the snake with the chicken stock and the vegetables from the stove. Cover the pan with foil and braise for 2 to 3 hours until the snake is tender. Carefully lift the snake out of the braising liquid. Debone and devein the snake. This portion should render 12 ounces of braised rattlesnake.

S E R V E S 6

"We wish to increase our licensed area to include the following balcony extensions and leasehold improvements to the Top Hat balcony and what is soon to become the loft of Croce-Rock Galleries," I wrote in a letter to my friend Donna Brisky at Alcoholic Beverage Control.

It was a phone call from Arlo and Jackie Guthrie that encouraged my letter. On Halloween, they called and asked if we knew of an art gallery that could exhibit their guru's paintings and I said, "Sure, Arlo." And to prove it, we opened the Croce-Rock Gallery in December 1990 for his guru's show.

Ingrid's catered a delicious opening for Ma Jaya's premiere San Diego art exhibit. As Arlo and many friends who attended were vegetarian, we made this wonderful veggie meatless-loaf, which has remained a favorite to this day.

ARLO AND MA'S VEGETARIAN NUTLOAF

1 cup coarse kasha (buckwheat groats)
4 large eggs, beaten lightly
4 cloves garlic, minced
2 tablespoons vegetable oil
4 cups water or vegetable stock
1/2 teaspoon kosher salt
1/8 teaspoon pepper, coarsely ground
2 cups mushrooms, thinly sliced
1/4 cup unsalted butter
2 cups onions, chopped

Salt and pepper, to taste
1 1/2 cups unsalted roasted cashews, ground
1/4 cup fresh parsley leaves, minced
1/2 teaspoon dried thyme
1/2 teaspoon dried sage
1/2 teaspoon dried rosemary
1/4 tablespoon olive oil or vegetable spray

1/2 cup celery, minced
1 carrot, coarsely grated

8 grape leaves, wet
Carrot shavings, for garnish

PLACE THE KASHA in a bowl and coat with 1 of the beaten eggs. Using a large, flat skillet, sauté 2 cloves of garlic in 1 teaspoon vegetable oil and add the buckwheat groats, toasting them until the grains separate and turn crunchy, 5 to 7 minutes. Add 2 cups of the vegetable stock or water. Add salt and pepper and bring to a boil. Cover and simmer for about 20 minutes. The kasha should double in volume.

In a separate pan, sauté 1 cup onions until golden in the remaining oil. Add the kasha and adjust with salt and pepper.

In a heavy skillet cook the mushrooms in 2 tablespoons of the butter over moderately high heat, stirring for 3 to 5 minutes. Add the kasha. Melt the remaining 2 tablespoons butter in the skillet, add the balance of the onions, celery, grated carrot, the remaining half of the garlic, and salt and pepper and cook the vegetables, stirring until the onions soften. Add the vegetable mixture to the kasha, toss until well combined, and let the mixture cool.

Add the cashews, eggs, parsley, dried herbs, and salt and pepper to the kasha mixture, and combine well.

Preheat the oven to 350°F. Coat a loaf pan with the olive oil or vegetable spray. Line the loaf pan with grape leaves, slightly overlapping each other all around the pan. Spoon the mixture into the prepared loaf pan. Fold the overhanging leaves over the top of the mixture, and cover with foil. Put the loaf pan in a baking pan, pour enough hot water into the baking pan to reach halfway up the sides of the loaf pan, and bake the loaf for 1 hour, or until a skewer inserted in the center comes out clean. Let the loaf stand on a rack for 10 minutes. Run a thin knife around the inside of the loaf pan, invert a platter over the pan, and invert the loaf onto the platter.

SERVES 4

Croce's restaurants and bars were not only offering dining, catering, and live music nightly, we now had our fine art gallery and a coach from Cinderella Carriage sitting outside the front door to take guests on tours of our wonderful historic Gaslamp district.

To add to our good luck, Arlo and Jackie's number-one daughter, Cathyeliza Guthrie, had moved west to go to college. Happily, she moved in with us, and Jim and I got the daughter we had always wanted when we became Cathy's "California Mom and Dad."

Then Cathy became our number-one hostess at Croce's Restaurant & Jazz Bar, just as Jackie had hosted in the sixties at Doug Westin's Troubadour in Los Angeles, where she met Arlo.

This is as good a place as any to boast that we know of over a hundred married couples who had the good luck to meet at Croce's. There's something to be said for that kind of magic. So just imagine your possibilities, Cathy!

PAPPAS FRITAS

1 tablespoon butter
1 medium potato, sliced
Salt and pepper, to taste
2 tablespoons Green Chile Sauce (see page 206) or Blackened Tomato Sauce (see page 212)
1 tablespoon green chiles, sliced
3 tablespoons Monterey Jack cheese, grated

1 tablespoon green onion, chopped
1 tablespoon tomatoes, diced
1 teaspoon sour cream
Two 9-inch-round flour tortillas
Optional: 2 eggs, fried

PREHEAT THE OVEN TO 250°F. Heat the butter in a medium nonstick sauté pan. Add the potatoes and season with salt and pepper. Turn with a spatula to the other side until both sides are lightly brown. Place the potatoes on a plate and top with Green Chile Sauce or Blackened Tomato Sauce.

Place the green chiles and Jack cheese on top of the sauce. Place the plate in the oven to melt the cheese. Remove from the oven and garnish with the green onion, tomatoes, and sour cream. Serve with the warm flour tortillas.

For Pappas Fritas with eggs, remove the plate from the oven. Fry 2 eggs over medium and place on top. Garnish with the green onion, tomatoes, and sour cream.

SERVES 1

For Christmas 1990 the first year Cathy lived with us, our California daughter bought us bowling balls. We were hooked on our hobby, even holding Croce's holiday party at the Aztec Bowl. About the same time, our son, A. J., his girlfriend, Marlo Gordon, and her six-month-old daughter, Camille, moved in together. A lot of us were on a roll. A. J. was hooked on Marlo and Camille, and during their courtship we met every Sunday before work to play a few games. Our unofficial Croce bowling team had shirts and balls, and at that time our Green Chile Macaroni and Cheese was our favorite lunchtime snack. It's the Cantina's version of mom's macaroni and cheese, with a great curve.

GREEN CHILE MACARONI AND CHEESE

16 ounces dry elbow macaroni
8 ounces ricotta cheese
1 cup heavy cream
2 cloves garlic, chopped
Salt and pepper, to taste
1/2 cup Parmesan cheese
1/2 cup mozzarella

1 large jalapeño pepper, minced
1/2 cup Green Chile Sauce
  (see page 206)
1 tablespoon dried red pepper
  threads, for garnish
1 bunch parsley or cilantro,
  chopped, for garnish

BOIL THE MACARONI until al dente and set aside.

Beat the ricotta, cream, and garlic together in a medium bowl. Transfer the ricotta-cream mixture to a large skillet. Over medium heat, stir in the Parmesan, mozzarella, jalapeño, and Green Chile Sauce. Add the cooked macaroni and stir the pasta until incorporated. Adjust the seasoning with salt and pepper and transfer to wide soup bowls. Garnish with red pepper threads and parsley.

Through all the interruptions, we kept working on the Jim Croce biography. In between goings and comings with our research, our restaurants, our son, and our bowling, Jim and I were still writing and sorting through it all. Along the way our publisher had insisted that we work with a collaborator, but from the time he came on the scene, things never felt quite right—and never got better.

Writing that book became a nightmare. Jim likened it to peeling an onion, layer by layer, and it was truly tearful. Our book was the story of a wonderful man of his times with a unique talent for creating stories and songs. It was not your typical "star" book about sex, drugs, and rock and roll, even though we were told that was what the public wanted to read about.

My husband and I had agreed from the start that if we weren't happy with the outcome of the book, we wouldn't publish it. So four years later, as we got ready to line our shelves with the manuscript pages, we bought back the rights to "The Jim Croce Story" and counted our blessings that we could.

The book has not yet been published, and I can't help but feel that Jim Croce had something to do with this outcome. He was a very private man, you know. He would have hated having his life exposed. I guess some things are just best left alone.

THE LIFE OF A RESTAURATEUR

Contemporary American Cuisine

Forty years ago, when I was enrolled in my third second-grade class, I started keeping a secret diary. By that time I'd already lived in four homes, attended five schools, and learned that change was something I could definitely count on.

The first week at my new school the gym teacher gave me a pair of stilts and challenged me to walk on them. Beyond her expectations, and even mine, I wasn't just walking high. Soon I was climbing steps, playing ball, and jumping double-dutch with them too.

But in the classroom, I was not as successful. It was a struggle for me to learn capitals, presidents, and such, and for the first time in my little life, I felt really dumb.

Then one day in history class, teacher Jean asked if anyone knew how to do the Irish jig. I was never very good at memorizing facts, but I felt sure I could dance.

"I can do it," I answered with certainty. It was my instant response to risk-taking that kicked right in. But my teacher wasn't buying it.

"I'm not pretending," I insisted. "I can do the Irish jig." And I wouldn't take no for an answer.

Teacher Jean put me to the test. She gave me a record of Irish music and said, "Come back to class tomorrow and show us your dance."

It was a dare, a quadruple dare. I was determined to teach my sister and my new friends Linda and Deenie how to do it too.

I listened to the music, improvised, and choreographed a routine that I imagined went perfectly with the songs. Somewhere from my collective unconscious, I pulled off the jig.

"Dear Luck," I wrote in my diary. "We danced today and everybody liked it, even teacher Jean. But, what's an 'Irish Jig' anyway?"

This story has been my parable for success ever since. For taking risks, putting people together for a common cause, and doing life with gusto.

So here I am running restaurants and bars and dancing the jig with our cooks, servers, and entertainers too. And to this day, I'm still not sure how the dance really goes.

🍴

When I opened Croce's, I soon realized I wasn't going to get rich owning a restaurant, but I believed I could be rich in other ways.

On some days, when everyone shows up for the shift, the guests arrive at a comfortable pace, the musicians start on time, and our chef is inspired to make her Spicy Grilled Shrimp with Wild Rice Pancakes and Honey Dijon Crème Fraîche, there's a brief moment for pause, and I'm happy for Croce's. But when the computer goes down on Saturday night, our cranky landlord complains about another leak in the basement, or the fire department decides that after eight years in business we need to put in a new exit through our back wall or cut our occupancy by 50 percent, I wonder what those other "rich" ways might be.

Spicy Grilled Shrimp
with Wild Rice Pancakes
and Honey Dijon Crème Fraîche

❧ ❧

30 shrimp, peeled and deveined, tails intact

1 teaspoon Sambol Oleek hot sauce
   (can substitute any hot sauce)

1 cup cilantro leaves, chopped

2 tablespoons fresh garlic, minced

1 teaspoon kosher salt

1/4 cup olive oil

1/2 cup fresh lime juice

1/4 cup soy sauce

18 Wild Rice Pancakes
   (see directions below)

6 tablespoons Honey Dijon Crème
   Fraîche (see directions below)

AN HOUR BEFORE SERVING, toss the shrimp with all the ingredients (except the pancakes and crème fraîche) in a nonreactive covered container and refrigerate.

Preheat the oven to Broil. Grill the marinated shrimp under the broiler until done, about 2 minutes on each side. Fill a squirt bottle with the crème fraîche and design each plate with squiggly lines. Stack 3 Wild Rice Pancakes on the center of the plate. Arrange the grilled shrimp on the pancakes. Garnish with additional Honey Dijon Crème Fraîche on top.

WILD RICE PANCAKES

1 cup wild rice

4 cups water

2 teaspoons kosher salt

1/2 teaspoon black pepper

2 tablespoons sugar

3/4 teaspoon baking powder

1 cup flour

2 eggs

3/4 cup heavy cream

1/4 cup whole milk

2 tablespoons soy sauce

1/2 cup green onion, chopped

1 tablespoon Clarified Butter
   (see page 174) or olive oil, to
   coat pan/griddle

Using a medium saucepot, cook the wild rice with the water. Bring to a boil, reduce the heat to a simmer, cover, and cook until the rice is tender, about 30 minutes. Remove from the heat and allow to cool.

In a medium mixing bowl, combine all the dry ingredients. In another bowl combine all the wet ingredients with a wire whip. Mix together the dry and wet ingredients. Add the wild rice and stir well.

Preheat the oven to 250°F. Using a nonstick sauté pan or griddle, heat 1/2 teaspoon Clarified Butter. Using a 3-ounce ladle or large spoon, ladle the batter for 3 small pancakes (1 ounce each) into the pan. When golden brown on 1 side flip over and finish cooking. Add butter for each set of pancakes. Hold on a platter in the oven to keep the pancakes warm.

This recipe makes 18 pancakes.

HONEY DIJON CRÈME FRAÎCHE

1/2 cup sour cream

1 tablespoon Dijon mustard

2 tablespoons heavy cream

1 tablespoon honey

Pinch salt

COMBINE ALL THE INGREDIENTS in a mixing bowl with a wire whip and mix well.

This recipe makes 1 cup of crème fraîche.

SERVES 6

Croce's, like the rest of the world, is in a state of endless change. While from the guest's eye it seems completely natural for the food to be served perfectly every time, I can assure you, it's not. A restaurant does not run itself. If it looks that way, you've made magic. Underneath the illusion there's so much hard work involved in keeping it up that at times I have to ask myself, Am I crazy to be a restaurateur?

To add to the difficulty, confusion, and expense of running my business, in the early nineties, all kinds of rule-making agencies, including the IRS and the INS, got the idea that restaurants were cash cows. They were all figuring out ways to shave off our fat. Croce's specialty being fresh fish and beautiful greens and vegetables, we had little fat to shave. But it certainly didn't stop them from trying.

Try Kathleen Daelemans's Sea Bass with Caramelized Onions and Figs, a wonderful remedy for the bureaucratic blues.

Santa Barbara Sea Bass
with Caramelized Onions and Figs, Blood Oranges, and Anchoiade Vinaigrette

&

4 medium yellow potatoes,
    such as Yukon Gold or Finnish
3 tablespoons olive oil
3 large sweet onions
4 ripe figs

3 sweet oranges
Eight 7-ounce portions sea bass
Salt and pepper, to taste
Anchoiade Vinaigrette
    (see directions below)

PREHEAT THE OVEN to 350°F. Wash the potatoes, cut them in half, and place them, cut-side down, on a cookie sheet that has been rubbed with 1 tablespoon of olive oil. Set them aside. Peel and slice the onions 1/3 inch thick. Lay the onion slices on another cookie sheet that has been rubbed with 1 tablespoon of olive oil. Put the onions and potatoes in the oven at the same time. After 15 minutes, turn the onions over with a spatula. Add the figs, meat-side down, to the cookie sheets to caramelize. The cooking times will be 30 to 35 minutes—check for doneness after 25 minutes or so. Make the vinaigrette and set it aside. When the potatoes, onions, and figs are done cooking, cover them with tinfoil to keep them warm and set them aside.

Peel the oranges with a knife, cut into slices, and arrange 3 slices on each serving plate. Season the fish with salt and pepper and place in a nonstick pan with

1 tablespoon of olive oil. Sear the fish over medium-high heat, skin-side up, for approximately 5 minutes. Turn the fish over and finish cooking. When the fish is completely cooked, place on individual serving plates. Arrange the potatoes, onions, and figs around the fish and ladle the vinaigrette over the plate.

ANCHOIADE VINAIGRETTE

1 1/2 cups loosely packed dried figs, minced

5 cloves garlic, minced

1 1/2 cups tightly packed anchovies, minced

1/2 cup walnuts, minced

2 tablespoons grappa or brandy

Juice of 1 orange

1/4 cup Champagne vinegar

1/2 cup extra virgin olive oil

PUT ALL THE INGREDIENTS in the bowl of a food processor and pulse until combined. The vinaigrette will be chunky, not smooth.

This recipe makes 3 cups of vinaigrette.

SERVES 8

I was anguished by the continual assaults on our meager returns. Risky business is one thing, but my whole investment was still perilously hanging out there, being ventured with no guarantees, and I was downright scared.

On a call from my wonderful new family, retired farmers on the plains of Iowa, I compared notes with Vernon, my father-in-law. He patiently listened to my concerns about business, and when I was done complaining he asked, "What would a farmer do if he won a million dollars?" He paused and then answered, "He'd farm until it was all gone."

The uncertain business of restaurateuring sure sounded a lot like buying the farm. You've simply gotta love it!

As the owner and general manager, I'm in charge of the "Croce puzzle." I'm the one with the big picture on the table, and my assignment is to keep track of our team players, all the pieces, and make the restaurants succeed.

This game may seem pretty easy on the surface, but it's a challenge. Besides all the tangible problems before us, we human beings have never done very well at working together.

Just when you think you've got every job filled with an excellent trained employee, someone decides to move back to Milwaukee, the bartender has twins, or the price of swordfish skyrockets off the menu and you need to replace it with shark. (This is Kathleen Daelemans's special recipe for shark.)

Vernon Rock, my father-in-law,
a retired farmer, Fourth of July, 1993.

Photograph by Evelyn Rock

GRILLED THRESHER SHARK WITH
WARM FRISEE SALAD AND YUKON GOLD POTATOES

⁊ ⁊

6 tablespoons Champagne vinegar

1 cup plus 2 tablespoons extra virgin olive oil

Salt and black pepper, to taste

Six 7-ounce portions thresher shark

1/2 pint cherry tomatoes, cut in half

1/2 pint yellow pear tomatoes, cut in half

Roasted Potatoes
   (see directions below)

18 pitted Niçoise olives

2 heads frisee

PREPARE A CHAMPAGNE VINAIGRETTE by whisking together the Champagne vinegar, 1 cup of olive oil, and salt and pepper. Set aside.

Heat the remaining 2 tablespoons of olive oil in a nonstick pan over medium-high heat and cook the fish until done, approximately 3 minutes per side. While the fish is cooking, heat 1/2 cup of the vinaigrette in a nonstick pan over medium-high heat until just warmed. Add the tomatoes, roasted potatoes, and olives to the pan. Heat. Add the frisee and toss until all the lettuce is coated with the vinaigrette. Do not let the lettuce wilt too much. Immediately serve over the fish. Drizzle the remaining vinaigrette over all.

ROASTED POTATOES

12 small potatoes, such as Yukon Gold,
   Finnish, or Bintje

Salt and pepper, to taste

1/4 cup olive oil

PREHEAT THE OVEN to 350°F. Wash the potatoes, cut them in half, generously coat with olive oil, season with salt and pepper, put them in a baking pan, and bake for 20 to 30 minutes, or until golden brown and completely cooked.

This recipe makes 6 servings of roasted potatoes.

SERVES 6

When someone loves you, they hear more than the words you say and find delight in the dumbest things you do. Without holding back, you can empty out your craziest thoughts to them, share your deepest, darkest feelings, and know your secrets are safe with them.

For more than twenty-some years since Jim and Maury Muehleisen died in that plane crash on September 20, 1973, I've felt that way with Judy Coffin. While the common experience of our

Judy Coffin
Photograph by Ingrid Croce

loved ones' deaths bonded us closely, it is our history and Judy's love affair with life that secures me to her.

I've never forgotten the laughter we shared on that bumpy ride in her jeep when I was ten months pregnant and Judy wanted to help me bring A.J. into the world on time. Or her bare-breasted attempt at one-upmanship, riding her Harley across the highway, half exposed, just to win a bet. The night we drank whiskey and wrote limericks that were so raunchy and memorable we still laugh at their first lines.

If you don't have a friend like my Jude, try our pork tenderloin with garlic Mashed Sweet Potatoes and Dried Cherry Chutney. It's never a disappointment, always a joy.

Seared Pork Tenderloin
with Garlic Mashed Sweet Potatoes and Michigan Dried Cherry Chutney

⁊ ⁊

Eighteen 2-ounce rounds pork tenderloin
2 teaspoons olive oil
2 medium sweet apples, sliced thin, skin on
2 sweet pears, sliced thin, skin on
1/4 cup chicken stock
3 cups Garlic Mashed Sweet Potatoes (see directions below)

1 1/2 cups Michigan Dried Cherry Chutney (see directions below)
Fresh cherries, cranberries, or blackberries (6 to 8 per serving)

POUND EACH ROUND OR PORK TENDERLOIN into a 5-inch-diameter "steak."

Heat the olive oil in a Teflon pan over a medium-high flame—do not burn. Add the pounded pork and sear it for approximately 1 minute on each side. Remove the pork from the pan and set aside.

Put the apples and pears in the pan and sear for 1 minute, then add the chutney and a touch of chicken stock. Reduce the sauce until it reaches the desired consistency and just before serving the pork throw the berries into the pan. Pile the mashed sweet potatoes in the center of the plate and arrange the pork around it, tepee style. Pour the chutney and fruit over the pork and around the plate.

Garlic Mashed Sweet Potatoes

3 large sweet potatoes
1 head garlic
2 teaspoons extra virgin olive oil

1 teaspoon fresh thyme
Salt and pepper, to taste

PREHEAT THE OVEN TO 350°F. Rub the sweet potatoes and the head of garlic with the oil and place on a cookie sheet. Bake for approximately 35 minutes or until very soft. Remove from the oven. While still warm, cut the head of garlic in half and squeeze out the garlic. Put in a mixing bowl. Cut the sweet potatoes in half length-wise and scoop out the potato. Put in the bowl with the garlic, add the thyme, and mix together with a wire whip. Season with salt and pepper.

This recipe makes 6 servings.

MICHIGAN DRIED CHERRY CHUTNEY

1/2 cup dried cherries	*2 tablespoons lemon juice*
(dried cranberries can be substituted)	*1/2 cinnamon stick*
1/2 cup sugar	*or dash cinnamon*
1/4 cup plus 2 tablespoons white vinegar	*1 whole dried chile pod or 1/2*
3 tablespoons apple juice	*teaspoon red pepper flakes*

COMBINE ALL THE INGREDIENTS in a microwavable quart container or a large bowl. Microwave on high until the mixture is saucelike and thickened, 5 to 10 minutes. Serve with turkey, chicken, or pork tenderloin.

This recipe makes 1 1/2 cups of chutney.

SERVES 6

I figure life gets you coming and going, so sometimes when I'm concerned about being a restaurateur, I consider the alternative and ask myself quite seriously: What else would you want to do, Ingrid, be a plumber?

🍴

In the early eighties when we began our business, everything was done manually. Then in 1987 we tediously switched over to a point-of-sale (POS) system in the restaurant and bar and to computer programs in the office for profit-and-loss statements, public relations, and daily correspondence.

The business was still small in 1987, but by the time we opened our second bar we had already outgrown the computers we started with. It was a difficult struggle to produce accurate numbers with the primitive machinery available.

Retaining staff who were completely frustrated by our inefficient equipment was also a drag. And we were going crazy trying to find effective POS systems that would interface with our office computers.

Then we found Positouch. It was flexible and user-friendly. This POS system spoke our language, answering questions about scheduling, customer count, sales percentages, and payroll. It even counted and priced the menu items we sold.

The good news was Positouch. The bad news was that the IRS liked our new system too. Positouch not only gave us the tools we needed to accumulate accurate figures, it was a perfect way to help the government keep track of our numbers.

As the POS systems became more sophisticated, we were able to account for the credit card sales tips. Of course, the IRS soon realized how much money the servers and bussers were receiving in tips, and it wanted some too.

While the IRS also had access to the number of swordfish sold, that wasn't as important to it as our charged tips. But you can never tell—it may hold those swords against us in the future.

Chargrilled Swordfish with a Hazelnut Glaze or a Dijon Ginger Butter

❧ ☙

6 to 8 swordfish steaks, sliced 1/2 to 3/4 inch thick (8 ounces each)
1 1/2 cups Hazelnut Glaze (see directions below)

Salt and white pepper, to taste
Dijon Ginger Butter (see directions below)

THOROUGHLY BRUSH each swordfish steak with the Hazelnut Glaze. Grill for 6 to 8 minutes on each side, or until the center is white, basting with the Hazelnut Glaze to avoid dryness.

Season each swordfish steak with salt and pepper, then coat with 2 tablespoons of the ginger butter.

Hazelnut Glaze

1/2 cup orange marmalade

1 tablespoon fresh ginger, minced

3 fresh cloves garlic, minced

1/4 teaspoon white pepper

1/3 cup lemon juice

1/3 cup water

3/4 cup Champagne vinegar

1 cup tangerine or orange juice

1/2 cup hazelnut oil

COMBINE ALL THE INGREDIENTS in a medium-size pot. Bring to a boil, reduce to a simmer, and reduce the liquid by half of the original volume.

This recipe makes 4 cups of glaze.

Dijon Ginger Butter

3 tablespoons fresh ginger, peeled and grated

1 teaspoon Dijon mustard

1 tablespoon parsley, chopped

1 cup butter, softened

Salt and white pepper, to taste

IN A MIXING BOWL, mix the ginger, Dijon mustard, parsley, and softened butter. Season with salt and pepper.

SERVES 8

In 1992, with the gift of distance and time off from the restaurant, my husband and I returned from a visit to Europe and the Middle East full of energy and ideas to build our third bar, Upstairs at Croce's.

Until that time we had used the second story for offices, but this space had a beautiful atrium with parlors flanking the main room. The ambience reminded us of a speakeasy or a turn-of-the-century saloon. After we built a counter, we trimmed the bar and cushioned the stools with the Turkish kilims we had purchased on our trip to Istanbul. With some limited decorating, we created the feeling of a Turkish-European coffee bar, and in no time the romantic Upstairs at

Croce's became our most sought-after private party room. It offered light meals, a full bar and in-house desserts.

Every new project reverberates change. So once Upstairs at Croce's was doing well, the rest of Croce's called out my name.

There was so much to examine: the changing climate of our industry, tax issues, new laws on sexual harassment, safety issues, insurance, and all sorts of discrimination laws. Before I could correctly answer the questions my staff and business were asking, I had to become more proactive than ever in gathering information.

When my friend John Campbell, then food and beverage manager at the Marriott Hotel, asked me if I would like to be on the board of the San Diego Restaurant Association, I was glad to be elected and very pleased to receive the most current information available. I was also happy to accept their award for the Best Bar in San Diego for the second time. It did great things for our employee morale and for our bottom line.

Our new bar, Upstairs at Croce's, was perfect for entertaining large parties, group sales and wedding rehearsal dinners. We also promoted wine and beer tastings and offered cooking classes for locals as well as conventioneers.

One night we catered a party for a group of professional women in the food and beverage industry. They invited me to speak about how I got into the hospitality industry.

I told them my story about the Pillsbury bake contest. How back in the early seventies my desire to help my husband do his music full time, and not have to work construction to pay rent, found me competing in the culinary arena for the $10,000 prize money with my blintz recipe. I explained how I had lost the contest but in the end, won "Time in a Bottle" and the gift of our son.

At the close of the event, a young woman handed me her card. She worked for Pillsbury and told me she'd be happy to get me an application so I could enter the contest again. Now, she informed me, the prize money was a million dollars. Wow, I thought, not bad for a blintz!

My favorite part of this business is the people. Nothing is more challenging than finding the right person for the right job. There's so much to consider. So much to be won.

Though it isn't kosher with today's stringent rules for hiring, I've often wished, when interviewing prospective employees, that besides filling out an application or submitting a résumé, they would bring along their family photos and share a picture of their pup or their favorite Thanksgiving dinner. I feel this way because when we hire people at Croce's, they don't stay strangers for long. It seems only right that we get to see a photochrome of their past in exchange for a part in our future.

🍴

In 1993, while little victories in our business were adding up, we were also ripe for reorganization. With 130 employees and about 200 musicians on the payroll, I felt my presence and direction were needed everywhere. But I couldn't clone myself, or do it alone.

So, while I needed to reinforce our structure from within, before we got any bigger, I depended on my Croce's supervisors and staff who already knew how to keep the dance going.

I was lucky that over the years, we conscientiously trained many wonderful, devoted people in a multiple of positions and we were able, therefore, to promote from within.

In 1994, college student Kristen Fullerton, who started as a clerk, and became a manager at our Horton Plaza coffeehouse, moved to hosting at Croce's Restaurant and then to our administrative offices where she practiced being our Human Resource Manager.

While I had always furnished the music for Croce's, I was lucky that my executive assistant Caroline Joyner was eager to take over my job. In time, Caroline became almost telepathic in handling my workload.

This book owes an enormous thank-you to Caroline Joyner. It would have been even harder to write without her. Her excellence gave me the freedom I needed to enjoy my job better and time for both of us to savor our Salmon Lova with Soba Noodles and Cucumber Salad.

Salmon Lova with Soba Noodles and Cucumber Salad

3 quarts warm water
8 spring roll wraps
Eight 5-ounce Norwegian salmon fillets
1/2 cup olive oil
2 teaspoons salt
1/8 teaspoon white pepper

1/4 cup Clarified Butter
  (see page 174)
1 cup Soba Noodles and Cucumber
  Salad (see directions below)
2 cups Spicy Orange Beurre
  Blanc (see directions below)

POUR THE WARM WATER into a medium mixing bowl. Place the spring roll wraps in the water, and press down until totally immersed. When the wraps are soft, remove from the water and using your fingertips, pat lightly with olive oil. Place the salmon fillet in the center of the wrapper and season with a pinch of salt and pepper. Fold the left and right sides of the wrap over the fish. Then fold the top and bottom. Turn over and pat with more olive oil. Repeat the process until all are completed.

Preheat the oven to 400°F. Using a nonstick pan that can be put in the oven, heat the Clarified Butter. Place the salmon fillets in the pan, lightly brown one side, turn over, and finish cooking in the oven for approximately 10 minutes. Put the Soba Noodles and Cucumber Salad on the top center of the plate, and the salmon on the front edge. Top the salmon with the Spicy Orange Beurre Blanc, approximately 1/4 cup per plate. Serve immediately.

Soba Noodles and Cucumber Salad

1 pound soba noodles
2 large cucumbers, peeled, halved, seeded,
  sliced 1/16 inch, salted, and squeezed

1 cup Japanese Vinaigrette
  (see directions below)
1 tablespoon dashi

COOK THE SOBA NOODLES according to the instructions on the package in boiling salted water until al dente, 6 to 8 minutes. Rinse and chill. Add the cucumbers, Japanese Vinaigrette, and dashi to the noodles and gently toss together.

This recipe makes 1 cup of noodles.

JAPANESE VINAIGRETTE

1/2 cup white vinegar
1/4 cup mirin (Japanese cooking wine)
8 teaspoons rice vinegar

1/2 teaspoon soy sauce
1 teaspoon sesame oil
2 tablespoons sugar

PUT ALL THE INGREDIENTS in a medium bowl and whisk together until thoroughly blended.

This recipe makes 1 cup of vinaigrette.

SPICY ORANGE BEURRE BLANC

1 cup white wine
1/2 cup rice wine vinegar
1/2 cup white vinegar
1 tablespoon shallots, minced
Juice from 2 oranges
1 teaspoon sugar
1 teaspoon chile oil

1 teaspoon sesame oil
2 teaspoons cracked black pepper
Juice from 1 lemon
1 tablespoon heavy cream
3/4 pound unsalted butter
*   (3 sticks), softened*
Salt, to taste

COMBINE ALL THE INGREDIENTS except the cream, butter, and salt in a saucepan. Bring to a boil and simmer until the liquid is reduced to approximately 3/4 cup. Add the cream and slowly whisk in the butter. The butter should be added a little at a time. Be sure to incorporate the butter thoroughly after each addition. Season with salt. Set the sauce aside near the warm part of the stove to keep it from separating.

This recipe makes 2 cups of beurre blanc.

SERVES 6

In 1994 Jim Rock and I and our favorite cowgirl and Willie's favorite ex-wife, Connie Nelson, formed Croce-Rock-Nelson Presents. We put on Generations, a concert to benefit local AIDS organizations in San Diego, at Copley Symphony Hall.

Connie's brother, Michael Koepke, had died of AIDS, along with many of my dear friends, like Tom Scheuring and our loyal employee Carmen Jorge Mendez. In tribute to their fight against AIDS and to all the people who survive it today, we decided to raise money to help educate people and prevent the spread of this deadly disease.

Singer-songwriter and friend Rita Coolidge donated her time and talent as master of ceremonies, and Willie Nelson, Arlo Guthrie, and A.J. Croce spanned the generations as our gracious and generous performers.

Our first joint venture took months of planning and enormous dedication from our staff and friends, but the concert raised thousands of dollars to donate to our cause. Bill Silva, Steve Redfearn, and Alison McGregor also earned our greatest respect for the enormous know-how they demonstrated in putting together the concert the right way. God knows we couldn't have done it without them.

🍴

Over the years, our Roundtable of managers met officially every Wednesday to discuss our short and long-term goals. Everyone who held a seat had a direct effect on the bottom line and in 1995 we played a game of musical chairs. Our finance manager, Kim Kovacs, who was hired on a part-time basis quickly worked her precocious way up to Controller and systems analyst.

In 1996, she passed the torch on to our accountant Kim Melchior, who brought our P&L and my trust and confidence to a brand new level. Kim embodies a true Christian spirit, and knock on wood, prosperity followed her to our door.

Deborah Ogburn, who once shadowed me as my personal assistant and manager of advertising and public relations, drew her extensive information about Croce's from working at my side at the office and restaurants for several years. With Deborah's professionalism, good heart and expertise, she interpreted visually the philosophy of our restaurants and bars and put all our business under one big wonderful umbrella.

Kathy Miller, once manager of "Croce's West" (formerly Ingrid's Cantina), took her time and patience to develop one of the best catering and group sales departments we ever had.

Then, Debra Andrade, promoted from waitress, to coffeehouse manager, to Kitchen Liaison and finally to Catering and Group Sales Director, took what Kathy Miller had started and made it even better. Today, our group sales encompass a great percentage of our business and we are throwing bigger and better parties than ever.

When Tom Fitzpatrick, our wonderful general manager, graduated from Croce University to open his Bayou Bar and Grill with partner Phillip Mossy, Mary Sullivan took over Tom's position.

During Croce's most successful years, Mary Sullivan, General Manager and Wine Director, has mastered the difficult job of overseeing Croce's Restaurant and Jazz Bar, Top Hat Bar and Grille, Croce's West, Upstairs at Croce's and our catering and group sales. She also helps Mary Rogers, our wonderful Human Resource Manager, and me to hire all the new members for our team. Mary Sullivan is a kind and caring person who runs all operations in my absence. Without her, my job would be too hard.

Mary Rogers, with patience and persistence continues to bring her growing capabilities to our Human Resource department. "The Dos Marias" as we now call them, have gained my confidence and friendship, and have given me peace of mind. Well, at least more peace than before!

Our first "Generations" local AIDS benefit at San Diego's Symphony Hall, 1994. *Left to right:* Paula Nelson with her dad, Willie Nelson, A. J. Croce, and Arlo Guthrie.

Photograph by Sandra Small

Pacific Rim Tamales
with Mousselline of Baguetta Sea Bass

⊱ ⊰

1/2 cup shiitake mushrooms, sliced
2 tablespoons olive oil
1/3 cup green onion, chopped
3/4 cup water chestnuts, chopped
Pinch salt

18-ounce sea bass,
    cut into 1-inch chunks
1/2 cup bay shrimp or
    4 large prawns, diced
1 1/2 cups heavy cream

1 teaspoon pepper	*2 teaspoon soy sauce*
2 ears of corn, kernels cut off the cob	*2 eggs*
1 teaspoon fresh ginger, minced	*12 corn husks*

SAUTÉ THE SHIITAKE MUSHROOMS in the olive oil in a Teflon pan over medium-high heat for 5 to 7 minutes. Add the green onion, water chestnuts, salt, pepper, corn, and ginger and cook for 5 minutes more. Cool completely.

Put the sea bass and shrimp into a food processor and puree. While the processor is running, add the cream and soy sauce. Scrape down the sides and add the eggs. Pulse 4 or 5 times. Transfer to a mixing bowl. Add the sautéed vegetable mixture. Mix thoroughly. Stuff the corn husks with the sea bass mousseline, dividing evenly. Steam the tamales in the corn husks in a steamer for half an hour.

SERVES 6

If 1994 had been a significant year for reinterpreting our organization, examining our mission, streamlining systems, and training staff, 1995 was going to be the year to enjoy the profit that our new and better systems would bring us. Less stress and more fun were on the agenda.

In December, at our roundtable meeting, all seven of us pledged to embrace our work as a team and to bring Croce's to new heights together. While the public knew we offered the "best bars," we believed we also offered the best restaurants. And our New Year was going to be devoted to bringing our chef and cuisine to the forefront.

Six months into the year, we began to move our guests' attention toward our kitchen. Newspaper and magazine articles boasted Croce's food and we had worked hard to get Chef Fay's picture in the press all over San Diego. There was a new buzz about Croce's Restaurants everywhere.

Then, in June of 1995, with our major campaign under way to promote our restaurants, Chef Fay told us, after seven and a half years at Croce's, that it was time for her to move on.

It was enormously difficult to get our arms around our company and console ourselves. The investment we had made in bringing our chef and kitchens to the forefront was a big one and having no leader to man or "woman" the kitchen was very tough.

We needed more than a professional executive chef to pick up the pieces—we needed a miracle!

So much for less stress in 1995. We now had a bigger job than ever to take a hold of our raging kitchen and guide it to safety. And believe me, Croce's was no chihuahua.

To temporarily cover the void, I took over as our administrative executive chef. We'd come a long way since I had cooked blintzes and lasagna. But despite the pressure, or maybe because of it, everyone in the kitchen worked very hard and the food went out to our guests with rave reviews.

Since then, I have continued to be the matriarch in our kitchen. Our talented culinary team enjoys working together like family. No matter how intense the pressure in our kitchen becomes, there's a lot of love that goes into the food, and it sustains the bittersweet refrain of change. Now that's a miracle!

INTENSE CHOCOLATE CAKE

1 cup pitted prunes
1 cup chocolate liqueur
1 cup sugar

1 teaspoon baking soda
1 tablespoon grated espresso
or instant espresso powder

1 cup skim milk

6 tablespoons canola oil

1 tablespoon white wine vinegar

1 teaspoon vanilla extract

1 1/4 cups all-purpose flour

1/3 cup cocoa powder

1 cup raspberry, mango,

or passion fruit puree

1/4 cup melted white chocolate

or 1/4 cup melted bittersweet

or semisweet chocolate

LINE THE BOTTON of a 9-inch springform pan with parchment paper and coat with cooking oil spray. In a heavy-bottomed pan over a medium-high flame, heat together the prunes and the chocolate liqueur for 20 minutes. Set aside and allow to cool to room temperature. When cooled, blend until smooth in a blender or food processor.

Preheat the oven to 350°F. Mix together the blended prunes, sugar, skim milk, canola oil, vinegar, and vanilla. In a separate bowl combine the flour, cocoa powder, baking soda, and the ground espresso. Mix the wet and dry ingredients alternately until they are thoroughly mixed. Spread the batter into the prepared springform pan. Bake for 30 to 40 minutes, or until a toothpick inserted in the center comes out clean. Allow the cake to cool in the pan for 10 minutes. Remove the sides of the pan and cool completely on a rack. To serve, place on a bed of fruit puree and drizzle with melted chocolate.

SERVES 12

In March of 1996, Jack McDavid invited me back east as a guest chef at Jack's Firehouse for Philadelphia's annual culinary event, "The Book and The Cook". Jack McDavid and Bobby Flay had just taped "Chillin' and Grillin'", their TV series for Food Network and Jack kindly encouraged me to talk with the people he knew at the television station about doing "Chef du Jour".

In mid-April 1997 I received a call from the producer at Food Network who wanted me to fly to New York City and tape seven shows the following week. I was absolutely thrilled by the opportunity to offer my recipes and stories nationally. At the same time, I was intimidated by the prospect of scripting and developing seven half-hour TV shows in only a week. Luckily Debra Andrade, Alfonso Morin and my husband, Jimmy Rock, helped me to prepare for the ordeal by staging the episodes in my own kitchen.

My first day on the set, I cursed my instant response to risk-taking. I was mortally afraid, and to add to my fear, I found Food Network's "low budget, one-take Jake" practice a freaking challenge. I completed four shows the first day, and I was anxious the next morning to walk into the studio and do my final three segments as scheduled.

Upon my arrival, however, I learned that the game plan had suddenly changed. My pre-scripted narratives and recipe descriptions became history when I was introduced to my unexpected co-host, Drew Nieporent, co-owner, and restaurateur of the world renown Rubicon, Montrachet, Nobu's, TriBecca Grill, Zeppole, Layla and more of the finest restaurants in the world. Drew could have made my experience miserable, but he was kind, engaging and a happy surprise.

For all my concerns about doing Chef Du Jour, I've received wonderful feedback from folks that saw me cooking on TV and as a result have come to dine with us at Croce's. Now, I can't wait to do it again!

🍴

In the summer of 1997, I received a call from Chuck Dalaklis, an independent producer working with VH-1, who wanted my approval and input to do a show on Jim Croce for a series called "Behind the Music".

We met, and after reading my book "Thyme In A Bottle" and going through Jim Croce archives and tapes, Chuck asked all kinds of questions. Intrusive as he was, nosey even, my husband and I liked him.

After turning down producers for over twenty-some years who had been anxious to do movies about Jim Croce, we finally felt that a VH-1 documentary would maintain the integrity we had held out for and reach the people who would appreciate Jim's story. We also believed that Chuck was resourceful, competent and the right guy for the job. As it turned out, he was!

Pursuing a list of people to interview, we started with Cheech Marin, whose heartfelt segment was done in San Francisco. Arlo Guthrie was doing a concert in L.A. and kindly took time with Chuck to give his great insights.

We traveled back to Pennsylvania with Chuck to interview some of Jim's and my old friends. On the way from the airport we stopped to have a Philadelphia cheese steak with our artist-friend Melvin Goldfield in South Philly. Judy Coffin kindly prepared a picnic feast for us when we did the shoot in Lyndell. And Chuck went on to do interviews and B-roll in Nachitoches, Louisiana where Jim Croce's plane went down on September 20, 1973. The final shoot and interviews with A.J. and me were done here in San Diego, at Croce's.

🍴

In November, VH-1's "Jim Croce; Behind the Music" aired for the first time. The response was sensational. And, with every additional replay, more and more people learned about Jim Croce, his music and his living tribute here at Croce's Restaurants and Bars.

🍴

In December, Roland Woerner, a producer for The Today Show, came to San Diego with his family for a relaxing weekend in Coronado. He had read that A.J. Croce was performing at Croce's Top Hat that night and he called me personally to see if he could get two tickets before the show sold out.

Roland and his wife, celebrating their anniversary, were thrilled with A.J.'s performance. Before they left, I signed their copy of "Thyme In A Bottle" as an anniversary gift.

A couple of days later I got a call from Roland. He told me that he had read my book cover to cover the night he received it. Serendipitously, he came upon the VH-1 special, "Jim Croce; Behind the Music" while channel surfing in his New York hotel room the next night.

After watching Jim's story, Roland had another Croce story he wanted to tell on the Today Show with Katie Couric. This segment was to be a portrait of how I had triumphed over adversity. It was to be a slice of the Ingrid Croce story. The segment aired in August and was a great success.

THE LIFE OF A RESTAURATEUR   263

The good fortune didn't stop with the Today Show. In the summer of 1998, TNN did a special called "Jim Croce; Life and Times" which aired in the summer of 1998. Before the year was up, Croce's Restaurants and Bars were honored with the Finest Service Award, I was inducted into San Diego's Business Hall of Fame and the San Diego Restaurant Association recognized me for special achievements as Restaurateur of the Year. It certainly was nice, after fifteen years of practicing my jig diligently, to be acknowledged by my peers and community.

The love and support I receive every day from my family and extended family here at Croce's is what truly keeps me going. In the end, it's those beginnings that really count the most. And one of my favorites at Croce's is Bruschetta with Sundried Tomato Pesto with Herbed Ricotta Cheese and our Baked Bread and Onion Soup.

BRUSCHETTA
WITH SUNDRIED TOMATO PESTO AND HERBED RICOTTA CHEESE

$\approx$ $\approx$

Twelve 1 1/2-inch-thick slices Italian bread
    (preferably whole wheat)
2 cloves garlic, peeled
1/4 cup extra virgin olive oil
Coarse salt

Sundried Tomato Pesto
    (see directions below)
Herbed Ricotta Cheese Spread
    (see directions below)
Fresh basil, for garnish

PREHEAT THE BROILER. Toast the bread on both sides under the broiler until lightly brown. Reduce the oven temperature to 350°F. While the bread is still warm, rub 1 side with a garlic clove. Brush each slice generously with olive oil and sprinkle with salt. Bake the Bruschetta in the oven for 10 minutes until crisp. Keep warm until ready to serve. Spread the Bruschetta first with the tomato paste and next with the cheese—do not mix the two spreads. Garnish with fresh basil.

SUNDRIED TOMATO PESTO

1 cup loosely packed sundried tomatoes
1/2 teaspoon garlic, roasted
2 teaspoons extra virgin olive oil

1/2 teaspoon fresh oregano
5 to 7 leaves fresh basil
Dash salt

IN A SMALL CONTAINER, barely cover the tomatoes with very hot water and soak until they start to plump, 10 to 30 minutes. Drain off the water and reserve. Put the tomatoes, garlic, olive oil, oregano, basil, and salt in a blender or food processor. Process until the mixture is rough-textured, not completely smooth. Add just enough of the soaking water to make a spreadable paste. Save the rest of the soaking water for soup stock.

Herbed Ricotta Cheese Spread

8 ounces skim milk ricotta cheese

1 teaspoon garlic, roasted

2 teaspoons fresh herbs of your choice:
  basil, thyme, parsley,
  oregano, or chives, chopped

2 teaspoons Parmesan cheese,
  freshly grated

Salt, to taste

Freshly cracked black pepper,
  to taste

COMBINE ALL THE INGREDIENTS in a small bowl and mix with a rubber spatula until blended.

SERVES 6

Baked Bread and Onion Soup

☙ ❧

Kathleen's Baked Bread and Onion Soup is a reminder of the "Archetypal" meal. The bread is an inseparable accompaniment to the broth. This soup is served at Croce's almost as a ritual. It reminds me how basic nourishment helps us to restore health and happiness too! And of how good soup can be!

1 loaf crusty country-style bread

2 medium onions, sliced

5 cloves garlic, slivered

1 teaspoon fresh thyme

1 cup loosely packed Parmesan
  cheese, freshly grated

2 medium tomatoes, sliced thin

6 cups chicken stock

SLICE THE BREAD 1/4 inch thick and dry out in a 200°F oven until crunchy. Cook the onions and garlic over medium heat in a stockpot with 1/4 cup of water or chicken stock until completely soft.

Preheat the oven to 350°F. Line a deep casserole dish with a layer of sliced bread. Place a layer of onions and garlic over the bread, sprinkle with half of the fresh thyme, add a layer of cheese followed by a layer of tomatoes. Continue layering the ingredients and finish with a layer of bread followed by a final layer of Parmesan cheese. Fill the casserole dish to the top with chicken stock and bake for approximately 40 minutes or until golden brown. Serve immediately.

SERVES 10 TO 12

The birth of our grandson Elijah Maxwell Croce on December 10, 1996 was calling me to take time away from work to get to know him. A.J. was off the road, preparing to go on tour to promote his third CD, "Fit To Serve". Marlo, our daughter-in-law, and Camille were happy for the chance to holiday in Tahiti. Judy Coffin, my best friend was ready for a trip to paradise. Mary Sullivan, our GM, and Eddie Perea Elias, our Bar Manager, were so much a part of our restaurants and our lives we just had to take them with us too. This was a brave move for Jim and me but we determined that Croce's would just have to survive without us all for a couple of weeks. Happily it did.

Tahiti's neighboring island, Moorea, French and sensual, was the perfect spot to indulge with family and friends for my birthday. Nine of us, spanning five decades, embarked on our adventure the day I turned fifty. I'm now determined to return to the island and turn fifty again, and again and again, until I turn 100!

MEYER LEMON TART

❧ ❧

1 1/4 cups all-purpose flour
1/4 cup almonds, finely ground
3 tablespoons sugar
1/4 teaspoon salt

1/2 cup cold butter, cut into pieces
2 1/2 tablespoons orange juice
Lemon Cream Filling
*   (see directions below)*

Kathleen's Meyer Lemon Tart is also dedicated to her wonderful friend and mentor, Richard Sax, who lived and died by his Classic Home

Desserts *and left us all his "bible" with his recipes for sweetness from around the world.*

TO CREATE THE DOUGH, combine the flour, almonds, sugar, and salt in the bowl of a food processor. Add the butter, and pulse briefly until it crumbles. Slowly add the orange juice as needed. (You may not need to add the full amount of orange juice.) Note: Do not overwork the dough. Mix only until all the ingredients are just combined. The dough will be smooth and form a ball.

Preheat the oven to 350°F. Roll the dough onto a floured surface. Butter a tart pan and arrange the dough in the pan, pressing it into the bottom and sides. Butter a piece of tinfoil cut to twice the size of the tart pan. Place the buttered side into the tart shell. Fill the tinfoil with 2 cups of dried beans to weigh the shell down and prevent it from rising. Bake for 8 minutes. Remove the foil and the beans, and cook for 8 minutes more. Let the tart cool while you prepare the filling.

Pour the Lemon Cream Filling into the prepared tart shells and bake at 350°F on a sheet pan. Check for doneness after 25 minutes and cook 10 to 12 minutes longer, if necessary. The top will just start to turn golden in color.

LEMON CREAM FILLING

5 eggs
1/2 cup sugar
5 tablespoons lime juice

5 tablespoons orange juice
6 tablespoons lemon juice
1 cup heavy cream

COMBINE THE EGGS AND SUGAR in a stainless-steel bowl and whisk until completely mixed. Add the fruit juices and, finally, add the cream.

Note: Use only the juice of fresh fruit—do not use bottled juices.

MAKES 1 TART

Procedural orderliness" is how I attempt to set up Croce's. As a compulsive organizer and facilitator, I'm either picking something up, moving it, or asking someone else to.

My two pet peeves are communication and employees stepping over trash on the floor. Jim's answer to this last dilemma was to put little messages on the trash to bring attention to the servers. For example, one piece of paper would say "This is worth five dollars in Croce Bucks" or "Coffee for two at Croce's." We actually did this and it worked. But once we stopped putting a cash value to the trash, we were back where we started.

The answer, ultimately, is finding people who take pride in themselves and therefore in Croce's. We constantly seek wonderful people who want to be a part of our "family." And if we don't have a job for them now, we will. We're still growing.

🍴

When our granddaughter Camille comes to visit for the night, we often prepare our meals together. And while she has already shown signs of being a natural born cook, she has told me emphatically that when she grows up she does not want to be a chef but a princess. For me she is already both.

CAMILLE'S ANGEL BANANA PANCAKES

It was Camille's idea, when she was four, to use our cookie cutters to fashion pancakes, and it works great. To begin, set three bowls on the counter: A Baby Bowl, a Ma-Ma Bowl, and a Pa-Pa Bowl.

1 1/2 cups ripe bananas, mashed
1 teaspoon sugar
1 teaspoon vanilla extract
1 cup all-purpose flour
1/4 teaspoon salt
1 teaspoon baking powder
1 egg, room temperature
1 cup buttermilk (low-fat if preferred)

3 tablespoons butter
(or 1 tablespoon butter and
2 tablespoons vegetable oil),
melted
3 tablespoons roasted walnuts,
chopped, for garnish
Maple syrup to serve

In the baby bowl mash the ripe bananas and add the sugar and vanilla. In the Ma-Ma Bowl combine the flour, salt, and baking powder. In the Pa-Pa Bowl beat the egg and stir in the buttermilk and melted butter until the mixture is smooth. (Prepare the griddle for the pancakes by melting the butter on the surface of the skillet over medium heat. Using a rubber spatula, put the butter into the bowl with the liquid.)

Add the Baby Bowl with the banana mixture to the Pa-Pa bowl with the buttermilk. Add the dry ingredients into the wet ingredients and stir until the batter is smooth.

Using large, uncomplicated metal cookie cutters, use vegetable spray to coat the inside of each form. For your first pancakes, heat the skillet with butter (see above instructions). Place the cookie cutters on a greased grill. Pour the batter by the spoonful into the cookie cutter to form a thin layer. When the pancake bubbles, use a spatula to flip both the hotcake and the cookie cutter. Push the pancake down onto the skillet, as it will rise inside of the cutter. When the pancake is golden, remove the cutter. Voilà. An "angel," "star," or "bear" banana pancake! To repeat the process, spray the cookie cutters each time. It is not necessary to rebutter the pan.

MAKES 12 TO 16 PANCAKES

(DEPENDING ON THE COOKIE CUTTER)

Our granddaughter, Camille, cooking animal pancakes at age five.

Photograph by Ingrid Croce

A.J., Marlo and Elijah Croce. 1998

Photograph by Elizabeth Fis

For all the hard work and trouble of operating a restaurant, at the end of the evening Jim and I get to sit down in the middle of Croce's magic and become guests in our own home away from home.

Our hard working culinary team prepares our delicious meals. The world's greatest bartender, Larry Lowy, a.k.a. "Kramer", works his magic on the crowd, turning Croce's customers into Croce friends and believers. Mary Sullivan, our cherished General Manager, pairs our wine and keeps balance on the floor and in the kitchen, while Bar Manager/Assistant GM, Eddie Perea Elias troubleshoots "emergencies" with a style and endearment that encourages us to declare "Eddie for President!"

Employee of the Year, Kitty Rice charms us with her service, as she does all her guests, transforming diners into family and making everyone feel at home.

I'm happy for my life as a restaurateur, for my husband and family, and for the pleasure I receive from providing a haven for great food, music, and fun. I don't know if I'm doing Croce's right, but as far as I can tell, it don't get much better than this.

Index

Adapted by Justine Korman
Illustrated by Rigol

Based on the Direct to Video
Pooh's Grand Adventure: *The Search For Christopher Robin*
by Karl Geurs and Carter Crocker

A GOLDEN BOOK • NEW YORK

Golden Books Publishing Company, Inc., Racine, Wisconsin 53404

It was the last day of summer in the Hundred-Acre
Wood. Pooh and Christopher Robin were having a grand
time playing on the Enchanted Hill.

   Christopher Robin had some important news, but he
wasn't quite sure how to tell it to Pooh.

Finally, Christopher Robin said, "Pooh, if you ever need me and I'm not around, you must remember this: You're braver than you believe, and stronger than you seem, and smarter than you think.

"And what's most important to know is that even if we're apart, I shall always be with you."

The next morning, Pooh rushed out to play in the leaves and found a honey pot. Of course, he wanted to eat all the honey right away. But he wasn't sure he should. So he set off to ask Christopher Robin.

But Pooh couldn't find Christopher Robin. Instead, he found Piglet high up in a tree, squeaking with fear.

"Whatever are you doing up there, Piglet?" asked Pooh.

"I'm learning not to be afraid of heights," Piglet explained—just as he started to fall.

Tigger tried to bounce up to catch Piglet.
But his tail wasn't strong enough for such a
big bounce. (Or so he thought.)
 Luckily, Piglet fell right into Tigger's arms!

Pooh went to see Rabbit, but Rabbit didn't know
where Christopher Robin was, either. Rabbit spotted a
note stuck to the honey pot, but he couldn't read it
because it was covered with honey.

Owl didn't let that stop him. He read around the honey. "The note is from Christopher Robin," said Owl. "He's gone away to a terrible place called SKULL! He needs our help!"

Pooh decided to rescue Christopher Robin. Owl drew a map of how to reach him in the Eye of the Skull, beyond the Forbidden Mountains.

Piglet didn't like the sound of that. "Are there monsters there?" he fretted.

"Oh, thank you, I nearly forgot!" Owl said, quickly adding monsters to his map. "There are heffalumps, woozles, jagulars . . . and the fabled Skullasaurus!"

No one knew what a Skullasaurus was (including Owl) and everyone was afraid of it. Still, for Christopher Robin's sake, his friends set off to save him. They crossed the bridge from the Hundred-Acre Wood into the Great Unknown.

Before long, Pooh said, "I wonder if those rather
forbidding-looking things up ahead might be the
Forbidden Mountains."

But Rabbit did not trust his eyes. "We must follow the
map," he declared.

Soon the friends were completely lost. They found themselves near a dark cave.

Piglet looked up. "Skuh-skuh-skuh—SKULL!" he stammered.

The friends suddenly realized they had reached Skull Cave! Pooh rushed inside to save Christopher Robin.

The others hesitated outside. Then they heard a horrible rumbling.

"The Skullasaurus!" Piglet squeaked. "It's getting c-c-closer!"

"And hungry!" added Tigger.

Without another thought, they all rushed into the cave.

It was a huge place, with tunnels leading everywhere. Pooh took a wrong turn, slipped, and rolled away from his friends. The shining, crystal-covered walls echoed with more terrible rumbling.

"The Skullasaurus got Pooh!" Tigger cried.

Then Rabbit spotted an opening high in the cave. "It's the Eye of the Skull!" he called.

"We must rescue Christopher Robin—for Pooh's sake," said Eeyore. "That is, if anybody has any idea how to get up there."

Rabbit looked at the map. "This is useless," he said in disgust. "I'm not smart enough to figure this out." But, after a moment, Rabbit came up with a plan. "Tigger, you bounce Piglet up to that ledge. And, Piglet, you toss that vine to us," he said.

Tigger didn't think his tail was strong enough
for the bounce.
Piglet was afraid of bouncing that high.
But they knew they had to do something to
save Christopher Robin and Pooh.

And—what do you know—the plan worked!
Christopher Robin's advice to Pooh was true for all of
them: Rabbit *was* smarter than he had seemed. Tigger
was stronger. And Piglet *was* braver.

The friends reached the Eye of the Skull and found
Christopher Robin. (Or, actually, he found them.) But
Christopher Robin was confused. "I wasn't in any danger.
I was just in school," he said.

Then a horrible growling rumbled from deep inside the cave.

"Oh," Piglet sobbed, "now the Skullasaurus wants to eat us, too!"

Christopher Robin shook his head. "I know that sound," he said.

Christopher Robin lowered a pot of honey into the cave. When he pulled it up again, the pot was empty of honey and full of bear.

The rumbling had stopped. The noise of the Skullasaurus had only been the grumbling of Pooh's tummy!

In fact, all the things the friends had been afraid of didn't seem scary any longer—now that they were together.

Pooh told his friends about being alone and afraid in the cave. Only one thing had made it better. He had remembered what Christopher Robin had said to him: "Even if we're apart, I shall always be with you."

Pooh put his paw on Christopher Robin's shoulder and said, "And I shall always be with you."